MW00827220

WORK PRESSURES

Work Pressures fills the void of research on the nature of pressures on individuals in the workplace. It offers a broad view of how work pressures can compromise the performance and vitality of individuals and their organizations. The contributions to this volume not only confirm communication's centrality to the problems work pressures pose, but also open an interdisciplinary conversation about how to learn from and, ultimately, manage them. Specific topics covered include the proliferation of communication technologies, organizational discourse, work overload, and generational differences in the workplace.

Dawna I. Ballard is Associate Professor in the Department of Communication Studies at The University of Texas at Austin.

Matthew S. McGlone is Associate Professor in the Department of Communication Studies at The University of Texas at Austin.

NEW AGENDAS IN COMMUNICATION

A Series from Routledge and the College of Communication at the University of Texas at Austin

Roderick Hart and Stephen Reese, Series Editors

This series brings together groups of emerging scholars to tackle important interdisciplinary themes that demand new scholarly attention and reach broadly across the communication field's existing courses. Each volume stakes out a key area, presents original findings, and considers the long-range implications of its "new agenda."

Recent series titles include:

Work Pressures
edited by Dawna I. Ballard and Matthew S. McGlone

Strategic Communication
edited by Anthony Dudo and LeeAnn Kahlor

Networked China: Global Dynamics of Digital Media and Civic Engagement
edited by Wenhong Chen and Stephen D. Reese

New Technologies and Civic Engagement
edited by Homero Gil de Zúñiga

The full list of series volumes is available at www.routledge.com.

WORK PRESSURES

New Agendas in Communication

Edited by Dawna I. Ballard and
Matthew S. McGlone

Routledge
Taylor & Francis Group

NEW YORK AND LONDON

First published 2017
by Routledge
711 Third Avenue, New York, NY 10017

and by Routledge
2 Park Square, Milton Park, Abingdon, Oxon OX14 4RN

Routledge is an imprint of the Taylor & Francis Group, an informa business

© 2017 Taylor & Francis

The right of the editor to be identified as the author of the editorial material, and of the authors for their individual chapters, has been asserted in accordance with sections 77 and 78 of the Copyright, Designs and Patents Act 1988.

All rights reserved. No part of this book may be reprinted or reproduced or utilised in any form or by any electronic, mechanical, or other means, now known or hereafter invented, including photocopying and recording, or in any information storage or retrieval system, without permission in writing from the publishers.

Trademark notice: Product or corporate names may be trademarks or registered trademarks, and are used only for identification and explanation without intent to infringe.

British Library Cataloguing in Publication Data
A catalogue record for this book is available from the British Library

Library of Congress Cataloging in Publication Data
Names: Ballard, Dawna I., editor. | McGlone, Matthew S., 1966- editor.
Title: Work pressures : new agendas in communication / edited by Dawna I. Ballard and Matthew S. McGlone.
Description: New York, NY : Routledge, 2017. | Series: New agendas in communication | Includes bibliographical references and index.
Identifiers: LCCN 2016031680| ISBN 9781138938236 (hardback) | ISBN 9781138938243 (pbk.) | ISBN 9781315675749 (ebook)
Subjects: LCSH: Job stress. | Information technology--Management. | Communication in organizations. | Work-life balance.
Classification: LCC HF5548.85 .W6676 2017 | DDC 158.7/2--dc23
LC record available at https://lccn.loc.gov/2016031680

ISBN: 978-1-138-93823-6 (hbk)
ISBN: 978-1-138-93824-3 (pbk)
ISBN: 978-1-315-67574-9 (ebk)

Typeset in Bembo
by Integra Software Services Pvt. Ltd.

CONTENTS

PREFACE

Work Pressures: New Agendas in Communication

Dawna I. Ballard and Matthew S. McGlone

Prevailing conversations on the issue of work pressures reveal a range of voices and vantage points on the topic—public and private, domestic and international, somber and humorous. The occupational challenges work pressures pose range from slightly irritating to completely immobilizing. Within reason, they are simply part of life—in both our work and personal affairs. Our concern in this book, however, is to offer a broad view of how work pressures can compromise the performance and vitality of individuals and their organizations over the long term. Based on any number of metrics documented in the literature and familiar to organizational members' lived experiences (e.g. higher rates of illness, absenteeism, turnover, industrial accidents, lower morale and decreased customer satisfaction), there are potential costs to the individual and the organization.

From recognition of the problem by the World Health Organization, to routine coverage of work pressures by news organizations around the globe, to legal statutes—both established and advocated—to protect citizens from undue work pressures, it is clear that a range of formal collectives (including inter-governmental entities, international news outlets, legislative bodies and advocacy groups) recognize the problem. Additionally, individual awareness of the problem is high and includes everything from advice for those wanting to learn how to work under pressure to cartoons that make light of the ways we manage the pressure to blogs about how to manage it wisely. Despite widespread acknowl-edgment of the problem, extant research has not offered a unifying approach for systematic investigation of a topic so central to our professional lives.

The present volume aims to fill this void in both practically and theoretically relevant ways through offering a multidisciplinary view of work pressures via the lens of communication. We consider how both contemporary and enduring work pressures are caused by, ameliorated through, and reflected in organizational members' communication patterns. While communication scholars are well suited to take a lead in addressing these matters, articulating the issues themselves requires an interdisciplinary approach as described below.

Pressure is defined simply as "the exertion of continuous force upon or against an object by something in contact with it; compression" (*Oxford English Dictionary*). The idea of what organizational members come into contact with that exerts this force (or buffers against it) is the focus of this volume. Our authors approach their area of research from different perspectives that allow the reader to understand the multilayered role of communication in shaping, deterring, or reflecting work pressures. We take this same set of interrelated concerns as an organizing framework for the chapters.

In the first section, we explore communication as the causal point of "contact" that exerts pressure on organizational members. In her chapter, Keri Stephens explores the history of communication overload as a concept and considers the work pressures that stem from the proliferation of communication technologies in contemporary (post)industrialized culture. She offers a novel biological framework for conceptualizing the "mixture" of people and technology that shapes our overload. Next, management consultant Christina Randle extends the discussion of overload by offering some practicable advice—gleaned from her work with clients navigating these challenges—about how to overcome the ill effects of communication technology and maintain one's effectiveness in work and life. Jamie Ladge then explores how the very messages that organizational members receive about work–life integration can create undue pressures in and of themselves. Fortunately, her findings indicate that this influence extends to positive messages as well: organizational messages can also bolster members' feelings of self-efficacy and support. In the final chapter of this section, Yoram Kalman poses a thought-provoking question that serves as his chapter title—*Why Do We Blame Information for Our Overload?* He points out that while communication and information are certainly culprits for the pressures we experience, communication is not our only source of compression in contemporary work.

In the second section, we develop the idea that communication can solve work pressures as well as create them. Rhetta Standifer and Scott Lester describe how the magnitude of perceived generational differences among Millennials, Generation X, and Baby Boomers are out of proportion to the actual differences among these cohorts. They discuss how an open exchange of communication initiated by managers can mitigate misunderstandings and miscommunication across groups. Next, Jennifer Gibbs focuses our attention directly on the communication-based tensions that both alleviate and add to our daily work pressures. Notably, she observes that such tensions are inevitable and actually productive for organizational members when managed properly. To close out this section, Dawna Ballard, Dina Inman Ramgolam, and Estee Solomon Gray examine how multiple interaction genres (relying upon both high-tech and low-tech communication strategies) can be enacted to manage the work pressures that members face. Specifically, they explore how varying our use of time and space can yield a variety of options for coping within the attention economy.

In the last section, we explore the role that communication research can play in diagnosing work pressure by investigating its reflection in organizational discourse. Stacey Passalacqua begins the section with an in-depth examination of research on burnout—a common response to work pressure—in healthcare contexts. She demonstrates that the fatigue traditionally associated with burnout induces an empathy deficit that is more subtle yet just as pernicious to doctor–patient interaction. Matthew McGlone, Joseph McGlynn, and Nicholas Merola mine a database of email correspondence between Enron executives to demonstrate how subtle differences in language use constitute an index of organizational change that occurred at the infamous firm. In particular, they introduce us to a concept called "temporal agency" in organizational discourse that gauges executives' affective reactions to the firm's meteoric rise and disastrous downfall. Finally, Mark Pfaff and Afarin Pirzadeh offer a methodological primer for studying a topic indirectly explored in most of the chapters in this volume—the role of emotion in computer-mediated communication. They report the empirical findings from three different studies examining how different communication platforms support the emotional expression needs of their users and offer useful advice for unobtrusively measuring emotional shifts.

Although work pressures may be inevitable in the organizational context, the adverse consequences we typically associate with them—anxiety, tension, burnout, turnover—need not be. The contributions to this volume not only confirm communication's centrality to the problems work pressures pose, but also open an interdisciplinary conversation about how to learn from them and ultimately manage them. We anticipate numerous constructive and important exchanges in this dialogue.

PART I

1

UNDERSTANDING OVERLOAD IN A CONTEMPORARY WORLD

Keri K. Stephens

UNIVERSITY OF TEXAS AT AUSTIN

It is the end of the semester, and students in a senior-level internship class are STRESSED OUT! Not only are they preparing to graduate, but they are finishing their internships, interviewing for jobs, and studying for final exams. While graduation is certainly a time in peoples' lives when they expect to be overwhelmed, these feelings also occur during our daily lives as well. Many people often report feelings of having too much information, pressures to respond to others, and overwhelming to-do lists. When was the last time you sat through a class and by the time it was over you had received ten, twenty, or even fifty text messages? All these messages could have made you happy, but they could also add to your feelings of being overloaded. This chapter explores issues of overload and centers on a specific type of excessive "load" defined as "the extent to which, in a given period of time, an organization's members perceive more quantity, complexity, and/or equivocality in the information than an individual desires, needs, or can handle in the process of communication" (Chung & Goldhaber, 1991, p. 8). By dissecting this common perception, you will learn how to consider different factors that can contribute to the feeling of being overloaded with information and communication. This knowledge can help you in college, graduate or professional school, and when you transition into the workplace.

Overload Research History

Overload seems to be a common perception now that our information society operates "under a more-faster-better philosophy of life" (Levy, 2009, p. 512). Not only do college students experience overload, but this phenomenon is highly relevant in the workplace today. Much of the past research on overload has been from the perspective of information overload found in the information sciences field (Edmunds & Morris, 2000; Eppler & Mengis, 2004; Hiltz & Turoff, 1985; Jones, Ravid, & Rafaeli, 2004) or organizational and decision-making research (O'Reilly, 1980; Speier, Valacich, & Vessey, 1999; Sutcliffe & Weick, 2008; Weick, 1970). In their comprehensive discussion of overload, Eppler and Mengis (2004) review a broad interdisciplinary literature that focuses on information overload and they find that when people are overloaded, they experience poorer decision-making and strenuous personal situations. Overload adversely affects individual performance and can lead to four types of outcomes: limited information search, arbitrary information analysis, suboptimal decisions, and strenuous personal situations (Eppler & Mengis, 2004). This means that people are more likely to collect less data and rush to finish a project instead of devoting the time needed to produce a quality product. In addition to individual performance degradation, Speier et al. (1999) found that when people are interrupted, they feel an increased sense of information overload which can result in decreased decision accuracy and increased decision time. Ultimately, if people are continuously overloaded at work, they report burnout (Maslach, Schaufeli, & Leiter, 2001), which often leads to job dissatisfaction and leaving a job.

Overload is a fundamental concept found in human communication because our field originated with information theory (Shannon & Weaver, 1949), and notions of load, communication channels, and noise were fundamental parts of that theory. Overload is also increasingly relevant for many subdisciplines of communication. Organizational communication, the study of workplace communication and how organizations are made up of communication processes and practices, has historically had the most pressing interests in this phenomenon—e.g., decision-making degradation—but the contemporary communication technology environment has expanded the relevance of overload. Now we see that interpersonal relationships and families are being impacted since people bring their mobile devices home and use them during family time or dinner (Mazmanian, Yates, & Orlikowski, 2006). We also find that overload is important in the study of health communication since people increasingly claim they are overloaded with health information (Kim, Lustria, Burke, & Kwon, 2007). Ultimately people's frustration with being overloaded illustrates a highly communicative concern— one that shares some similarities with the concept of information overload, but also introduces new people-related, communicative issues that are highly relevant in a contemporary society. Let us examine some of the issues next.

Technology and Accessibility

The rise in mobile phones, more broadly described as personal communication technologies or PCTs (Campbell & Park, 2008), and the increase in communication accessibility have created new opportunities and expectations for interacting with others, a practice associated with higher overload (Rafaeli, 1988). Today's young adults are likely to receive text messages, emails, phone calls, face-to-face conversations, and social media messages, all interspersed throughout their day. The knowledge that people can be reached immediately through a mix of technologies can create what has been called an electronic leash (Jarvenpaa & Lang, 2005) and a feeling of needing to be accessible anytime and anywhere (Jarvenpaa & Lang, 2005; Middleton, 2007). Consider the following example provided by a student we will call John:

> "You see I have my iPhone with me all the time, and my friends know this about me. The problem is that when my friends text me, they don't know if I am in class or busy, and they always expect an immediate response. If they don't get one, they keep texting and calling me. I've tried turning off my phone, but I feel like I'm punished if I am not always available. I'd rather handle messages as I get them than be overwhelmed with hundreds of texts."

This scenario is common with college students and young adults entering the workforce. The real paradox, identified by Jarvenpaa and Lang (2005), is that people enjoy and need their technologies, but they also depend on mobile devices. Jarvenpaa and Lang (2005) studied 222 urban mobile users in four countries and their independence/dependence paradox describes people's reliance on communication technology and their struggle to be free of the constant connection to others. They call this the difficulty to "break the 'always on' habit" (p. 12) and they stress that mobile phone use appears to be habitual, meaning that people do not actively consider why and how they use these devices.

In a course taught at the University of Texas at Austin, *Workplace Technologies*, we assign students the task of going twenty-four hours with no access to communication technologies. This means no mobile phone, no computer, no social media, and no electronic music. It forces students to use pen and paper to take field notes about their experiences and all their communication occurs face-to-face. These students have to plan ahead and download class notes and electronic textbook resources prior to their deprivation experience. While very few students report joy from this experience, most of them learn two key things: they are living as always accessible people, and they are not using their time as wisely as they probably should. Most students also relate these two key realizations to the fundamental reasons they feel overloaded. While we will explore both of these observations in detail in this chapter, these realizations help us understand a core argument: people, both self and others, not information, are a frequent cause of overload perceptions.

Understanding Overload by Using Biology Metaphors

Past research has established that overload is important to study because it leads to serious personal and organizational problems (Eppler & Mengis, 2004; Farhoomand & Drury, 2002). Furthermore, many causes of overload have been identified and there are attempts to measure this phenomenon (e.g., Eppler & Mengis, 2004; Ballard & Seibold, 2006). Yet there is still a large gap to fill in this body of research because we have inadequately considered the role that other people play in the perception of overload. We need to understand that overload is best defined on a continuum of severity and that overload is in a constant state of flux because "both the creation and reduction of overload, as parallel processes, can occur at the same time" (Weick, 1970, p. 85). So people tend to end up in situations that cause them to feel overload, sometimes just an annoyance, but sometimes a debilitating experience. This is why overload is in a state of flux; people are constantly adjusting their practices to cope. People change both their physical practices and their beliefs concerning their perceived state of overload.

Equating Load to Biology

To better understand how overload functions, let's take a trip to our entry-level biology classes that discussed cells and the human body. Even though we are social scientists studying people and work practices in this type of overload research, it is often helpful to borrow metaphors from fields that are studied by students of all majors and backgrounds. Thus biology and basic science courses provide these helpful examples.

Communication load functions much like cells in the human body because our goal is to maintain internal system health while living and interacting in a constantly changing environment. This maintenance goal of living cells is called homeostasis, a term also common in cybernetics and organizational systems (Katz & Kahn, 1966). A homeostatic system (a cell, an organization, or the process of communication load) maintains its functions by constantly adjusting to internal and external demands. While equilibrium is desired, there are times when homeostatic imbalance occurs and the system is compromised. In the human body, homeostatic imbalances can lead to diseases such as diabetes and dehydration; thus some of these imbalances can be corrected, yet some are permanent. In communication load, this imbalance is called overload or underload. Much like a living cell undergoing homeostatic imbalance, people under conditions of load imbalance also experience negative effects and they adjust themselves and their environment to return to a state of homeostasis. Homeostatic load varies between people because overload is a perception and people have different tolerance levels for how they interpret and respond to load imbalances.

Through communication processes, load is constituted and it involves constant negotiation of the human components of self and others along with technological considerations. In the process of communication, people are interacting with others (social) and using tools, often technology-based (material), to facilitate and interpret the load they experience in the communication process. For example, as people try to respond to text messages, they have decisions to consider such as their own time management strategies to only check text messages once an hour, the power that the sender of the text message has over them, and whether or not they will join groups that send copious group texts. When people adjust combinations of technological and social concerns to maintain homeostasis, overload is fleeting and the concept is more accurately depicted as communication load, instead of permanent overload.

Mixtures and Solutions of People and Technology

If we sit back and analyze our own overload situations, we can often identify the unique social and technology issues that lead us to feel overloaded. In these situations, we can think of the social and material components as a type of physical change. Some mixtures are like combinations of red gravel and white gravel, items that do not change form or take on new properties when they combine and they are clearly separable. Yet there are other times when we have no idea how we ended up overloaded, and the social and material components are irreversibly entangled much like a chemical change. In using the terms "physical change" and "chemical change," I refer to a commonly understood distinction in the chemical sciences where components are combined and become a single entity, yet have varying properties that allow for separation or permanent chemical change.

One type of matter combination, helpful for understanding how overload occurs, is when two materials undergo a physical change such as salt dissolving in water. The new mixture looks different, but if we work hard enough, we can identify that salt and water constituted the saltwater mixture. Furthermore, the saltwater has different properties—e.g., freezing temperature—than the salt and water had individually. Let us apply this physical change metaphor to overload. We might own an iPhone (material component), and we might be a member of a very active student organization (social component). Separately, each of those components has unique properties. But after we decide to join a group text from this highly active organization, we find ourselves receiving over fifty texts an hour, and now we view both our phone and our organization as problems, not opportunities for communication.

Yet combinations of material and social issues in human communication are often not simple, because people, like cells and organizations, change their practices over time. Therefore, in addition to clearly separable mixtures, there are irreversible chemical changes—e.g., iron reacting with air to form rust. Once rust is formed, we cannot change it back to usable iron and we only know what created the rust if we are knowledgeable about that chemical reaction. This irreversible chemical change is similar to the argument for entanglement between social and material concerns because once we experience this type of overload, we can no longer tell the individual compounds used to create our situation.

Combinations of social and material components create changes in perceptions of communication load. For example, the literature on overload often reports that people define themselves as overloaded and they tend to place blame on material objects (as in their iPhone) or social objects (their student organization). By examining material and social components together, we can understand how our decision to join a group text, combined with our use of a mobile device, created a new practice that made us feel overloaded.

The Constitution of Communication Overload

Multiple Agencies

When deciding how to dissect our own overload perceptions, we need to think broadly about people and technologies. A communicative term often used to describe these types of components is an agent. Agency is defined in many ways, but we will borrow a definition that originated in structuration theory (Giddens, 1984), that defines agency as human action or the notion that humans actively construct their worlds. When we think about agents, scholars stress that there are often "a plenum of agencies" (Cooren, 2006)—meaning multiple agents—that include both material and human agency. This is likely the case with communication overload as well. There are multiple types of material agency and human agency that come into play as people experience perceptions of communication overload. If we understand these combinations of agencies, we can begin to understand our own overload situations. For example, overload can be constituted through requests from a significant other, requests from a manager, receiving forty emails in an hour, and having a computer crash. This example represents at least two different types of human agency and two types of material agency. To depict this visually, assume that O_1 represents one type of social agency, requests from a significant other, and O_2 represents a request from a manager. For material considerations, assume that Z_1 represents one type of materiality, receiving forty emails in an hour, and Z_2 represents another type of materiality, having a computer crash. The load constitution at that time is represented by:

$O_1O_2Z_1Z_2$: load constitution for two types of social agency and two material agencies.

Types of Human Agency

There are two major categories of human agency that play a role in communication overload. The first is the individual and his or her agency in the creation and management of overload—students know that the end of the semester is very busy and they have some control over managing their time to either spread out the workload or to procrastinate. The second major category of human agency is other human communicators and their agency in making requests and providing materials—teammates are not always on time providing their information to you, and managers occasionally wait until the last minute to notify people of deadlines. There is interplay between these categories of human agency that must be considered when understanding overload. For example, individuals have *human* agency in terms of how they manage their time or choose to communicate with others. People can decide to use email extensively and have all voicemail messages converted to email to streamline their messages.

There are also additional *social* influences that contribute a different form of human or social agency. Others can initiate conversations that interrupt, they can influence technology adoption, they can provide needed information, and they can communicate their demands for attention. To depict these visually, we will use O_X to represent multiple types of social agencies involved, and Y_X to represent the combinations of individual human agency involved. These multiple types of material (Z_X), individual (Y_X), and social (O_X) considerations function together, yet their collective constitution is changing over time. Thus let us consider the fluidity of agencies constituting overload.

Acknowledging the Fluid Nature of Communication Overload

Communication overload is ambiguous, not an easily identified data point on a graph that indicates when people cross a line into a state of overload. Less process perspectives on information overload exist (e.g., Himma, 2007) and can be valuable, but a communicative perspective must view overload in a more fluid manner, much like a homeostatic system, that changes over time. For example, data taken from an undergraduate internship program at the University of Texas at Austin has consistently shown that interns experience a higher degree of overload as they begin their new positions. Over time, the overload level decreases, and in some situations, it rises again as students are completing their internships. The students explain this finding by acknowledging that they have so much information and new working relationships thrown at them early in their internship that they feel overloaded. Over time, they learn to handle the people and the information, and their overload becomes more manageable. See Figure 1.1 for a graphical representation of this overload situation.

Overload is often fleeting since material and social agencies are constantly interacting. An unanticipated request can change a person's overload perceptions in an instant, and seconds later a colleague's willingness to handle the request can return the person to homeostasis. Communication overload is constantly re-negotiated between people and their environment, and this perception varies between individuals. When the load process is chained out over time, a series of graphical representations of overload can be depicted.

Figure 1.2 depicts three social factors and two material factors constituting load at time one and time three. At time two, an additional social factor (unexpected request from coworker) occurs and temporarily raises the perception of a higher communication load.

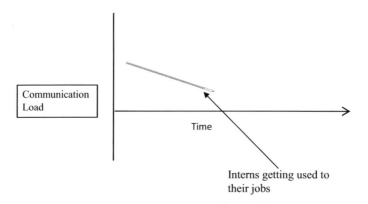

FIGURE 1.1

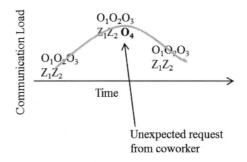

FIGURE 1.2 Fluid Nature of Communication Overload.

Shifting Influencers

Communication load changes occur under two primary conditions. First, as depicted in Figure 1.2, a social, material, or individual agent can function as a catalyst, enter the system, create a homeostatic imbalance, and people sense a change in communication load. In the prior example, that catalyst was the social agent of a coworker with an unexpected request. The second way to conceptualize a load change is that one of the agents grows in importance and creates such an imbalance that the other components in the model cannot compensate and people perceive a load change. Figure 1.3 illustrates how a person, working on a request from a team member (O_3), is doing fine until right before the deadline, and that request becomes the driver in the load imbalance that results.

   While the example in Figure 1.3 contains a social influencer, there is a practical reality that under certain conditions any one of the three components—social, material, or individual—can drive the overload relationship. This does not mean that the other components go away, but the influencer increases in relevance when load is constituted. These dominant influences likely change over time

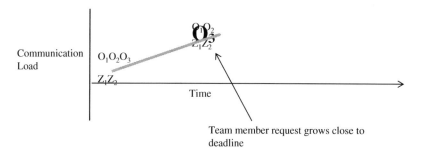

FIGURE 1.3

(Leonardi, 2010). The concept of an influencer in this load system acknowledges that under varying conditions, each of the three model considerations might expand in importance and dominate the load situation. Let us explore examples of these influencers next.

Material Influencers

Some of the more obvious types of material influencers are things like ICT features such as synchronicity of communication, combinations of ICTs, and accessibility to ICTs in terms of portability. For example, people who do not own a smartphone or those who cannot access the Internet with their phones will not receive their email until they are located in front of a computer. While material features like synchronicity are often associated with specific types of ICTs— e.g., smartphones—social and individual agency can still play a role in how these ICTs are used. Just because people own a smartphone does not mean that they will answer every call or text as it is received. People determine how their ICTs are actually used.

Another material agent example concerns features of the messages communicated, specifically message quantity and quality. For example, short and clear messages typically are not perceived as overloading, but long and ambiguous messages can overload us quickly. Yet once again, human agency will play a role in how the messages are interpreted because some people prefer more details in their messages and they can tolerate longer messages.

Individual Influencers

Human agency is certainly involved in the production of communication load imbalances because people can be poor time managers or set their boundaries wide enough to allow others to encroach on their limited time. Do you ever turn off your phone and allow yourself to focus on studying? This is an example of a time management strategy—an act of individual agency—that can change how the smartphone is used.

Another related example concerns people's practices of self-interrupting, stopping a current focused activity spontaneously, with no influence from others. Mark, Gonzalez, and Harris (2006) and Jin and Dabbish (2009) have identified that people self-interrupt themselves quite often when they work. One way to view these interruptions is a type of sequential use of multiple sociomaterial agents. For example, people who allow their computer to check their email every five minutes and display the latest messages (as in a study by Jackson, Dawson, and Wilson, 2003) are using a material agent to help them self-interrupt themselves.

A final individual influencer example concerns how communication load from one life sphere (e.g., school) relates to the load perception in another life sphere (personal life). For example, when we have a week full of tests and our significant other is angry with us, this can lead us to be more overloaded than if both of those major issues had not happened. It is plausible that agents from different spheres interact and accumulate communication load, like the example above, but it is also possible that these agents help balance one another. Sometimes we deliberately overload ourselves in one life sphere, like work, to help us forget that we are overloaded in our personal lives.

As mentioned earlier, in our *Workplace Technologies* course at UT Austin, when students were deprived of communication technologies, they realized they were being inefficient with their time. A key inefficiency they identified was their use of ICTs to self-interrupt and waste time. One student reported finishing all of her homework for an entire week during the twenty-four hours of the exercise. She said, "I cannot believe how many times I normally check Facebook. Without that distraction, I was efficient and focused." The class discussion that ensued after her statement confirmed that having limited technology distractions helped the students realize that not only did they self-interrupt themselves, but they were causing their own perceptions of overload by being so responsive to others. These students also acknowledged that this is not an easy problem to fix. While the individual influencers are often related to time management, the social influencers are much more complex.

Social Influencers

The fact that people are an active part of communication practices is a fundamental assumption in communication research, and people also serve an important role in the constitution of communication load. Some overload researchers claim that other people are a major cause of overload (i.e., interruptions as in Karr-Wisniewski & Lu, 2010) or ignore the impact of others by focusing on the message structures (Lee & Lee, 2004) or technology features (Stephens & Rains, 2011). This chapter reminds us that *people* are an integral part of communication and thus of load, and the requests from others can significantly influence our overload perceptions. For example, one of the most common issues that students in our

Workplace Technologies course had with the twenty-four-hour communication technology deprivation experience was handling frustrated and confused friends and family. When students told their friends and family that they had to be "off the grid" for twenty-four hours, there were reports of mothers being shocked, roommates being unsupportive, and professors forcing students to log into a class website or risk grade deductions. One student explained how her furious roommate threw rocks at her window because she had locked herself out of their house and could not reach the student on her phone. Obviously, other people now expect us to be connected and accessible when they need us, a situation that makes overload an issue not easily under individual-level control.

Entangled Influencers

While I have argued for the value of focusing on how the social, individual, and material agencies can be identified in the production of communication load, there will be times that they are what Orlikowski (2007) calls constitutively entangled; thus, they cannot be separated. This is what I equated to the irreversible reaction earlier in this chapter. This type of relationship is represented in the model as an $(Z_x O_x)_x$ and agents are so entwined that we cannot identify the material component(s) or the social component(s); we simply know that a mix of influencers created our overload perceptions. Think back to math class when you learned about subscripts and parentheses because this explanation follows those same rules. The inclusion of an x subscript is an acknowledgment that as the social and material become entangled, it is possible for there to be more than one material and social component that constitutes overload. The parentheses surrounding the material and social entanglement (ZO) indicate that these entangled practices function as a single unit, and the x subscript outside the parentheses indicates that there can be multiple groupings that have become entangled.

Example of the Constitution of Communication Load Model

In pulling these conceptual ideas together it is helpful to examine an example. Grace is a twenty-one-year-old college student at the end of her junior year. She has had some ups and downs in her college career, but her semester is going well and it has reinvigorated her. She is on a team where 50 percent of her final grade will be determined by a team presentation. She has described her team as fairly functional and they have a solid chance to earn an A on this major project. She likes many of her team members, but there is one who fails to read instructions carefully and asks the same questions over and over. Grace is leading the project that is due the next day, so her team members know that they can reach her on her iPhone any time day or night. As Grace is working on the project, she begins getting text messages from the problematic teammate who is asking the same questions Grace had answered the day before. Then Grace gets a message that her mother is being hospitalized for some heart-related tests and her family needs her to travel home as soon as possible. Grace is very frustrated and describes this situation as the ultimate in feeling overloaded in her life.

In this situation, it is fairly obvious that overload is a combination of social, individual, and material agencies. Let us next move to the empirical utility of this model by identifying the various social and material agencies at play in the development of Grace's overload perceptions.

First, we will define the factors:

Material: Z_1 = Quantity of messages, Z_2 = ICT features (portability of the iPhone)

Social: O_1 = Expectations of team members for a quick reply, O_2 = Parental issue

Entangled Social and Individual: (O_2Y_1) = Quality of interpersonal relationships between Grace and her team members

Individual: Y_2 = Grace's time management skills, Y_3 = Grace's life sphere complexity.

Next, we will model how her communication load changes over a brief period of time. You will notice that the load situation begins at a slightly elevated level. Then, with the introduction of an additional social agent (parental issue) and the relevance of her life sphere complexity, her load rises further to a point where she defines her state as "the ultimate in feeling overloaded in her life." See Figure 1.4 for an example of this overload depicted over time.

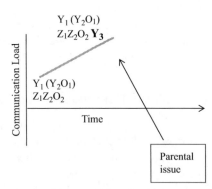

FIGURE 1.4

Discussion and Future Directions of Research

Understanding that overload is not simple and that different components constitute overload can help you make sense of situations in your life. Research on overload foregrounds the role that people and technology play in fluctuating communication load patterns and how we seek equilibrium. This dissection of load explains why this issue is not easily "fixed." Overload is not simply a failure in people's abilities to manage their time or to cope with a complex environment. Even if individuals or organizations change their practices, policies, laws, or technology tools, the pressure exerted by other communicators can push people back into a perceived state of overload. Even if software developers create tools to refine search capabilities or email filters, the material changes will not necessarily reduce overload if people use technology in unproductive ways. For decades scholars have warned that people need to be responsible for creating structures that control overload, rather than rely on software (Hiltz & Turoff, 1985).

While many of the examples provided here explain how load can become overload, this model also explains how communication load becomes reduced. Through the reduction in the number of agents or the introduction of different types of agent or driver, communication load can decrease and these agent changes can have a positive effect. For example, a coworker could leave the company and through the reduction in the quantity of messages sent by that coworker, communication load can reduce. Sometimes this reduction can even create a perception of underload, a situation that is not typically positive because people feel they do not get enough communication, which can also lead to dissatisfaction. This balanced perspective on communication load is a strength of this perspective on overload.

Advancing Directions for Future Research

Applying the Model to an Organizational Level of Analysis

Overload is not only an individual-level phenomenon; it also occurs at a more macro, organizational level. For example, student organizations often need to communicate with many audiences including internal members and external speakers. The overall health of the organization depends on its ability to communicate through appropriate technologies and communication channels to reach and inform its membership. Imagine attending a student organizational meeting for the first time and during the meeting you receive twelve pieces of paper and you are assigned to four different work groups. Unless you are incredibly enthusiastic about this organization and have copious time, you will probably not return.

It takes a mix of people and technology to maintain organizational communication load, and at any given time, homeostasis can be interrupted by an imbalance of material or social agencies and the over-dominance of material or social considerations. The resulting communication overload or underload can have devastating effects. If people are overloaded by group texts or excessive social media messages, they may leave the organization as a way to cope with excessive messages. Yet if the organization underloads people by providing them very little information, members might skip meetings and eventually drop out of the organization because they don't know how to be a member.

Overload Might Not Matter in Some Situations

As the interest in overload has increased, recent research has begun to speculate that the importance of overload will likely change depending on context. For example, there are times that people expect to be overloaded, and this expectation changes their perceptions of whether they are overloaded or not. Two examples are during new employee orientation and when people receive emergency messages. Research by Stephens and Dailey (2012) focused on new employee orientation because people receive copious information about benefits, their job, their coworkers, training, and their work environment. This study found that the new employees in this particular organization did not report being overloaded, despite receiving a flood of information. A similar finding resulted from a study conducted by Stephens, Barrett, and Mahometa (2013) where they examined people receiving multiple emergency response messages through different communication channels. In both of these studies the authors speculate that the expectation or desire for information might buffer the perception of overload. When people want the information or communication, they do not feel as overloaded.

Speculating On Changing ICT Practices

Now that we understand the important role that technologies and other people play in overload, we can begin to speculate on how overload perceptions could be shaping contemporary communication practices. For example, it is possible that a coping mechanism for overload could be partially responsible for the rise in text messaging and the use of social networks. Studies are now showing that some of the advantages of text messaging include the time savings of not having to engage others in lengthy conversations (Baron, 2008). The material limitations of text messaging and the norms surrounding text messaging use mean that people can process many more brief messages from a wide variety of people than they could if the messages and interaction times were longer.

Social media move beyond brevity—a materially relevant feature of text messaging—and demonstrate that social concerns have become more relevant. For example, research has demonstrated that many people rely on their social networks for news and other types of information (Greenhow & Robelia, 2009). Perhaps social media are functioning as filters because they are another coping mechanism of overload. Twitter might take this example to an extreme because it combines the rigid material limitations of limited characters along with the social implications of allowing others to filter through copious amounts of information.

If these changes in practices are reducing people's overload perceptions, people will likely continue to rely on succinct information and the communication channels that provide this form of information. These practices raise serious concerns about the credibility of the sources of this information, especially since people are relying on unknown others to synthesize disparate data into pithy forms. Think about your reliance on social media. To what extent do you get your news from social media, and do you know the credentials of the people providing you that information? It is possible that we are simply trading contemporary problems. We devour the concise information and that reduces our overload, but is that information correct?

Conclusion

This chapter invited you to think more deeply about what shapes overload. Hopefully you realize that you have some control over how your overload develops and how it is brought under control. This chapter also should have made you think about the material features of the technologies you use and how those might help or hinder your overload. Finally, other people can be a key contributing factor to your overload. As you finish this chapter, think about the graphs from this chapter and see if you can graph your own communication load. Be sure to identify all the material, social, and individual components that constitute your load. Consider which of these components induce the most overload for you and actively brainstorm ways to bring those factors under control. Everyone experiences work pressures and school pressures at some points in their lives; hopefully you have a better understanding of overload and how to find solutions to bring them under control.

References

Ballard, D. I., & Seibold, D. R. (2006). The experience of time at work: Relationship to communication load, job satisfaction, and interdepartmental communication. *Communication Studies, 57*, 317–340. doi:10.1080/10510970600845974.

Baron, N. S. (2008). Adjusting the volume: Technology and multitasking in discourse control. In J. E. Katz (Ed.), *Mobile communication and social change in a global context* (pp. 117–194). Cambridge, MA: The MIT Press.

Campbell, S. W., & Park, Y. J. (2008). Social implication of mobile telephony: The rise of personal communication society. *Sociology Compass, 2*, 371–387. doi: 10.111/j.1751-9020.2007.00080.x.

Chung, C. J., & Goldhaber, G. (1991, May). Measuring communication load: A three-dimensional instrument. Paper presented at the Internal Communication Association Meeting, Chicago.

Cooren, F. (2006). The organizational world as a plenum of agencies. In F. Cooren, J. R. Taylor, & E. J. Van Every (Eds.), *Empirical and theoretical explorations in the dynamic of text and conversation* (pp. 81–100). Mahwah, NY: Lawrence Erlbaum.

Edmunds, A., & Morris, A. (2000). The problem of information overload in business organizations: A review of literature. *International Journal of Information Management, 20*, 17–28. doi: 10.1016/S0268-4012(99)00051-1.

Eppler, M. J., & Mengis, J. (2004). The concept of information overload: A review of literature from organization science, accounting, marketing, MIS, and related disciplines. *The Information Society, 20,* 325–344. doi: 10.1080/01972240490507974.

Farhoomand, A. F., & Drury, D. H. (2002). Managerial information overload. *Communications of the ACM, 45,* 127–131.

Giddens, A. (1984). *The constitution of society.* Berkeley: University of California Press.

Greenhow, C., & Robelia, B. (2009). Old communication, new literacies: Social network sites as social learning resources. *Journal of Computer-Mediated Communication, 14,* 1130–1161. doi: 10.111/j.1083-6101.2009.01484.x.

Hiltz, S. R., & Turoff, M. (1985). Structuring computer-mediated communication systems to avoid information overload. *Communications of the ACM, 28,* 680–689.

Himma, K. E. (2007). The concept of information overload: A preliminary step in understanding the nature of a harmful information-related condition. *Ethics and Information Technology, 9,* 259–272. doi: 10.1007/s10676-007-9140-8.

Jackson, T., Dawson, R., & Wilson, D. (2003). Reducing the effect of email interruptions on employees. *International Journal of Information Management, 23,* 55–65.

Jarvenpaa, S. L., & Lang, K. R. (2005). Managing the paradoxes of mobile technology. *Information Systems Management, Fall,* 7–23.

Jin, J., & Dabbish, L. A. (2009). Self-interruption on the computer: A typology of discretionary task interleaving. *CHI 2009 Proceedings* (pp. 1799–1808). Boston, MA: ACM.

Jones, Q., Ravid, G., & Rafaeli, S. (2004). Information overload and the message dynamics of online interaction spaces: A theoretical model and empirical exploration. *Information Systems Research, 15,* 194–210. doi: 10.1287/Isre.1040.0023.

Karr-Wisniewski, P., & Lu, Y. (2010). When more is too much: Operationalizing technology overload and its impact on knowledge worker productivity. *Computers in Human Behavior, 26,* 1061–1072. doi: 10.1016/j.chb.2010.03.008.

Katz, D., & Kahn, R. L. (1966). *The social psychology of organizations.* New York: Wiley.

Kim, K., Lustria, M. L. A., Burke, D., & Kwon, N. (2007). Predictors of cancer information overload: Findings from a national survey. *Information Research, 12,* paper 326. Retrieved from http://InformationR.net/ir/12–4/paper326.html.

Lee, B. K., & Lee, W. N. (2004). The effect of information overload on consumer choice quality in an on-line environment. *Psychology & Marketing, 21,* 159–183. doi: 10.1002/mar.20000.

Leonardi, P. M. (2010). Digital materiality? How artifacts without matter, matter. *First Monday, 15.* Retrieved from: http://firstmonday.org/htbin/cgiwrap/bin/ojs/index.php/fm/article/view/3036/2567.

Levy, D. M. (2009). Information overload. In K. D. Himma and H. T. Tavani (Eds.), *The handbook of information and communication ethics* (pp. 497–516). New Jersey: Wiley & Sons.

Mark, G., Gonzalez, V. M., & Harris, J. (2006). No task left behind: Examining the nature of fragmented work. *CHI 2006 Proceedings* (pp. 321–330). Portland, OR: ACM.

Maslach, C., Schaufeli, W., & Leiter, M. (2001). Job burnout. *Annual Review of Psychology, 52*(1), 397–422.

Mazmanian, M., Yates, J., & Orlikowski, W. (2006). Ubiquitous email: Individual experiences and organizational consequences of BlackBerry use. *Proceedings of the 65th Annual Meeting of the Academy of Management, 66,* Atlanta, GA.

Middleton, C. (2007). Illusions of balance and control in an always-on environment: A case study of BlackBerry users. *Continuum: Journal of Media & Culture Studies, 21,* 165–178.

O'Reilly, C. A. (1980). Individuals and information overload in organizations: Is more necessarily better? *Academy of Management Journal, 23*, 684–696. Retrieved from: http://www.jstor.org/stable/255556.

Orlikowski, W. J. (2007). Sociomaterial practices: Exploring technology at work. *Organizational Studies, 28*, 1435–1448. doi: 10.177/0170840607081138.

Rafaeli, S. (1988). Interactivity: From new media to communication. In R. P Hawkins, J. M. Wiemann, & S. Pingree (Eds.), *Advancing communication sciences: Merging mass and interpersonal processes* (pp. 110–134). Newbury Park, CA: Sage.

Shannon, C. E., & Weaver, W. (1949). *The mathematical theory of communication.* Urbana, IL: University of Illinois Press.

Speier, C., Valacich, J. S., & Vessey, I. (1999). The influence of task interruption on individual decision making: An information overload perspective. *Decision Sciences, 30*, 337–360.

Stephens, K. K., Barrett, A., & Mahometa, M. L. (2013). Organizational communication in emergencies: Using multiple channels and sources to combat noise and capture attention. *Human Communication Research*, articles in advance. doi: 10.1111/hcre.12002.

Stephens, K. K., & Dailey, S. (2012). Situated organizational identification in newcomers: Impacts of preentry organizational exposure. *Management Communication Quarterly, 26*, 402–422.

Stephens, K. K., & Rains, S. A. (2011). Information and communication technology sequences and message repetition in interpersonal interaction. *Communication Research, 38*, 101–122. doi: 10.1177/0093650210362679.

Sutcliffe, K. M., & Weick, K. E. (2008). Information overload revisited. In G. P. Hodgkinson & W. H. Starbuck (Eds.), *The Oxford handbook of organizational decision making* (pp. 56–75). New York: Oxford University Press.

Weick, K. E. (1970). The twigging of overload. In H. B. Pepinsky (Ed.), *People and information* (pp. 67–129). New York: Pergamon Press.

2

24/7: MANAGING CONSTANT CONNECTIVITY

Christina Randle

Ping! Bing! Chime! Sit in any office for more than a few minutes and you will hear a cacophony of notifications alerting people that they have new e-mails, chats, text messages, tweets and posts. You can see workers flinch at their desk as they are assaulted by the alarms.

We are constantly connected, pecking out messages on our smart phones in meetings, at the dinner table, even waiting in line for coffee. While the Internet and mobile devices have given us the freedom to not be chained to a desk, they have also resulted in us being perpetually tethered to the office. The average professional in the US works 46.5 hours per week, the most of any country in the world (Chui, Manyika, Bughin, Dobbs, Roxburgh, Sarrazin, Sands, & Westergren, 2012).

And it's making people miserable. In a 2009 survey by The Conference Board (Franco, Gibbons, & Barrington, 2010), only 45 percent of respondents said they were happy with their job, the lowest satisfaction rate in twenty-two years. It's also hurting performance with long hours, diminishing the ability to think. A study published by Virtanen, Heikkila, Jokela, Ferrie, Batty, Vahtera, & Kivimaki (2012) found that workers who put in fifty-five hours per week scored lower on vocabulary tests than those who worked a forty-hour week, and workers ran a greater risk for cardiovascular disease, diabetes, and depression as well as developing dementia later in life.

For some, staying connected borders on addiction. In a survey of eighteen- to thirty-year-olds in Cisco Connected World Technology Report (2012), one in three people considered the Internet to be as important as air, water, food and shelter, and more than half claimed they could not live without the Internet, citing it as an integral part of their lives. Some respondents said it was even more essential than owning a car, dating and socializing with friends.

The persistent connectivity means that we are constantly interrupted. Czerwinski, Horvitz, & Wilhite (2004) found Microsoft employees were interrupted almost every time they tried to complete a task and that it took almost fifteen minutes to return to the work they were doing previously. The disruptions also tempt us to multitask, trying to answer phone calls and e-mails simultaneously, or even worse, texting or e-mailing while driving.

Multitasking is not only counterproductive because it takes longer to complete each individual task, but it can actually lower your IQ. Dr. Glenn Wilson, a psychiatrist at King's College London University, studied the work styles of eighty professionals and found the IQ of people who tried to multitask fell by ten points throughout the day—the equivalent to missing a whole night's sleep and more than double the four-point fall seen after smoking marijuana, according to a CNN.com interview (2005).

Dr. Wilson said during a CNN interview, "This is a very real and widespread phenomenon. We have found that this obsession with looking at messages, if unchecked, will damage a worker's performance by reducing their mental sharpness."

Very little gets our **full attention**, the most significant of all of the assets that we bring to our work, families and lives.

At Effective Edge, we have trained and coached thousands of professionals around the world for over twenty years, with the goal of increasing individual and organizational productivity, creativity and innovation. We have discovered tried and true behaviors and practices that can be used to break the cycle of workplace stress:

- Take charge of the technology instead of letting the devices control the tempo of the day.
- Keep priorities front and center to cut through the fluff and irrelevant demands on time in a day.
- Maintain a reliable system for managing outstanding tasks.
- Create a life that is meaningful and about more than work.

If we can master these best practices, we can thrive in our personal and professional lives without unnecessary pressure.

Take Control of Our Devices

The constant flood of information blurs our ability to discern what is important versus what is meaningless chatter, swamping us with minutiae and making it difficult for us to focus on the right things. The average professional, according to Chui et al. (2012), now spends over a quarter of their day just managing e-mail, which eats up valuable time that could be used to deliver on goals and objectives.

To stop the avalanche of information, some are taking bold steps. In an article in *Forbes*, Shayne Hughes,[i] CEO of Learning as Leadership, banned internal company e-mail for a week (Hughes, 2012). Realizing that he and his employees were mistaking urgent e-mail activity for productivity, they turned instead to phone calls and meetings to take care of tactical issues and to give more time for strategic and creative work.

After the initial panic of making change wore off, the team quickly found that they were less stressed and more productive. In his article about the experience for *Forbes*, Hughes related, "This was when I grasped the most damaging cost of thoughtless e-mail: It prevents us from doing our best work."

While turning e-mail off completely might seem drastic, gaining perspective on where e-mail fits into our priorities is key. Too many professionals have let e-mail take over their day at the sacrifice of things they promised to deliver to their team and customers. Giving oneself permission to unplug and create space for focus and contemplation can both lower stress and increase productivity.

Many professionals are looking for ways to create boundaries which might include scheduling an unplugged day on the weekend to give them time to rest and refresh their mind. Others turn off their devices after a certain hour in the evening so that they can give their full focus to their home life. It is these small changes that add up to achieve a positive impact.

Keeping the Big Picture in Sight

When constantly plugged in, it is easy to become distracted by unimportant tasks and irrelevant information, losing focus of our priorities. Deliberately unsubscribing or opting out of insignificant conversations helps us focus on the material that supports our main work. Having what is needed at our fingertips is helpful; drowning in superfluous data is not.

This daily focus on priorities is key. We are energized by our goals and objectives. Curtis (2012) in *Forbes* reported the optimal things professionals wanted from their work. At the top of the list were being able to do meaningful work and move things forward every day. Working from the e-mail inbox may get those communications answered, but it doesn't fulfill the need to do meaningful work.

Saying yes to something is the equivalent to saying no to something else. And saying yes to everything guarantees that nothing will be delivered 100 percent. When an individual is focused on what is important, the yeses matter most. This minimizes the pressure of overcommitment.

Many professionals struggle with focusing on their priorities because they are unclear, or don't understand how they fit within the larger organization's needs. That lack of vision creates stress as they try to prioritize and manage their day, creating tension with colleagues as they struggle to collaborate and communicate. This amplifies the negative experience of constant connectivity.

To relieve the stress of the mundane, professionals need clearly defined priorities that connect to the larger goals of the organization and are visible as part of their daily work. From those goals, they can evaluate how and when to spend their time.

Maintain a Reliable System

Professionals are given many tools and often not trained on which best practice or approaches will get the desired outcomes we want. It's hard to get the right thing done at the right time with relaxed control when attempting to deliver on goals. And if the systems in use on a daily basis cannot be trusted entirely, individuals certainly cannot get results when the stakes are high. This leads to the experience of a crisis.

Individuals need a methodology that supports them in making smart and fast decisions, whether that be an online task list, a smart phone app that organizes to-dos or a reliable paper-based system. This tool must be paired with repeated behaviors that maintain that system—whether those practices occur daily, weekly, monthly or yearly.

One of the most effective best practices involves keeping a clear head so that the task at hand can be given complete and focused attention. During the study of interruptions and task switching for Microsoft employees, Czerwinski et al. (2004) found that 40 percent of the interruptions, the largest category, were self-created.

Interrupting oneself is often caused by trying to manage outstanding work from mental recall. The challenge is that the average professional now receives at least 200 new pieces of information, but can only hold between three to seven items in their conscious mind at one time. When something new pops into one's head, something old drops into the unconscious mind. These items are not forgotten; individuals go unconscious, not remembering until the mind is prompted or the mind is clear of other things.

When one's head is too full of the things that need to get done, one's perception is impaired and the individual does not respond appropriately—overreacting to things that aren't that important or missing things that need real attention. By taking a few minutes once or twice a day to place everything that needs to get done into a centralized list or task management system, individuals can stop managing from their heads and more easily focus on what actions need to be managed next.

Creating a Compelling Life

Controlling the flood of information, focusing on priorities and maintaining a system can help alleviate a great deal of workplace stress, but that must be done in conjunction with making time for leisure—not working! In an article for the *Washington Times*, Janati (2012) noted that three of the countries with the lowest average work hours per week—Germany, Norway and the Netherlands—also ranked as the world's happiest countries in Gallup polls.

The average American worker only takes 85 percent of their vacation. Twenty-five percent of Americans don't take any vacation at all, according to Expedia.com (Harris Interactive Media Poll, 2012). And yet Dries (2011) reports 35 percent of Americans said they feel better about their job and are more productive after a vacation. Something is not adding up here!

Some corporate cultures brand those who take time for themselves as "slackers," not realizing that they are putting their employees' health at jeopardy. People who don't take vacation are more likely to be unhealthy and unhappy (Gump & Matthews, 2000).

The Millennials, or Generation Y (those born after 1980), are constantly connected, but place a high value on their personal time, asking for more flexibility in scheduling their work hours and additional, even unlimited, vacation. Companies have begun incorporating changes to accommodate their youngest workers so as not to lose their valuable contributions to the team (Kwoh, 2012).

Once on vacation, take a vacation from your devices as well. After conducting a survey in which they learned that 85 percent of their guests had been bothered by someone else talking loudly on a phone, Marriott created tech-free zones for seven of their Caribbean and Mexican resorts (Marriott News Center, 2012). These public spots banned cell phones, tablets and laptops to encourage their guests to live in the moment and disconnect. It's more than a small warning sign when a hotel has to force its patrons to enjoy the view.

Deliberately disconnecting creates time to refresh one's mind and spirit, and rejuvenates one's creativity. That vital downtime makes the individual not only a better person but a better employee. Companies that invest in and encourage employee downtime reap the rewards in increased productivity.

Henry Ford was one of the first to discover that worker productivity diminished after forty hours in a work week and permanently set the five-day work week for his company. More companies need to remember that working longer doesn't necessarily result in getting more work done.

And as individuals back away from work, they must make sure that they are not just living in the busyness of the day, but that they are looking at the big picture and making sure that their life is going in the direction that they want. Individuals must live intentionally, not floating like reed on water, but moving with purpose and direction. Reflecting on the previous year's accomplishments, carving out time for vacation and giving time for contemplation and planning throughout the year help create that meaningful life most individuals seek.

And What Does the Future Hold?

The contributors to this book will lay out the sources and costs of workplace stress. The challenge is that the future promises to be more connected, not less. With the prevalence of cloud computing (Microsoft recently released its Office 365 cloud-based office suite, and Google Apps continues to grow its computer base), information is available from any computer or smart phone. Individuals are rarely farther than a few keystrokes or swipes away from their e-mail, spreadsheets and presentations.

Conclusions and Future Study

More than ever it will be incumbent upon us to choose how and when we engage and work, because the work will always be there, chained to us through our portable devices. The benefits of having information at our fingertips come with a cost that, left unchecked, can have serious, detrimental long-term effects. We must learn to wield the double-edged sword of 24/7 constant communication carefully, or risk taking the joy out of work and life.

The busy, frenetic sense of overwhelm that we feel is how our bodies and minds signal us that it is time to pause and take stock. Are you listening? What will you do differently to move from a place of pressure and stress to relaxed control and purpose?

References

Chui, M., Manyika, J., Bughin, J., Dobbs, R., Roxburgh, C., Sarrazin, H., Sands, G., & Westergren, M. (2012). The social economy: Unlocking value and productivity through social technologies. Report McKinsey Global Institute, 30, 151.

Cisco Connected World Technology Report (2012), Gen Y: New dawn for work, play, identity.

Curtis, L. (2012, January 23). Happiness is the new success: Why Millennials are reprioritizing. Forbes/ForbesWoman.

Czerwinski, M., Horvitz, E., & Wilhite, S. (2004). A Diary Study of Task Switching and Interruptions. *Microsoft Research.*

Dries, N. (2011). The meaning of career success: avoiding reification through a closer inspection of historical, cultural and ideological contexts. *Career Development International 16(4)*, 364–384.

Franco, L., Gibbons, J. M., & Barrington, L. (2010, January). I can't get no … job satisfaction, that is. Conference Board.

Gump B. B., & Matthews, K. A. (2000, September–October). Are vacations good for your health? The 9-year mortality experience after the multiple risk factor intervention trial. *Psychosomatic Medicine 62(5)*, pp. 608–612.

Harris Interactive Media Poll (2012). The French take 30 days off, Americans take 10: Expedia's 2012 vacation deprivation study reveals stark differences in national attitudes towards vacation. Retrieved from http://www.expediainc.com/news-release/?aid=122977&fid=785&yy=2012.

Hughes, S. (2012, October 25). I banned all internal e-mails at my company for a week. Forbes/Leadership.

Janati, M. (2012, April 22). U.S. abandoning happiness and health for paychecks. *Washington Times.*

Kwoh, L. (2012, August 22). More firms bow to Generation Y's demands. Retrieved from http://www.wsj.com/articles/SB10000872396390440443713704577603302382190374.

Marriott News Center (2012, December 12). Marriott and Renaissance Caribbean & Mexico resorts offering tech-free zones for travelers who crave a braincation. Retrieved from http://news.marriott.com/2012/12/page/3/.

Virtanen, M., Heikkila, K., Jokela, M., Ferrie, J. E., Batty, G. D., Vahtera, J., & Kivimaki, M. (2012). Long working hours and coronary heart disease: A systematic review and meta-analysis. *American Journal of Epidemiology 176*(7), pp. 586–596.

Wilson, G. (2005, April 22). E-mails "hurt IQ more than pot." Retrieved from http://www.cnn.com/2005/WORLD/europe/04/22/text.iq/.

3

COMMUNICATING WORK–LIFE SUPPORT

Implications for Organizations, Employees, and Families

Jamie Ladge

Introduction

A father rushes out of the office to his infant's day care before it closes at six p.m. A marathon runner finds time to run ten miles before heading off to work. A government employee hurries to catch the shuttle from Washington D.C. to get home on time for his mother's eightieth birthday. A young executive steals an hour of her lunch break to handle a few last-minute wedding arrangements. A college student juggles employment, a full-time course load, and several extracurricular activities. All of the examples are representative how most of us live and work today. We are seeking to strike a balance between our work and non-work lives. The term "work–life balance" is defined as the ability of an individual to be "equally involved and satisfied" with their work role and family (or other significant non-work) role (Greenhaus & Singh, 2003).

The concept of work–life balance was made popular in the United States during the 1970s when organizations were instituting new government mandates which paved the way for a host of organizational policies to aid working mothers, as societal norms shifted from traditional single-income households to dual-income households (Bianchi & Milkie, 2010; Coontz, 2000; Hochschild, 1989). In addition to societal shifts, a number of other factors led to the work–life conversation, including increasing use of technology, effects of globalization on competition and productivity, company layoffs and the rise of women and minorities in the workplace (Boswell & Olson-Buchanan, 2007; Hall & Hall, 1976; Hammer et al., 1997). In response to these changing demographics and societal shifts, organizations became increasingly pressured to adopt policies and practices to assist workers with their work–life needs. "Work–life balance practices in the workplace are therefore those that, intentionally or otherwise, increase the flexibility and autonomy of the worker in negotiating their attention (time) and presence in the workplace, while work–life balance policies exist where those practices are intentionally designed and implemented" (Gregory & Milner, 2009, pp. 1–2).

Some forty years later, the work–life balance conversation continues to evolve giving rise to numerous books, research reports and academic articles on the subject. Work–life scholarship has focused largely on the balancing of an individual's work and life domains, and what organizations can do to facilitate this process. Recently, the terminology has been debated among researchers suggesting that the term "work–life balance" is seemingly outdated, suggesting the term "work–life integration" is more fitting and encouraging (Gregory & Milner, 2009). Balance implies that something has to give on either side or that one "can't have it all," while integration implies a mutual and positive support between the two domains (Lewis & Cooper, 2005; Rapoport et al., 2002). Where the two sets of terms converge is on the notion that each sphere impacts the other, for better or worse. We use the term "work–life integration" throughout the chapter.

Most of the attention regarding issues of work–life integration has been focused on the conflict that arises when pressures from work roles are incompatible with pressures from non-work roles (Greenhaus & Beutell, 1985; Parasuraman et al., 1996). However, the spillover effects between work and non-work spheres in both directions are not always negative, as more recent studies have shown. Positive work-to-family or family-to-work spillover (also referred to as enrichment) arises when elements of work roles positively influence elements of non-work roles, and vice versa (Carson et al., 2006; Greenhaus & Powell, 2006, 2010). Rothbard (2001) found instances of both depletion and enrichment among individuals' work and family domains. Interestingly, some gender differences have been observed in these spillover effects. Women experienced depletion in the work-to-family direction, while men experienced enrichment in this direction. In the family-to-work direction, women experienced enrichment.

Much has changed in the dynamics of the workforce since the concept of work–life balance and integration came into existence. While work–life balance was initially viewed as an issue for parents, demographic and generational shifts, technological advances and the globalization of the workforce have fostered a need for all types of workers to strive for better integration between work and non-work spheres. The drivers of these changes have pushed organizations to make work–life integration a global concern for all workers, in their efforts to support the whole person. For example, the millennial generation desires flexibility—it's no longer something that only working women with young children request (Schwabel, 2011; MomCorps Study, 2012). Increasingly, employees want to be held accountable not "for where or when they work, but for the results they produce" (The 2012 Guide to Bold New Ideas for Making Work Work, 2012, p. 6). Additionally, working fathers are reporting just as much work–family conflict as ever before, according to a recent study by the Families and Work Institute (Aumann, Galinsky, & Matos, 2011).

In response to the changing demographics, many organizations have established a wide range of policies and programs to support work–life integration. Such policies include flexible work arrangements, reduced work schedules, family and medical leaves, paid vacations and other time-off programs, health and wellness programs including reduced rates at fitness facilities and health screenings, access to on- or off-site child- or eldercare, job sharing and telecommuting. These examples are among the more popular policies and programs organizations offer to support their employees. Despite these widespread offerings of work–life policies and programs, studies show that utilization rates remain low. That is, although employees have access to these benefits, they often don't use them (Allen, 2001; Thompson et al., 1999). Now we will explore why work–life integration policies tend to fall short, and suggest that companies' use rates are low as a result of the organization's problematic communication of these programs and policies.

Why Organizational Policies Fall Short—Ideal Worker Norms

While work–life integration issues are a concern for individuals all over the world, workers in the United States face an even greater concern of trying to meet ideal worker expectations. According to a report by the Sloan Work–Family Policy Network:

> *Workplaces continue to be structured around the image of an ideal worker who starts to work in early adulthood and continues uninterrupted for forty years, taking no time off for child bearing or child rearing, supported by a spouse or family member who takes primary responsibility for family and community. In the last half century, we have moved from a division of labor depending generally on men as breadwinners and women as family caregivers to a way of life in which both men and women are breadwinners. But we have done so without redesigning work or occupational career paths and without making new provisions for family care.*
>
> *(Bailyn, Drago, & Kochan, 2001, p. 6)*

Essentially, this is an American industrial model of work norms that is based on assumptions that face time is necessary, and that in order for employees to be productive they must by observed and supervised.

In general, the social policies in U.S.-based organizations that are shaped by the same societal ideals are lagging social changes, a situation that fosters conflicts between work and non-work domains, particularly when non-work domains include family/childcare. In contrast to the U.S. pattern of work, many other industrialized nations have shorter workweeks and recognize various family needs through employment law (Schor, 1992). For example, in many European countries, paternal leave of fifty-two weeks or above is the norm (Norway, Finland, Sweden, Germany, Czech Republic, Austria and Slovakia), often for each parent

TABLE 3.1 Comparison of Parental Leave and Paid Vacation Policies, Five Countries.

Country	Parental Policy	Paid Vacation
China	No paid parental leave	1–1.9 weeks
France	26–51 weeks	4 or more weeks
Japan	26–51 weeks	1–1.9 weeks
Sweden	52 weeks or more	4 or more weeks
United States of America	No paid parental leave	No paid vacation

Source: World Legal Rights Data Center (http://raisingtheglobalfloor.org)

sequentially, while in the U.S., there is no guaranteed parental paid leave (World Legal Rights Data Centre, http://raisingtheglobalfloor.org/policies/map). Americans may be surprised to learn that the U.S. is one of four nations in the world that do not guarantee paid family leave for maternity, paternity or adoption (Fass, 2009). Table 3.1 illustrates further contrasts between U.S. labor conditions and those of other industrialized economies on guaranteed parental leave that may include both maternal and paternal leaves and paid vacation.

The contrasts reinforce the U.S. ideal worker standard, and thus the limited level to which Americans can maintain a successful integration between work and family life as compared to other nations.

Who Is Responsible for Work–Life Integration?

Increasing the level of work–life integration is a complex challenge that requires input from all stakeholders in the organization. The fundamental requirements for such efforts to be successful include an organizational culture in which trust levels are high, a culture in which there is significant respect and reciprocity among all stakeholders and a culture with high levels of inclusiveness (Ryan & Kossek, 2008). Such a culture is one that values individual differences, supports blending work and non-work demands, and promotes involvement of all employees where employees feel accepted regardless of their non-work identities (Ryan & Kossek, 2008). While organizations may strive for a family-friendly climate, a debate looms over who is ultimately responsible for work–life integration: the employer, the employee or both.

We argue both the organization and employee are responsible for work–life integration programs. Organizations are responsible for developing universal programs that support individual needs. When organizations implement work–life programs, such as compressed workweeks or part-time benefits, the organization must rethink and retrain the performance evaluations within these programs. Rather than the number of hours and company face time, the employee's productivity and results are held more accountable. It's the organization's responsibility to inform and train employees utilizing these programs. However, work–life programs need to be universal and should be designed in such a way that they can be customized to fit individual needs.

Individual employees are responsible for using work–life programs appropriately, designing their programs so that they do not hinder the organization, and working so that they add value to the organization. Most importantly, individuals must feel comfortable to ask for changes without fear their request will be denied, or that they will be stereotyped for using work–life integration programs. Such stereotyping does exist, and often it is a manifestation of resistance to the implementation of work–life integration programs. For example, employees who utilize flexible work arrangements or work part-time may be stereotyped as someone who is less dedicated or committed to his/her job (Allen, 2001). While it's the individual's responsibility to take initiative towards achieving work–life integration, it may also be difficult for him/her to achieve without the support of a mentor and/or advocate inside the organization. Individuals need to witness role models or work peers in their organization who have successfully integrated work and family. Role models and/or mentors can extend guidance and/or tips on integration, as well as strategies on asking for help, managing alternative schedules or any other changes that result in utilizing work–life programs. By witnessing other employees integrating work–life programs, individuals will understand what programs to ask for and how to correctly ask for them.

Beyond the organization and employees, the U.S. government plays a significant role in the evolution of work–life integration. Presently, the government's contributions to work–life integration at federal and state levels tend to be scattered among different agencies and actors; they are uncoordinated with other governmental programs and targeted at low-income workers or, as is the case with the Family Leave Medical Act (FMLA), applicable to only a part of the labor force. There is no clear government vision or set of objectives on the work–life relationship (Bailyn et al., 2001, p. 40). Yet both state and federal governments could play an important catalytic role in building work–life integration in the private sector. Currently, the government ensures that the most basic work–life standards are available to all citizens such as in the case of parental leave.

MIT professor and work–life expert Lotte Bailyn recommends that government take actions on seven initiatives:

1. Fund care leave programs, as is done in other industrialized economies;
2. Provide incentives for high-quality part-time employment;
3. Mandate employee participation in the design of work–life balance programs;
4. Establish incentives for flexible hours;
5. Mandate portable benefits;
6. Establish quality child- and eldercare work; and
7. Establish national-level work and family councils (Bailyn et al., 2001, p. 51).

At this point of the chapter we have looked at the context in which work–life integration exists and the vast set of challenges and opportunities it presents in organizations, in individuals and in public policy. We now move to a discussion that focuses specifically on how U.S.-based organizations have traditionally fostered work–life support and the impact of communications these supports have had on an employee's work and non-work selves, health and well-being.

Fostering Work–Life Support in Organizations

We think of work–life integration programs as collections of both formal policies and procedures (structural) and the informal supports (cultural) employees have in the work context. Here we look first at the formal aspect of these programs and their communication, and then at the informal cultural communication that surrounds these same programs.

Structural support consists of formal policies and procedures that organizations develop to shape the programs, usually communicated in writing and available to all employees, although employee knowledge of the existence of these policies is sometimes lacking. Recent surveys suggest that 25 percent of employers make "a real and ongoing effort to inform employees of available assistance for managing work and family responsibilities" (Families and Work Institute, 2012 National Study of Employers, 2012).

Such formal policies are used by organizations to recruit and retain workers and also to minimize work–family conflicts for employees. For example, some family responsiveness programs might include compressed workweeks, family and medical leave, onsite/backup childcare and other programs designed to reduce work–family conflict. How these programs affect workers is explored in a recent study (Ladge, 2008) of women's work re-entry after the birth of their first child. Women's re-entry experiences indicate that the organization's formal policies and programs designed to target work–family responsiveness were a critical component of women's re-establishment of their professional selves.

Organizations communicate structural support through formal institutionalized methods such as written documentation (human resources manuals and SOPs) and seminars (human resources training programs, work–life seminars, company website and company emails). Such documentation may be readily available to the employees, or they may learn of it by word-of-mouth and then have to ask for it. How changes in programs are communicated is part of the structural support system. Often work–life integration programs are available to a subset of employees, such as those classified as exempt workers (Fair Labor Standards Act), those in professional graded positions, and those classified as permanent full time. The written documentation that constitutes structural support for work–life integration programs tends to be formal in tone and downward in direction.

We now address a brief review of the benefits of these formal work–life programs, which are many and broadly dispersed, since they have the potential to reach all stakeholders, especially organizations, individual employees and employees' family members. One of the major benefits, beyond the more evident employee benefits, is the fostering of inclusive workplaces or the perception of inclusion (Gasorek, 2000; Mor Barak, 2005; Ryan & Kossek, 2008). This benefit is in part because when an individual's needs are recognized and addressed, the individual is "likely to feel accepted and valued (Pelled et al., 1999; Robertson, 2006) regardless of whether they are single or partnered, have children or not, are hetero-sexual or not, work full-time or a reduced load, or are present daily or tele-commute" (Ryan & Kossek, 2008, p. 296). Work–life integration programs also foster positive employee attitudes and behaviors (Lee et al., 2002), improve quality of life and health and wellness (Greenhaus & Allen, 2011) and increase overall engagement and productivity (English, 2010). All of these benefits are argued to be in the business interest of the organization.

Formal work–life integration programs also have several deficits that we should recognize. First, as mentioned previously, utilization rates are low. This hesitancy to use programs has been explained as a result of employee fear of not meeting ideal work norms (Allen, 2001; Williams, 2000). In a comprehensive global study, potential program users report negative consequences and fear including: unfavorable job assignments, negative performance reviews, negative comments from coworkers or supervisors, exclusion from business or social networks, being denied promotion, exclusion from consideration for career-advancing assignments and having commitment to job questioned (Linkow, Civian, & WFD Consulting, 2011).

Another deficit of formal work–life integration programs is their frequent standardization across portions of the organization. We hold that if work–life integration is to make its most robust impact on the organization, a one-size-fits-all approach will fall short. There needs to be a wide array of programs because there is a wide array of individual needs and family situations (Friedman, 2008; Harrington & Ladge, 2009). Standardization for work–life integration programs should only serve as a baseline and it works only when aligned with an employee's specific work–life needs. Programs should be designed with flexibility so that individual requirements based on a range of work–life circumstances can be met. Finally, there is one last deficit to mention: work–life integration programs may counteract cultural norms and may differ from managerial and peer expectations.

The communication of work–life integration programs is not limited to formal organizational communication. It also is carried throughout the organization informally, in the organization's culture and through informal communications among colleagues. In the study of women returning to work after the birth of their first child, cultural communication around work–life support was shown to affect how women began to conceptualize what it meant to be a mother, a pro-fessional and a working mother, and how effective they would be in these roles (Ladge, 2008). In fact, research has shown that the informal culture within organizations may shape employees' behaviors and experiences within their organizations to a greater extent than do formal policies (Bailyn, Rapoport, Kolb, & Fletcher, 1996; Eaton, 2003).

Unlike the formal communications in support of work–life integration programs, an organization's cultural communications may be multidirectional and iterative, with patterns of informal communications including personal exchanges with colleagues and supervisors at work about matters that are non-work related. These patterns of informal communications may be highly positive and include encouragement and advice from colleagues and supervisors. Conversely, they may invoke negative judgments and expectations from individuals at work related to, in the case of returning new mothers, ideal mothering and professional norms and expectations. These judgments and expectations often get communicated to women through passing comments, through implicit actions of others, such as leaving women out of decision-making processes or social events, or through explicit remarks that are derogatory towards working mothers. So, while organizations may espouse various norms and expectations towards working mothers, patterns of informal interactions from organizational members may contradict the goals of more formal organizational norms and policies that support work–life integration. For example, an organization may have formal support for working mothers by offering flexibility and other formal work–family responsive policies and pro-grams, yet direct supervisors may informally denounce the usage of such programs by making disparaging statements about people who use them (Allen, 2001; Thompson et al., 1999).

Unfortunately, often these informal modes of communications can counteract any positive effects from the formal efforts, and even worse, they have the potential to influence an employee's sense of self, creating a greater sense of work–life conflict for the individual. Several recent studies have described the ways in which informal communications at work influence the extent to which fathers and mothers grapple with their roles as parents and professionals.

One study (Ladge, Clair, & Greenberg, 2012) found that comments from peers at work that were seemingly negative caused anxiety and self-questioning of a mother's ability to balance work and family roles. As reported by one woman in the study, *"a few of my staff members are like 'well, how are you going to do that?' And I was like 'I don't know, we'll figure it out when it happens.' I mean (they were) not just being a jerk about it, but they were just kind of wondering 'how are you going to do that and this.' I'm like 'it's called babysitter, I don't know, we'll figure it out, don't worry about it, don't stress me out'"* (016). These comments perpetuate stereotypes and assumptions around working mothers and whether they can do it all. However, not all informal communications of work–life support and programs are perceived as negative. The same study of pregnant working women showed that seemingly positive comments facilitated a sense of empowerment. As another participant from the pregnancy study pointed out, *"because I have such great support, Company XX has assumed that I can make it work. I can find a way to make it work"* (021).

Similarly, another study of new mothers recently returning from maternity leave found that as women transition back to work, their supervisors, work peers and other colleagues may more subtly impose their own ideologies and norms about working mothers. Such patterns of informal communications have been described as a means to test a re-entrant's role commitment (Millward, 2006). Organizational members may use language that implies lack of support for work–family needs in ways that may leave women feeling conflicted about how they should prioritize their roles as mothers and professionals (Buzzanell & Liu, 2005). Sturm (2001) refers to these subtle, hidden messages as *second-generation bias*. The bias is manifested in an individual's beliefs about mothers and their place in society. In some instances, peers who are also working parents may offer guidance, support and coping strategies while others may make negative comments or evidence-biased assumptions about working mothers and their maternal commitment. For example, a female boss who has no children and works extensive hours repeatedly reminds the new mother about her own concerted decision to stay focused on her career rather than on a family. Or a male boss who constantly reminds the new mother that his wife is a stay-at-home mom. Both scenarios may send negative signals suggesting that a woman is not fully committed to her career or that a woman's place is in the home once she has children. Also, colleagues may inquire of women upon their return why they came back to work, assuming that most women prefer to stay at home. These communications actually were vocalized by supervisors, peers and even other mothers at work. Table 3.2 provides examples of these subtle biases that may be inferred from such informal communications.

Interestingly, fathers have very different informal communications with their supervisors, peers and coworkers that are perceived predominately as positive. This was evident in an interview-based study of thirty-one men, all of whom were relatively new fathers. As one dad explained his interaction with his boss, *"So, one time … [my new boss] ran into me leaving at four o'clock with my son in the*

TABLE 3.2

Communicated by:	Comment	Perceived Bias
Supervisors	"She was like, 'Now are you sure; you don't want to be one of those women who come back for a month and then leaves because you can't give the best.'"	Assumption that all working mothers are less committed or leave after having a baby
Peers	"There were comments like, 'Oh, you're back; oh, you're back full-time?' And, 'oh, they won't let you come back part-time? I'm sure they'll let you come back part-time.'"	Assumption that working mothers only work part-time
Other moms at work	"But everyone around me just said, 'It must be so hard … oh, when I came back, I cried and cried,' but I didn't."	Assumption that new mothers are emotional and can't have a life outside of work

stroller. And you know his reaction was not you know 'Where are you going? You know you have work to do.' It was like: 'oh ... congratulations. Is this little Gerald?' You know ... because in his mind, it was completely fine." Other men described how in their interactions with peers, becoming a father lends itself to an established sense of credibility and maturity. Sam, an executive from a financial services firm who became a first-time father at an age slightly older than the norm, explained, *"They looked at me as 'Sam's finally getting serious' and 'he's finally one of us now.'"* To Sam, this meant that he was now part of a club of other parents in his workplace, and he now had a special bond (of having kids) with them. Another participant from this same study claimed that becoming a father meant, *"I think certain people get some level of respect when folks have a family and they are able to balance both work and family obligations and it's something that makes them successful."*

Impact of Formal and Informal Communication of Work–Life Support On Individual Identity and Well-Being

How organizations communicate about work–life integration programs, through both formal and informal means, can influence how those who desire to take advantage of such policies feel about themselves. In particular, new parents may already be feeling a sense of identity threat and vulnerability around their work and non-work identities. As described above, the transition to motherhood in an organizational context has been described as a process of individual sense-making through interactions with others (Bailey, 1999; Ladge, 2008; Millward, 2006). In the study of new mothers re-entering their workplaces after maternity leave, many of the women described certain interactions with peers that seemed like tests of their commitment to roles as mothers and professionals. Such comments tended to be based on traditional ideals of "good mothering" as intensive and child-centric, because this is the dominant mothering ideology in North America (Hayes, 1996). Some interactions and communications with colleagues signaled an expectation that mothers should stay at home and that career-oriented women are bad mothers, nonconformists (Hattery, 2001) or reluctant mothers (Gerson, 1985). It appears that these more subtle interactions had a significant psychological impact on women during the re-entry by altering their thoughts, feelings and images ascribed to being a mother. These comments invoked certain ideals of motherhood that influenced how women defined and evaluated themselves as mothers, particularly at a time when their identities were in flux, and how they thought about work–life integration options.

The degree to which these patterns of informal communications that are part of the organizational culture are perceived as positive or negative has implications for how individuals think about their work and non-work identities. And in this way, it influences how they think about the organization's work–life integration programs. Jenny's experience represents one example of how patterns of informal interactions perceived as negative can diminish women's professional self-concept.

Jenny negatively perceived the comments her peers made about her coming back to work full-time. She explained that her colleagues were drawing inaccurate assumptions about working mothers in her institution—"It was almost as if anyone who had a baby went part-time," but that wasn't in fact the case. It also wasn't an option that Jenny had considered until it was raised by her colleagues, and this led her to begin questioning her choices. Conversely, Amy's positive experience and interactions with colleagues and supervisors made her feel welcome and less pigeonholed as a working mother: "My mothering identity has had an impact on my professional identity in the way that now I'm in the club with mothers and fathers at work, so we can talk about that. Almost everybody has kids so I think in some ways it makes me feel less threatening to people." The fathers from the dads study largely expressed experiences similar to Amy's experience. All of the communications they had with colleagues around their child or non-work life were perceived as very positive. Thus, a gender divide appears to exist.

The vulnerability of a woman's identity and the struggles she faces may also lead her to internalize comments from others as negative even when they are meant to be supportive. For example, Sarah, a nonprofit manager who would bring her son to work one day a week, explained, "I do still feel like, when he's here with me, some guilt sometimes about what the staff think and if I'm not fully doing my job. Not that they've ever made any [negative comments] other than they want to see him and they think it's great, and they want to come and play with him and take him around for a few minutes. So it's not that they're actively [critiquing], it's just self-imposed." Additionally, patterns of informal interactions also destabilized maternal and professional identities in such a way that created conflict between the two identities for women but not for men. When women were confronted by others who questioned their commitment levels, especially if they came back in a reduced-schedule capacity, they began to feel a greater sense of conflict about who they were or should be as mothers and professionals. In response to others' reactions at work, women reflected on how things "used to be" before they had their child (e.g., the amount of time and effort they could spend at work before) or considered the current state of how they were handling the balance of childcare and work. For example, the comments that Danny received from other mothers about how they cried and she didn't during re-entry led her to feel confused about who she should be as a working mother. On one hand, she felt relieved that she was able to transition back to work without feeling guilty about leaving her child behind, but on the other hand these comments made her question whether she had made the right choices and whether she was a good mom. The pressure from her peers had built up in such a way that she decided to leave the firm several months following her re-entry to take on a more senior-level position at a different firm where she chose not to reveal that she was a mother.

These informal communications from supervisors and peers, while seemingly harmless, may invoke stereotypes and biases about working mothers that may be interpreted as a lack of work–life support. While unintentional, these patterns of informal communications from supervisors and peers at work have the power to influence one's efficacy beliefs, in other words, how good a working parent feels he/she is and can be as both a parent and a professional. This process is likely to be facilitated by social comparisons made with other working parents in their organization (Festinger, 1954). A common source of self-efficacy is role modeling or learning vicariously from others (Bandura, 1997). When there are working parents at work whom they view as good mothers or fathers, these working parents may serve as role models helping to facilitate a greater sense of parenting efficacy.

It was evident from the study of mothers and pregnant women that their return to work fostered a change in how supervisors were treating them now that they were mothers, which led them to question their abilities to perform their work roles. Men did not experience any negative treatment with respect to becoming a father in their organizational contexts. The differential treatment experienced by the mothers was evident in the comments that their supervisors made about the re-entrant's commitment levels and the assumptions about their work ethic. For example, Andrea, who worked for a recording studio and had come back part-time, analyzed her situation: *"The interoffice jokes still mostly don't include me, but the ones that do all seem to culminate in some remark about my being a new mom. For example, my boss apologized in an email for saying something disparaging about an old studio ad that I designed. I jokingly responded, 'No worries, I'll just go about quietly developing a complex.' He replied, 'Good, good. You're becoming a mother already.' It was innocuous on the surface, but I think I correctly interpret it as subtle evidence that my being a mom has affected how I'm perceived at work."* For Andrea, these comments had a profound influence on her ability to do her job effectively, giving way to a Pygmalion effect whereby expectations of others subtly shaped her behavior (Livingston, 2003). In other words, managers or peers who treat or perceive new mothers at re-entry as less capable based on their new home roles can cause new mothers to actually feel less efficacious and begin to call into question how good a job they can do in their professional role, particularly when others may view them as less committed or ambitious, as was the case with Andrea.

On the flip side, when patterns of informal communications at re-entry were viewed in a very positive light, they had the power to make the re-entry experience much better. Several of the women took cues from others during re-entry, and any positive feedback from others fostered their efficacy beliefs. One participant described that she hadn't realized she was doing a good job until she heard it from other people at work. When women heard from others at work that they were doing well, they tended to feel better about themselves and their working mother status. Robin explained, *"But I got a really warm welcome when I came back. People were excited to see me and they said that the consultant who was here did a great job but they really missed me, and that felt good. It felt like maybe it doesn't matter that I don't remember everything. They are really glad I am here."* Additionally, many expressed the difficulty in getting positive feedback from taking care of an

TABLE 3.3: Identity and Efficacy Questions Raised by Parents in Response to Formal and Informal Communications of Work–Life Support

	Identity Questions	Efficacy Questions
Formal Communication of Policies and Programs	How do I maintain my professional image while developing a parent self?	Can I do it all?
Patterns of Informal Communications	Who am I? Who should I be?	Am I an ideal parent? Am I an ideal worker?

infant and the desire to get encouragement at work. As Ginny put it, *"Professionally, you just get instant feedback about doing a good job whereas at home you don't, and just the interaction you have with colleagues and conversation with peers and adults on a consistent basis is refreshing and nice to come back to, as well as to be intellectually challenged because you don't get that with an infant."*

Table 3.3 above shows how various communications can influence the degree of questioning individuals experience around their sense of self as parents and professionals. When communications around structural work–life supports are perceived as positive, parents should experience less self-questioning because taking advantage of such policies and programs is seen as a nonissue. That is, the informal communications actually serve to facilitate work–life integration. Conversely, when communications around structural work-life supports are perceived as negative, employees feel less confident in their work and personal selves due to a need to preserve and protect their work self over their non-work self identities. They also are more likely to question whether they can "do it all" with respect to integrating work and non-work lives.

Positive interactions among peers and managers will facilitate less questioning around one's sense of self as a professional and parent, and will foster a sense of value as an ideal worker and ideal parent. Conversely, informal interactions perceived as negative will have detrimental effects on one's sense of self and efficacy, leading individuals to question who they are, who they should be and how they can fulfill ideal worker and parent expectations.

Work-Life Support Communication Effects: A Summary

Formal and informal communications of work–life supports send both direct and indirect signals to individuals. From the studies we draw from in this chapter, it appears that women are more influenced by the informal communication in the organization than are men, because of perceived stereotypes and assumptions that mothers "can't do it all." However, just because men don't feel the informal threat, it's not good news for fathers. Fathers are not always viewed as targets for such integration programs, so if working fathers want to utilize such programs, they will be less likely to because it's seen as something that is "not for them."

Such perceptions may increase their level of work–family conflict and the inability to integrate work and family domains effectively.

Research has long supported the idea that perceived organizational support strongly influences job satisfaction (Eisenberger, Fasolo, & Davis-LaMastro, 1990; Holtzman & Glass, 1999) and overall employee health and well-being (Allen, 2001; Anderson, Coffey, & Byerly, 2002). New parents and others experiencing significant work–life challenges need to feel supported by their organizations in order to feel confident and identify with their multiple roles both inside and outside their work organizations. When employees lack the confidence or struggle to reconcile their work and non-work identities, they will experience greater conflict. In turn, they will also be more likely to lower their career aspiration, change or quit their jobs (Bailey, 1999; Waite et al., 1986). Thus it is in the organization's interest to ensure the communications of its work–life practices are effectively meeting employee needs and expectations and, as it is able, to influence the organization's informal culture's support of work–life programs. In the last section of the chapter, we will explore ways that organizations can improve communication of their work–life practices such that employees and employers can reap mutual gain.

Going Forward

We offer several suggestions for organizations to improve their communication of work–life support. First, organizations and managers need to develop an awareness of how institutional forces can shape employees' experiences and non-work identities (Ramarajan & Reid, forthcoming). Second, while many organizations have programs and policies to aid employees with work–life integration, many of these programs fall short in helping employees actually address the individual challenges. One-size-fits-all policies don't work. Organizations need to consider the whole person, meeting the demographic and generational shifts in the workplace. Frequent needs assessments are a way to stay in touch with evolving employee needs.

One recent study actually debunked the need for organizations to provide any format for work–life balance for employees (Bloom et al., 2009). Instead, the authors argued that what is necessary is good management (Bloom et al., 2009). Certainly good management is a necessary ingredient, but we wonder if it alone is sufficient. Additionally, managers and coworkers need to provide support for work–life integration in ways other than the formal programs. They need to be aware in offering advice or comments that may alter women's beliefs, values, emotions and behaviors. Managers may be unaware of their subtle biases, so organizations may benefit from developing extensive training and mentoring programs to raise awareness of the impact such manager biases may have on employees. We recommend that managers work with individuals to develop an individual plan for re-entry rather than follow a one-size-fits-all strategy. The plan should be revisited on a regular basis to ensure that the employee is satisfied with the plan and that the manager is following through on the program.

Lastly, there is a bias that persists within organizations against those individuals who take advantage of work–life policies. The roots of these role expectations need to be challenged within organizations. In the case of new mothers, women are torn between the gendered expectations and the suggested competitive nature of their maternal and professional roles. Organizations would benefit in recognizing that they play a significant role in shaping how women react to these expectations. In the study of new mothers, the majority of women only began to question their decisions to return to work when they perceived others were implicitly or explicitly raising the issue. A general shift in the organizational mindset of how people view working women needs to occur, not in a way that ignores the internal challenges that women are facing, but instead in a way that deals directly with the employee. Additionally, although we may assume that organizations and individuals are well past stereotypes of working mothers because there is a high degree of women represented in the workforce, that is not the case. Many studies suggest a bias still exists. Organizations and managers need to be aware of the different forms of bias, particularly in their subtle forms.

For organizations to truly be effective in communicating support for the work–life integration of their employees, a cultural shift is needed that moves away from simple implementation of policies and programs that accommodate employee needs (Harrington & Ladge, 2009). Instead, organizations should consider the external environment, including the changing demographics of the workforce. Organizations would do well to develop work–life initiatives that are part of a broader strategy to create a culture of flexibility that can withstand the constantly changing environment in which they now operate.

References

Allen, T. D. (2001). Family-supportive work environments: The role of organizational perceptions. *Journal of Vocational Behavior, 58*, pp. 414–435.

Anderson, S. E., Coffey, B. S., & Byerly, R. T. (2002). Formal organizational initiatives and informal workplace practices: Links to work–family conflict and job-related outcomes. *Journal of Management, 28*(6), pp. 787–810.

Aumann, K., Galinsky, E., & Matos, K. (2011). *The new male mystique.* New York, New York: Families and Work Institute.

Bailey, L. (1999). Refracted selves? A study of changes in self-identity in the transition to motherhood. *Sociology, 33*(2), pp. 335–352.

Bailyn, L., Drago, R., & Kochan, T. A. (2001). Integrating work and family life: A holistic approach. *Sloan Work–Family Policy Network, MIT Sloan School of Management*, pp. 1–66.

Bailyn, L., Rapoport, R., Kolb, D., & Fletcher, J. K. (1996). Re-linking work and family: A catalyst for organizational change. *Unpublished manuscript, Working Paper #3892–96, MIT Sloan School of Management*, Cambridge, MA.

Bandura, A. (1997). *Self-efficacy in changing societies.* New York, New York: Cambridge University Press.

Bianchi, S. M., & Milkie, M. A. (2010). Work and family research in the first decade of the 21st century. *Journal of Marriage and Family, 72*.

Bloom, N., Kretschmer, T., & Reenen, J. V. (2009). Work–life balance, management practices, and productivity. In R. B. Freeman & K. L. Shaw (Eds.), *International differences in the business practices and productivity of firms* (p. 15–54). Chicago: University of Chicago Press.

Bloom, N., & Van Reenen, J. (2006). Management practices, work-life balance and productivity: A review of recent evidence. *Oxford Review of Economic Policy, 22(4)*, pp. 457–481.

Boswell, W., & Olson-Buchanan, J. (2007). The use of communication technologies after hours: The role of work attitudes and work–life conflict. *Journal of Management, 33.4*, pp. 592–608.

Buzzanell, P.M., & Liu, M. (2005). Struggling with maternity leave policies and practices: A poststructuralist feminist analysis of gendered organizing. *Journal of Applied Communication Research, 33*, pp. 1–25.

Carson, E., Ranzijn, R., Price, D., & Winefield A. (2006). On the scrap heap at 45: The human impact of mature-age unemployment. *Journal of Occupational and Organizational Psychology, 79*, pp. 467–479.

Catalyst. (2012). Catalyst quick take: Work–life: Prevalence, utilization, and benefits. New York, New York: Catalyst.

Coontz, S. (2000). *The way we never were: American families and the nostalgia trap*. New York, New York: Basic Books.

Correll, S. J., Benard, S., & Paik, I. (2007). Getting a job: Is there a motherhood penalty? *American Journal of Sociology, 112*, pp. 1297–1338.

Eaton, S. (2003). If you can use them: Flexibility policies, organizational commitment, and perceived performance. *Industrial Relations, 42*, pp. 145–167.

Eisenberger, R., Fasolo, P. M., & Davis-LaMastro, V. (1990). Effects of perceived organizational support on employee diligence, innovation, and commitment. *Journal of Applied Psychology, 53*, pp. 51–59.

English, L. (2010). *Enhanced employee health, well-being, and engagement through dependent care supports*. A study by Bright Horizons. Watertown, MA.

Families and Work Institute. (2012). *2012 National Study of Employers*. From http://familiesandwork.org/site/research/reports/NSE_2012.pdf.

Fass, S. (2009, March). Paid leave in the States: A critical support for low-wage workers and their families. *National Center for Children in Poverty*. From http://www.nccp.org/publications/pub_864.html.

Festinger, L. (1954). A theory of social comparison processes. *Human Relations, 7*, pp. 117–140.

Friedman, S. (2008). Be a better leader, have a richer life. *Harvard Business Review, 86*, pp. 112–118.

Gasorek, D. (2000). Inclusion at Dun & Bradstreet: Building a high-performing company. *The Diversity Factor*, pp. 25–29.

Gerson, K. (1985). *Hard choices: How woman decide about work, career and motherhood*. Berkeley, California: University of California Press.

Greenhaus, J. H., & Allen, T. D. (2011). Work-family balance: A review and extension of the literature. *Handbook of Occupational Health Psychology, (2)*, pp. 165–183.

Greenhaus, J. H., & Beutell, N. J. (1985). Source of conflict between work and family roles. *Academy of Management Review, 10*, pp. 76–88.

Greenhaus, J. H., & Powell, G. (2006). When work and family are allies: A theory of work–family enrichment. *Academy of Management Review, 31*, pp. 72–92.

Greenhaus, J. H., & Powell, G. (2010). Sex, gender and the work-to-family interface: Exploring negative and positive interdependencies. *Academy of Management Journal, 53,* pp. 513–534.

Greenhaus, J. H., & Singh, R. (2003, February 25). Work-family linkages. A Sloan Work and Family Encyclopedia *entry.* Chestnut Hill, MA: Boston College.

Gregory, A., & Milner, S. (2009). Trade unions and work–life balance: Changing times in France and the UK? *British Journal of Industrial Relations, 47 (1),* pp. 122–146.

Hall, D. T., & Hall, F. S. (1976). What's new in career management. *Organizational Dynamics,* Summer, 17–33.

Hammer, L. B., Allen, E., & Grigsby, T. D. (1997). Work-family conflict in dual-earner couples: Within-individual and crossover effects of work and family. *Journal of Vocational Behavior, 50,* pp. 185–203.

Harrington, B., & Ladge, J. J. (2009). Work-life integration: Present dynamics and future directions for organizations. *Organizational Dynamics, 38,* pp. 148–157.

Hattery, A. J. (2001). *Women, work, and family: Balancing and weaving.* Thousands Oaks, California: Sage Publications Inc.

Hayes, S. (1996). *The cultural contradictions of motherhood.* New Haven, Connecticut: Yale University Press.

Hayman, J. R. (2009). Flexible work arrangements: Exploring the linkages between perceived usability of flexible work schedules and work/life balance. *Journal of Community, Work and Family, 12(3),* pp. 123–138.

Hochschild, A. R. (1989). *The second shift: Working parents and the revolution at home.* New York, New York: Viking.

Hock, E., Gnezda, M. T., & McBride, S. L. (1984). Mothers of infants: Attitudes toward employment following birth of the first child. *Journal of Marriage and the Family, 46,* pp. 435–431.

Holtzman, M., & Glass, J. (1999). Explaining changes in mothers' job satisfaction following childbirth. *Work and Occupations, 25,* pp. 365–404.

Ladge, J. J. (2008). *Becoming a working mother: Identity, efficacy and re-socialization following re-entry.* Retrieved from ProQuest Digital Dissertations.

Ladge, J., Clair, J., & Greenberg, D. (2012). Cross-domain identity transition during liminal periods: Constructing multiple selves as "professional and mother" during pregnancy. *Academy of Management Journal, 55(6),* pp. 1449–1471.

Lee, M. D., Hourguet, P. G., McDemid, S. M., Cooper, C. L., & Burke, R. J. (2002). Reduced-load work arrangements: The changing nature of professional and managerial work. In C.L. Cooper & R.J. Burke (Eds.), *The new world of work: Challenges and opportunities* (pp. 137–156). Malden, MA: Blackwell Publishers Ltd.

Lewis, S., & Cooper, C. (2005). *Work–life integration: Case studies of organizational change.* Chichester: Wiley.

Linkow, P., Civian, J., & WFD Consulting. (2011, May 18). Global Study of Men and Women Work-Life Integration. *Worlds Work.com.* Retrieved from: http://www.worldatwork.org.

Livingston, J. S. (2003). Pygmalion in management. *Harvard Business Review, 81(1),* pp. 97–106.

Millward, L. J. (2006). The transition to motherhood in an organizational context: An interpretative phenomenological analysis. *Journal of Occupational and Organizational Psychology, 79,* pp. 315–333.

MomCorps. (2012). Momcorps study. New York, New York: MomCorps.

Mor Barak, M. E. (2005). *Managing diversity: Toward a globally inclusive workplace.* Thousands Oaks, California: Sage Publications Inc.

Parasuraman, S., Purohit, Y. S., Godshalk, V. M., & Beutell, N. J. (1996). Work and family variables, entrepreneurial career success and psychological well-being. *Journal of Vocational Behavior, 48,* pp. 275–300.

Pelled, L. H., Eisenhardt K. M., & Xin, K. R. (1999). Exploring the black box: An analysis of work group diversity, conflict, and performance. *Administrative Science Quarterly, 44(1),* pp. 1–28.

Ramarajan, L., & Reid, E. (forthcoming). Shattering the myth of separate worlds: Negotiating non-work identities at work. *Academy of Management Review.*

Rapoport, R., Bailyn, L., Fletcher, J. K., & Pruitt, B. (2002). *Beyond work–family balance: Advancing gender equity and workplace performance.* San Francisco, CA: Jossey Bass.

Robertson, I. (2006). Family-friendly policies: Help or hindrance? The International Employment Relations Association Conference. Hong Kong: June 19–23.

Rothbard, N. P. (2001). Enriching or depleting? The dynamics of engagement in work and family roles. *Administrative Science Quarterly,* pp. 655–684.

Ryan, A. M., & Kossek, E. E. (2008). Work-life implementation: Breaking down or creating barriers to inclusiveness? *Human Resource Management, 47,* pp. 295–310.

Schor, J. B. (1992). *The overworked American: The unexpected decline of leisure.* New York, New York: Basic Books.

Schwabel, D. (2011, December). The beginning of the end of the 9-to-5 workday? *Time.* Retrieved January 2, 2013, from http://business.time.com/2011/12/21/the-be ginning-of-the-end-of-the-9-to-5-workday/#ixzz2J1MP7auZ.

Sturm, S. (2001). Second generation employment discrimination: A structural approach. *Columbia Law Review, 101,* pp. 458–568.

The 2012 guide to bold new ideas for making work work. (2012). New York, New York: Families and Work Institute.

Thompson, C. A., Beauvais, L. L., & Lyness, K. S. (1999). When work–family benefits are not enough: The influence of work–family culture on benefit utilization, organizational attachment, and work–family conflict. *Journal of Vocational Behavior, 54,* pp. 392–415.

Valcour, P. M., & Ladge, J. J. (2008). Family and career path characteristics as predictors of women's career success outcomes. *Journal of Vocational Behavior, 73(2),* pp. 300–309.

Waite, L. J., Haggstrom, G. W., & Kanouse, D. (1986). The effects of parenthood on the career orientation of young adults. *Social Forces,* 65: 43–73.

Williams, J. (2000). *Unbending gender: Why family and work conflict and what to do about it.* New York, New York: Oxford University Press.

World Legal Rights Data Centre at McGill Institute for Health and Social Policy. (May 2011). Global Policies. *Raising the global floor: Adult labour.* From http://raisingthegloba lfloor.org/policies/map.

4

WHY DO WE BLAME INFORMATION FOR OUR OVERLOAD?

Yoram M. Kalman

DEPARTMENT OF MANAGEMENT AND ECONOMICS, THE OPEN UNIVERSITY OF ISRAEL

It's Not My Fault; It's Information Overload!

> "This is why I am not getting anything done. I am suffering from information overload!" This has been the salvation of writing-blocked tech journalists for 15 years. When you don't know what to write, you can always go down the hall to your editor and say "Hey, I want to do a story about information overload." And the editor, looking up from their overflowing email inbox, says "That's brilliant!" And you always get to do that story, and so for 15 years we've been reading the *same* story about information overload
>
> *(Shirky, 2008).*

This chapter discusses the concept of information overload. Information overload is often cited by researchers, as well as by journalists and consultants, as one of the main causes of work-related pressures. My goal in this chapter is to explore what we refer to when we talk of "information overload," and to suggest that although the workplace pressures attributed to information overload are very real, the concept itself is vague and poorly defined. I then try to isolate the actual causes of the workplace pressures that currently fall under this all-inclusive term, and to unveil two underlying fallacies that hamper our ability to identify and address these causes. These lead me to propose a new agenda for researching and dealing with these causes of workplace pressure.

Information Overload—One Concept, Many Definitions

As already alluded to in the quote by Clay Shirky used at the beginning of this chapter, information overload is a term often used and misused by both laypeople and professionals. What, then, is information overload? An excellent review of the academic literature on the concept of information overload was published by Eppler and Mengis (2004). It reviews dozens of articles that deal with information overload and organizes the findings. I will use the framework offered by Eppler and Mengis to present the concept of information overload: situations in which information overload occurs, definitions of information overload, its causes and symptoms, as well as countermeasures that were suggested to deal with it.

Information Overload Situations

In what situations do people experience information overload? Eppler and Mengis (2004) divide these into three useful groups: (1) information retrieval, organization and analysis processes; (2) decision processes; and (3) communication processes. Let's explore examples from each of these groups. The most obvious example of overload associated with retrieving information, organizing it and analyzing it is that of using search engines for finding information on the Internet (Berghel, 1997). Other publications relate to additional information-seeking activities (Case, 2012) such as analyzing accounting information for signs of financial distress (Chewning & Harrell, 1990), staying up to date on medical articles and guidelines (Hall & Walton, 2004), or marketing activities such as competitor analysis and advertising media decisions (Meyer, 1998). Decision processes that lead to overload range from decisions taken by highly trained professionals such as air traffic controllers (Sperandio, 1978), to the challenge of choosing between the large numbers of alternative products consumers encounter as they shop for everyday items such as breakfast cereals or gourmet jams (Iyengar & Lepper, 2000; Jacoby, 1984). Finally, information overload occurs during all communication processes including emailing (Whittaker & Sidner, 1996; Kalman & Ravid, 2015) and online discussions (Jones, Ravid, & Rafaeli, 2004), as well as during other forms of face-to-face and mediated communication events (Hudson, Christensen, Kellogg, & Erickson, 2002; Sparrow, 2002) such as face-to-face meetings, video conferences or phone-based teleconferences.

Definitions of Information Overload

Eppler and Mengis (2004) identify seven general definitions of information overload which appear in the literature. All of the definitions focus on a specific excess of information which exceeds a given capacity and which leads to a negative consequence. The definitions differ in the capacities and the consequences to which they pay attention. Several of them focus on the limitations of human information processing capacity. They suggest that information overload occurs when this capacity is exceeded, leading to negative consequences such as (1) not utilizing all of the available information for the decision; (2) not utilizing all of the required information in the decision-making process; and (3) stress and confusion. Others focus on time as the limiting factor and suggest that overload occurs when there isn't enough time to process the information. Others still focus on the subjective negative experience of decision-makers who suffer stress, overstimulation and anxiety, which they attribute to being overloaded with information.

As is evident from these attempts to make sense of the many different definitions of information overload, the concept is not well defined. Consequently, it is not surprising that information overload is difficult to measure and study. The concept has several objective components such as the amount of information and the time consumed processing the information. It also has some subjective components such as decision quality, sense of stress or satisfaction. Moreover, some of the components are not independent and might be influenced by the amount of information. For example, it is not clear how information processing ability is influenced by the amount of information available (e.g., Streufert, Suedfeld, & Driver, 1965).

One of the more useful illustrations of the information overload concept is the inverted U-curve (e.g., Hwang & Lin, 1999). Figure 4.1 illustrates how information overload occurs when a specific desired outcome requires the input of information, and when the quality of the outcomes improves, at least initially, as the amount of information increases (region a). Like most processes that have inputs and outputs, information processing too exhibits the phenomenon of decreasing returns (or decreasing marginal returns), namely that as inputs are added, the quality of the output does not increase linearly and shows saturation (region b). Finally, more input actually has the harmful effect of negatively impacting the output, and the direction of the graph starts to drop (region c).

This phenomenon of "too much of a good thing" is not unique to information. An obvious example would be food consumption and health. Living creatures require an adequate amount of food in order to sustain their health, and lack of food leads to malnutrition and hunger. Nevertheless, too much food leads to obesity and health hazards. Similarly, when it comes to weather, a lack of sufficient precipitation leads to drought damages, while too much precipitation leads to flood damages.

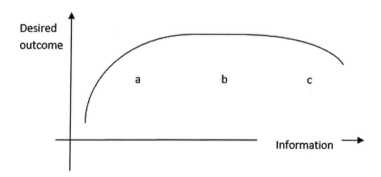

FIGURE 4.1 The inverted U-curve of information overload, detailing region a (decreasing returns), region b (saturation) and region c (inversion).

A good demonstration of the ambiguity of the information overload concept is the large number of concepts used synonymously with it or which are closely associated with it. These include: information fatigue syndrome (McCune, 1998); cognitive overload (Kirsh, 2000); technostress (Ayyagari et al., 2011); data smog (Shenk, 1997); technology crowding (Karr-Wisniewski & Lu, 2010); sensory overload (Lipowski, 1975); information anxiety (Wurman, 2000); info(rmation) glut (Denning, 2006); continuous partial attention ("Continuous Partial Attention," n.d.); attention deficit trait (Hallowell, 2005); infomania (Zeldes, Sward, & Louchheim, 2007); infobesity (Bell, 2004; Morris, 2003); and communication overload (Franz, 1999). A quick search using Google's Ngram viewer ("Google Ngram Viewer," n.d.) reveals that the usage of many of these terms has been on the rise since the 1960s, and that the top two most popular ones are information overload and sensory overload. A close reading of the academic and popular literature reveals significant inconsistencies in the use of these terms and of "information overload." In some cases the terms are used interchangeably, and in other cases specific distinctions between the terms are made by particular authors, only to be disregarded by later authors.

This brief review of the concept of information overload demonstrates that the term "information overload" is poorly defined and inconsistently used. In this chapter I suggest that despite this vagueness, the ubiquity of the term and of related terms in scientific literature, in books and in the popular press implies that it signifies something real, and that this thing is a stress experienced by citizens of the information society. This stress is linked to "information" since it is closely associated with the ever-increasing amounts of information delivered via a constantly rising number of information and communication technologies (ICTs). Nevertheless, as I discuss in the following section, the current conceptualizations of information overload need to be carefully evaluated if we wish to make further progress towards overcoming the ubiquitous stress attributed to "information overload."

What's Wrong with the Information Overload Concept?

The weakness of current perceptions of information overload stems from the fact that many of them are *technologically deterministic* and that they are based on a false *utopian/dystopian dichotomy*. Let's explore these two concepts, technological determinism and the utopian/dystopian dichotomy. Technological determinism is a concept developed by proponents of social construction of technology (SCOT) (Bijker, Hughes, & Pinch, 1987). Determinists describe technology as an entity that develops autonomously and that determines, to a large extent, societal development (Bijker, 2010). SCOT researchers have shown that the evolution of technology is not deterministic and that the many decisions involved in its development are influenced by society and by societal values. They have also shown it is naïve to assume that technology influences society without acknowledging that society influences technology. They go on to show that one of the main consequences of a deterministic view of technology is that it often leads to the false dichotomy of classifying specific technologies as "good" or "bad"—the utopian/dystopian dichotomy (Kalman, Raban, & Rafaeli, 2013). SCOT researchers make convincing claims that show the futility of arguing whether a specific technology (e.g., guns, nuclear power or social networking services) are "good" or "bad." They also show that the societal benefits (or harms) of technologies are not intrinsic to the technologies, but rather are a consequence of the way the technology is developed by society, and the way it is adopted and used by society.

An Example of Dystopian Technological Determinism

In what way is the common conceptualization of information overload deterministic? And how does it exhibit the characteristics of the utopian/dystopian dichotomy? A good demonstration of this conceptualization is a study of technostress published in the prestigious *MIS Quarterly* (Ayyagari et al., 2011). Technostress is one of the terms used synonymously or in close association to information overload, and it describes "a modern disease caused by one's inability to cope or deal with ICTs in a healthy manner" (Ayyagari et al., 2011, p. 832). In their study, the authors focus on workplace technostress and identify a list of five workplace stressors that might be linked to ICTs. They are: work overload, role ambiguity, job insecurity, work–home conflict and invasion of privacy. Then, they measure how each of these are related to other constructs and to technostress.

The study is carefully designed and controlled, and its findings are important and interesting. What I focus on is how the five workplace stressors are operationalized in the study. For example, the work overload construct comprises three items which the study participants are asked to provide their agreement to: (1) "ICTs create many more requests, problems, or complaints in my job than I would otherwise experience"; (2) "I feel busy or rushed due to ICTs"; (3) "I feel pressured due to ICTs." The work–home conflict comprises items such as "Using ICTs blurs boundaries between my job and my home life." And the role ambiguity construct comprises items such as (1) "I am unsure what to prioritize: dealing with ICT problems or my work activities" and (2) "I can NOT allocate time properly for my work activities because my time spent on ICTs activities varies."

If one looks at all these items, it is clear that these stressors that lead to technostress are operationalized by "blaming" technology and suggesting that ICTs create requests, make us feel busy, rushed or pressured, and that they blur boundaries and take away time from work activities. But a SCOT researcher would point out that it is not the ICTs that create the requests, but rather people who use the ICTs to send messages or to assign tasks. It is not the use of ICTs that blurs the boundaries between work and home, but rather the managers, colleagues or clients who expect work to be carried out at home (or family and friends who expect employees to divert attention to them during the workday). And it is unclear priorities set by managers and organizations that lead to role ambiguity in regards to the balance between ICT-related activities and other work activities. Blaming ICTs for work pressure, work–home conflicts or role ambiguity does not make sense, and is a good example of technological determinism and the false utopian/dystopian dichotomy.

Overload: Perception vs. Reality

Nevertheless, the sense that ICTs are to blame for these stresses is pervasive, and the Ayyagari et al. (2011) study reflects this widely held belief. This belief is elegantly demonstrated in a study by Barley, Meyerson, and Grodal (2011). In this study, the researchers studied the communicative activities of employees in a high-tech firm. Their goal was teasing apart the impact of two categories of influencers of workplace stress and sense of overload. The first category, often studied in the past, is the material properties of the communication technologies the employees used. The second category, which received much less attention in prior literature, is social forces. This research perspective, which accepts that both social forces and material properties of technologies influence experiences such as the stress of information overload, is the sociomaterial approach (Orlikowski, 2007). It asserts that these two categories of influencers, social and material, are entwined and interdependent, and that studying one without regard to the other leads to a partial understanding and to debatable conclusions.

Barley et al. (2011) tried to understand how email and other ICTs contribute to workplace stress and overload by examining the technologies used by the employees, and how these are entangled with social norms, interpretations and the daily workflow. They tried to understand why the same technologies that are perceived as adding flexibility and bolstering the employees' sense of being able to cope with their workload are also perceived as the cause of stress and overload. Their findings were instructive. They reported that about two-thirds of the employees' average workdays (6.4 hours out of 9.4 hours) were spent communicating. These 6.4 hours were spent about equally on meetings and face-to-face encounters (34 percent), email (31 percent) and phone calls or teleconferences (30 percent). The remaining 5 percent were spent using various other technologies such as instant messaging, video conferencing and voicemail. Note that of these three major modes of communication, email is the only asynchronous mode of communication, a mode of communication that does not require an immediate response and that offers some flexibility in regards to timing.

The researchers examined the participants' communication logs and the surveys and interviews that evaluated the attitudes, stresses, perceptions and interpretations of the employees who participated in the study. The examination revealed an important gap between participant perceptions and reality. The participants believed that the more they used email, the longer they worked, and that this increase in work time led to an increased sense of overload. Nevertheless, the findings of the study show that the assumption that the increase in time devoted to email is the major source of the overload was overly simplistic. In fact, email use was related to stress regardless of how much time participants worked. Moreover, the participants were not aware that teleconferences and phone calls were also associated with longer working hours, and that time spent in meetings also increased workload. In other words, it seems like people focus on email as the cause of increased work hours and of increased sense of overload, and ignore other time sinks and causes of overload. The authors conclude that "rather than attending to how much time teleconferences and meetings consumed … interviewees focused on their inboxes as the salient source of overload and the target of their complaints" (Barley et al., 2011, p. 901). Thus, email is perceived not only as the single source of workplace stress but also as its symbol.

In light of these findings, is it surprising that ICTs[1] are blamed for workplace stress in a technologically deterministic and dystopian manner? In fact, it seems as if the same material properties of ICTs, such as email that provide users with more control and flexibility, are the properties that make email stand out from the crowd of other communication activities as the one that leads to overload and stress. It is easier to focus on email work during off-work hours than on the face-to-face meetings and teleconferences that consumed a large part of the workday, leaving the employee with little time for other tasks. This is somewhat analogous to complaining about the high cost of gasoline and ignoring the impact of insurance, car payments, maintenance and repairs on the high cost of car ownership.

The findings that there is a gap between the perceived causes of overload and stress and the real causes are not unique to the Barley et al. (2011) study. For example, Kock, Parente and Verville (2008) identified gaps in the perception of information overload that stem from nationality (US versus New Zealand). Gaps in the perception of information overload that stem from differences in the perception of email as a "business critical" tool have been described by Sumecki, Chipulu and Ojiako (2011). And gaps that stem from different email management tactics have been described by Dabbish and Kraut (2006). Furthermore, it was shown that activities that increase overload, such as multitasking, might not improve performance, but still satisfy other needs, for example, by providing emotional gratifications (Wang & Tchernev, 2012).

In the first part of this chapter we reviewed the academic literature on information overload and saw that the concept is poorly defined and its usage is inconsistent. In the second part of the chapter we reviewed several studies of people's perceptions of workplace overload and of the attributions they make in regards to the causes of these pressures, and saw that people's understanding of these pressures and of their causes is also vague, highly subjective and often lacking and not in line with empirical evidence. Nevertheless, it is also clear that the pressures and sense of overload described in the studies are real and that they have a negative impact on the well-being of knowledge workers. The question is how to move away from the deterministic dystopian attitude to ICTs and workplace stress and develop a research agenda that will further our understanding of these pressures. The next section proposes an answer to this question.

Different Loads for Different Folks

I propose that the pressures that fall under the category of "information overload" and which are experienced by workers in general, and by information workers in particular, arise from three separate but overlapping loads that characterize the typical workplace of the knowledge society. These three loads are work load, communication load, and information load (Figure 4.2). Each of these loads is different, but they overlap to varying extents and are thus interdependent. Because of these interdependencies, treating or studying only one of them is not fruitful. An unreasonable amount of any of these three loads will lead to overload, and this overload can lead to stress, but it is important not to confuse the three terms: a load is different from overload, and both of these are different from stress.

In order to demonstrate the need to distinguish between the three loads, as well as between load, overload and stress, let's take the way a knowledge worker— for example, a manager—uses email in the workplace. This manager uses email extensively to carry out her job responsibilities. She uses it to communicate with her managers, subordinates, clients and other organizational stakeholders. A lot of the information she needs arrives via email, though she also uses many other information sources. Now, let's examine what could increase each of the three loads on this manager. The work load could increase as a result of the manager being assigned new duties that have in the past been assigned to a colleague who is no longer employed by the company. The communication load could increase as a result of the company adding a new company-wide communication tool,

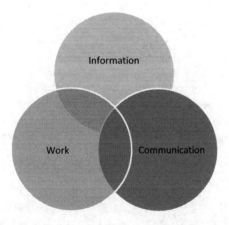

FIGURE 4.2 The three loads that characterize the workplace.

such as instant messaging to all company computers, and requiring employees to monitor it during the workday, or as a result of an increase in the number of company-wide messages that originate from the human resources department, messages updating employees about new procedures, events and benefits. The information load could increase as a result of the company purchasing a license for the manager to access a database that includes large amounts of valuable information about competitors.

Each of these increases in load would either be an increase that the manager could absorb, or an increase that leads to overload—i.e., to a situation where the resources that the manager has are no longer enough in order to deal with the increased load. In the case of the new duties, the result of the increased work load would be considered work overload if, for example, her ability to perform her old duties were diminished, as well as her ability to perform the additional duties. In the case of the increased communication load, we would consider her to experience communication overload if as a consequence of the new medium or the additional messages, she were no longer able to stay on top of all her incoming messages and to provide timely responses. In the case of the new license for the valuable database, we would consider the consequence to be information overload if, for example, the manager found herself spending a lot of her research time in the new database, but ending up with less actionable information to assist her decisions than she had in the past.

In addition to these three examples of possible overloads, each of them could cause stress for the manager, or not. For example, in the case of communication overload, the manager might overcome the overload by taking a training session that will improve her ability to deal with large amounts of workplace email (e.g., Soucek & Moser, 2010) and consequently avoid the stress. Or she could decide to filter all the incoming messages from human resources and read them at home over the weekend. If this does not result in a home–work conflict, this might be a solution that prevents the manager from experiencing the stress associated with communication overload.

Identifying Root Causes

The goal of the manager example was to demonstrate the differences between the three main sources of workplace loads: work, communication and information, as well as the difference between "load," "overload" and "stress." The different sources of load could lead to overload and stress, and if we wish to deal with these negative consequences, we need to be clear about the source of these negative consequences. In other words, we are looking for the *root cause* of the overload and stress the employee is experiencing. For example, if an employee experiences stress since he or she is dealing with ever-increasing numbers of emails during unusual hours (early in the morning, late at night, over weekends and holiday, and during vacations), it is essential to identify the root cause of this situation.

The root cause might be work overload that leads to less time to "do email" in the office, or simply added work responsibilities that lead to more email correspondence. Alternatively, the root cause might be information overload—for example, if the employee joined a very active mailing list that is an important source of information. Finally, the root cause might be communication overload, since there is a significant increase in the exchange of email messages within the company. Unless we understand the root cause of the stress the employee experiences, it is unlikely that our solutions will help overcome the stress. For example, if this employee who reports stress due to unmanageable amounts of email is working for a manager who feels that when a subordinate is not working evenings and weekends, that subordinate is not productive enough, then the root cause of the employee's overload and stress is work overload. In this case it is unlikely that providing such an employee with tips and technologies on dealing with emails more effectively would help. The only consequence of more effective handling of emails by this employee would be that the manager would continue adding tasks and assignments until the workload again forces the employee to work evenings and weekends.

Information Overload, Then and Now

Having made the distinction between the possible root causes, as well as between load, overload and stress, it is important to note that these distinctions are very difficult to make, especially in the case of knowledge workers. For knowledge workers, *information* and *communication* comprise a significant part of the *work* they do, and it is difficult to separate their effects. A rise in the workload leads in many cases to increased communication and an increase in the amount of information required to carry out the new tasks. Nevertheless, despite the difficulty, disentangling the roles and impacts of these loads in the contemporary workplace remains an important challenge to researchers and practitioners.

Information overload is not a new phenomenon. The biblical Ecclesiastes already complained that "of making books there is no end, and much study is a weariness to the flesh" (Ecclesiastes, 12:12, 1917 JPS edition), and we hear concerns about the difficulties of dealing with the ever-increasing amounts of information throughout recorded history. Nevertheless, the amount of information we deal with on a daily basis at home and at work is constantly on the rise (Neuman, Park, & Panek, 2012; "Special report—Managing information," 2010), and we are constantly finding new ways to use this information (Weinberger, 2012). Russell Neuman, cited above, tells the story of a panel of experts that was convened in the early days of trains, to study the possible psychological effects trains might have on passengers. They concluded that as trains increase their speed, we will reach a psychological speed limit above which the passengers will no longer be able to look out the windows. The reason would be that the amount of information that will flood them from the fast-changing scenery outside will overload their brains and cause psychological damage. The experts recommended that when those speeds are achieved, the transparent windows should be covered or replaced.

History teaches us that all of the dire predictions about our inability to deal with an ever-increasing amount of information were disconfirmed. On the contrary: society succeeds in leveraging knowledge to advance science, improve living standards, fight illness and increase lifespans. This effect is most apparent in the postindustrial rise of the knowledge economy, or information society (Machlup, 1962; Porat, 1977), where an increasing percentage of the workforce comprises knowledge workers who produce knowledge goods (Kalman et al., 2013).

Although the discussion of information overload is not new, information overload is now a widespread phenomenon that permeates much wider audiences. What has changed in the last few decades? What are the forces that encourage work, information and communication overload in our society? The rise of the information society and knowledge economy created an environment where information is both the chief economic input and output. Unlike the industrial age, which gradually developed optimization methods that steadily improved the ability to turn physical inputs and labor into tangible outputs, the relationship between inputs and outputs in the knowledge economy is more difficult to measure and to optimize.

Despite interesting first steps towards the understanding of value creation by knowledge workers (Spohrer, Maglio, Bailey, & Gruhl, 2007; Spohrer, Vargo, Caswell, & Maglio, 2008), we are still far from understanding at what point the three workplace loads we discuss here—information, work and communication—become overloads, and negatively impact outputs. It is an economy where innovation and creativity are important, but also the ability to plan and to execute according to plan; it is an economy based on information which can, once digitized, be duplicated indefinitely and almost at no cost; it is an economy that is not based on scarcity, but rather on the abundance of information which is its main input and output; and it is a highly competitive economy where change is the only constant. While we might be making progress in our ability to optimize the productivity of help-desk personnel and sales representatives, we are far from this level of understanding in regards to employees for whom the relationship between inputs and outputs is more complex, employees in roles such as managers, marketers, researchers, instructors or designers.

One of the common solutions to the difficulty of assessing the required inputs for these employees, and the value they create, is to use crude heuristics and rules-of-thumb such as "the more the better," "keep them busy," or "idleness is the mother of evil." In other words, overload the employees with tasks and with information. The rationale is that if we can't measure the employees' productivity, at least we can ensure they are busy all day emailing, flooded and complaining about overload and stress. Needless to say, this is not an effective approach, and often it is counterproductive. The fallacy of the assumption that keeping employees busy all the time is a key to productivity has been refuted even in regards to traditional industries (e.g., Ronen, 1992), and this certainly applies to knowledge work, where employee creativity, innovation and motivation are cherished.

Unloading the Future

So far in this chapter we saw that information overload and related terms are poorly defined but widely used, and that this wide usage reflects a ubiquitous sense of stress related to knowledge work and to usage of information and communication technologies. We learned that this stress is a result of at least three main categories of loads—work, information and communication—and that although these three are highly interdependent, it is important to identify which of them is the root cause of the stress the employee experiences. How can these insights guide future research on workplace pressures, and how can they assist practitioners such as managers and employees better cope with these pressures?

The first step is to distinguish among the root causes of the stress attributed to information, communication or technology overload, and identify the causal chain that leads to these stresses. Even if people feel, for example, that their stress is a consequence of too much email, researchers need to explore deeper and see whether they can identify causes that lead to the excessive email: is it work overload, information overload or communication overload? Based on anecdotal evidence, it is more likely that most of these cases are a result of work overload: too many tasks and insufficient resources. Identifying root causes is not an easy challenge (Andersen & Fagerhaug, 2006), especially in regards to the complex ecosystems in which knowledge workers find themselves (e.g., Ahuja, Chudoba, Kacmar, McKnight, & George, 2007). Nevertheless, until these are identified, probably through a combination of qualitative and quantitative methods, the fruitfulness of efforts to lower stress levels will be limited.

Once the root causes are distinguished from effects that are further down the causality chain, the next step is to better understand the incentives that promote the different types of loads and overloads. Different types of loads and overloads will be associated with different incentives—some more obvious, such as the belief of managers that overloading an employee is the way to increased productivity (Brown & Benson, 2005), and some less obvious. A good example of a covert incentive is the phenomenon of self-interruptions by knowledge workers who stop in the midst of working on one task to engage in another task such as checking for new email and browsing news websites or social networking sites. What do they gain by breaking their concentration and diverting it to another unrelated task? One possible incentive to self-interrupt in order to check for new messages might be the mechanism of variable interval reinforcement, which was shown to reward brains through the release of dopamine (Freeman, 2009). More research is required to understand the motives to self-interrupt (Adler & Benbunan-Fich, 2012; Jin & Dabbish, 2009).

Finally, once we have a better understanding of the root causes of the stresses, and of the explicit and implicit incentives that perpetuate the loads and the overloads that lead to these stresses, it should be possible to devise more effective solutions to the stresses and to evaluate their efficacy. The solutions could be organizational as well as technological. Moreover, the most interesting solutions would probably combine organizational changes and technology. A good example of the complex relationship between organizational attitudes and practices that use technology to reduce stress is provided in a study by Leslie, Manchester, Park and Mehng (2012). The study showed that flexible work practices such as telecommuting can have either a positive or negative impact on the career of employees who utilize them. They demonstrated that the impact varies based on the attributions made by the managers of the employees who utilize flexible work practices. When managers attribute the utilization of flexible work practices to a desire to increase productivity, the utilization led to positive career outcomes. However, when the same utilization was attributed to a desire for personal life accommodation, it led to negative career outcomes. This study demonstrates that finding the technological solution to a specific load is not necessarily a solution to the organizational challenge, and that organizational context needs to be taken into account when applying these solutions.

Conclusion

The stress attributed to information overload in the knowledge society is pervasive and ubiquitous. Nevertheless, a close examination of the literature shows that information overload is poorly defined and that its conceptualization and usage exhibit technological determinism and a false utopian/dystopian dichotomy. Knowledge workers who suffer from workplace pressures, as well as researchers who study them, tend to blame information and ICTs for the stress and are likely to disregard other causes such as work overload. Researchers and practitioners still find it difficult to identify whether the root cause of the stress is information overload, work overload or communication overload. Failing to distinguish between these root causes prevents us from finding solutions that will effectively alleviate the stress. This is exacerbated by the many processes, forces and incentives of the information society that promote a constant increase in the amount of information we have access to, in the amount of communication we are engaged in and in the amount of tasks and assignments we attempt to accomplish.

Workplace pressures and stress are not an inevitable consequence of the knowledge society. We need to carefully analyze the causal chain that leads to these stresses, and the incentives that encourage practices that eventually lead to overload and stress. This analysis needs to avoid technological determinism and to acknowledge the subjectivity and context dependency of these workplace pressures and loads, and of the stress they cause. Consequently, we will be able to devise solutions that harness information technologies not only to optimize traditional measures such as throughput and short-term productivity, but also measures such as employee satisfaction and sense of accomplishment. There is no reason why the same technologies that facilitate the constant rise in the productivity of knowledge workers cannot be employed to also decrease the workplace stresses discussed in this book, and lead to outcomes such as better work–life balance, increased workplace diversity and a decrease in workplace stress and burnout.

Note

1   The Barley et al. (2011) study is based on data collected in 2001–2, before the wide use of ICT's such as smartphones and applications associated with them.

References

Adler, R., & Benbunan-Fich, R. (2012). The effects of positive and negative self-interruptions in discretionary multitasking. In *CHI '12 Extended Abstracts on Human Factors in Computing Systems* (pp. 1763–1768). Austin, Texas, USA: ACM.

Ahuja, M. K., Chudoba, K. M., Kacmar, C. J., McKnight, D. H., & George, J. F. (2007). IT road warriors: Balancing work–family conflict, job autonomy, and work overload to mitigate turnover intentions. *MIS Quarterly, 31*(1), 1–17.

Andersen, B., & Fagerhaug, T. (2006). *Root cause analysis: Simplified tools and techniques.* ASQ Quality Press.

Ayyagari, R., Grover, V., & Purvis, R. (2011). Technostress: Technological antecedents and implications. *MIS Quarterly, 35*(4), 831–858.

Barley, S. R., Meyerson, D. E., & Grodal, S. (2011). E-mail as a source and symbol of stress. *Organization Science, 22*(4), 887–906. doi:10.1287/orsc.1100.0573.

Bell, S. J. (2004). The infodiet: How libraries can offer an appetizing alternative to Google. *The Chronicle of Higher Education, 50*(24), B15.

Berghel, H. (1997). Cyberspace 2000: Dealing with information overload. *Communications of the ACM, 40*(2), 19–24.

Bijker, W. E. (2010). How is technology made?—That is the question! *Cambridge Journal of Economics, 34*(1), 63–76. doi:http://dx.doi.org/10.1093/cje/bep068.

Bijker, W. E., Hughes, T. P., & Pinch, T. J. (1987). *The social construction of technological systems: New directions in the sociology and history of technology.* Cambridge, Mass.: MIT Press.

Brown, M., & Benson, J. (2005). Managing to overload? Work overload and performance appraisal processes. *Group & Organization Management, 30*(1), 99–124. doi:10.1177/1059601104269117.

Case, D. O. (2012). *Looking for information: A survey of research on information seeking, needs, and behavior.* Emerald Group Publishing.

Chewning, E. G., Jr., & Harrell, A. M. (1990). The effect of information load on decision makers' cue utilization levels and decision quality in a financial distress decision task. *Accounting, Organizations and Society, 15*(6), 527–542. doi:10.1016/0361–3682(90)90033-Q.

Continuous Partial Attention. (n.d.). *Linda Stone.* Retrieved January 18, 2013, from http://lindastone.net/qa/continuous-partial-attention/.

Dabbish, L. A., & Kraut, R. E. (2006). Email overload at work: An analysis of factors associated with email strain. In *Proceedings of the 2006 20th anniversary conference on computer supported cooperative work* (pp. 431–440). Banff, Alberta, Canada: ACM. doi:10.1.1.83.9750.

Denning, P. J. (2006). Infoglut. *Communications of the ACM, 49*(7), 15–19. doi:http://dx. doi.org/10.1145%2F1139922.1139936.

Eppler, M. J., & Mengis, J. (2004). The concept of information overload: A review of literature from organization science, accounting, marketing, MIS, and related disciplines. *The Information Society, 20*(5), 325–344. doi:10.1080/01972240490507974.

Franz, H. (1999). The impact of computer-mediated communication on information overload in distributed teams. In *Proceedings of the 32nd annual Hawaii international conference on systems sciences, 1999. HICSS-32* (Vol. Track 1, p. 15). Presented at the Proceedings of the 32nd Annual Hawaii International Conference on Systems Sciences, 1999. HICSS-32. doi:10.1109/HICSS.1999.772712.

Freeman, J. (2009). *The tyranny of e-mail: The four-thousand-year journey to your inbox.* Simon and Schuster.

Google Ngram Viewer. (n.d.). Retrieved January 18, 2013, from http://books.google. com/ngrams.

Hall, A., & Walton, G. (2004). Information overload within the health care system: A literature review. *Health Information & Libraries Journal, 21*(2), 102–108. doi:10.1111/ j.1471–1842.2004.00506.x.

Hallowell, E. M. (2005). Overloaded circuits: Why smart people underperform. *Harvard Business Review,* (January).

Hudson, J. M., Christensen, J., Kellogg, W. A., & Erickson, T. (2002). I'd be overwhelmed, but it's just one more thing to do: Availability and interruption in research management. In *Proceedings of the SIGCHI conference on human factors in computing systems: Changing our world, changing ourselves* (pp. 97–104). ACM. doi:10.1145/503376.503394.

Hwang, M. I., & Lin, J. W. (1999). Information dimension, information overload and decision quality. *Journal of Information Science, 25*(3), 213–218. doi:10.1177/0165551599 02500305.

Iyengar, S. S., & Lepper, M. R. (2000). When choice is demotivating: Can one desire too much of a good thing? *Journal of Personality and Social Psychology, 79*(6), 995. doi:10.1037/0022–3514.79.6.995.

Jacoby, J. (1984). Perspectives on information overload. *The Journal of Consumer Research, 10*(4), 432–435. doi:10.1086/208981.

Jin, J., & Dabbish, L. A. (2009). Self-interruption on the computer: A typology of discretionary task interleaving. In *Proceedings of the SIGCHI conference on human factors in computing systems* (pp. 1799–1808). Boston, MA, USA: ACM.

Jones, Q., Ravid, G., & Rafaeli, S. (2004). Information overload and the message dynamics of online interaction spaces: A theoretical model and empirical exploration. *Information Systems Research, 15*(2), 194–211.

Kalman, Y. M., Raban, D. R., & Rafaeli, S. (2013). Netified: Social cognition in crowds and clouds. In *The social net: Understanding our online behavior, 2nd edition.* Oxford University Press.

Kalman, Y. M. and Ravid, G. (2015), Filing, piling, and everything in between: The dynamics of E-mail inbox management. *Journal of the American Society for Information Science and Technology, 66:* 2540–2552. doi:10.1002/asi.23337

Karr-Wisniewski, P., & Lu, Y. (2010). When more is too much: Operationalizing technology overload and exploring its impact on knowledge worker productivity. *Computers in Human Behavior, 26*(5), 1061–1072. doi:10.1016/j.chb.2010.03.008.

Kirsh, D. (2000). A few thoughts on cognitive overload. *Intellectica, 30*(1), 19–51.

Kock, N., Parente, R., & Verville, J. (2008). Can Hofstede's model explain national differences in perceived information overload? A look at data from the US and New Zealand. *IEEE Transactions on Professional Communication, 51*(1), 33–49. doi:10.1109/TPC.2007.2000047.

Leslie, L., Manchester, C., Park, T. Y., & Mehng, S. A. (2012). Flexible work practices: A Source of career premiums or penalties? *Academy of Management Journal.* doi:10.5465/amj.2010.0651.

Lipowski, Z. J. (1975). Sensory and information inputs overload: Behavioral effects. *Comprehensive Psychiatry.* doi:10.1016/0010-440X(75)90047-4.

Machlup, F. (1962). *The production and distribution of knowledge in the United States.* Princeton University Press.

McCune, J. C. (1998). Data, data everywhere. *Management Review, 87*(10), 10–12.

Meyer, J. A. (1998). Information overload in marketing management. *Marketing Intelligence & Planning, 16*(3), 200–209. doi:10.1108/02634509810217318.

Morris, J. H. (2003). Tales of technology: Consider a cure for pernicious infobesity. *Pittsburgh Post-Gazette.* Retrieved January 18, 2013, from http://www.post-gazette.com/stories/business/news/tales-of-technology-consider-a-cure-for-pernicious-infobesity-517925/.

Neuman, W. R., Park, Y. J., & Panek, E. (2012). Info capacity| Tracking the flow of information into the home: An empirical assessment of the digital revolution in the U.S. from 1960–2005. *International Journal of Communication, 6.* doi:http://ijoc.org/ojs/index.php/ijoc/article/view/1369.

Orlikowski, W. J. (2007). Sociomaterial practices: Exploring technology at work. *Organization Studies, 28*(9), 1435–1448. doi:10.1177/0170840607081138.

Porat, M. U. (1977). *The information economy: Definition and measurement.* U.S. Dept. of Commerce, Office of Telecommunications.

Ronen, B. (1992). The complete kit concept. *International Journal of Production Research, 30* (10), 2457–2466. doi:10.1080/00207549208948166.

Shenk, D. (1997). *Data smog: Surviving the information glut* (1st ed.). HarperOne.

Shirky, C. (2008). Clay Shirky. It's not information overload. It's filter failure. Retrieved December 16, 2012, from http://blip.tv/web2expo/web-2-0-expo-ny-clay-shirky-shirky-com-it-s-not-information-overload-it-s-filter-failure-1283699.

Soucek, R., & Moser, K. (2010). Coping with information overload in email communication: Evaluation of a training intervention. *Computers in Human Behavior, 26*(6), 1458–1466. doi:10.1016/j.chb.2010.04.024.

Sparrow, P. (2002). Strategy and cognition: Understanding the role of management knowledge structures, organizational memory and information overload. *Creativity and Innovation Management, 8*(2), 140–148. doi:10.1111/1467–8691.00128.

Special report—Managing information. (2010). *The Economist.* Retrieved January 23, 2013, from http://www.economist.com/printedition/2010–02-27.

Sperandio, J. C. (1978). The regulation of working methods as a function of work-load among air traffic controllers. *Ergonomics, 21*(3), 195–202. doi:10.1080/00140137808931713.

Spohrer, J., Maglio, P. P., Bailey, J., & Gruhl, D. (2007). Steps toward a science of service systems. *Computer, 40*(1), 71 –77. doi:10.1109/MC.2007.33.

Spohrer, J., Vargo, S. L., Caswell, N., & Maglio, P. P. (2008). The service system is the basic abstraction of service science. In *Hawaii international conference on system sciences, proceedings of the 41st annual* (p. 104). Presented at the Hawaii International Conference on System Sciences, Proceedings of the 41st Annual. doi:10.1109/HICSS.2008.451.

Streufert, S., Suedfeld, P., & Driver, M. J. (1965). Conceptual structure, information search, and information utilization. *Journal of Personality and Social Psychology, 2*(5), 736–740. doi:10.1037/h0022679.

Sumecki, D., Chipulu, M., & Ojiako, U. (2011). Email overload: Exploring the moderating role of the perception of email as a "business critical" tool. *International Journal of Information Management, 31*(5), 407–414. doi:10.1016/j.ijinfomgt.2010.12.008.

Wang, Z., & Tchernev, J. M. (2012). The "myth" of media multitasking: Reciprocal dynamics of media multitasking, personal needs, and gratifications. *Journal of Communication, 62*(3), 493–513. doi:10.1111/j.1460-2466.2012.01641.x.

Weinberger, D. (2012). *Too big to know: Rethinking knowledge now that the facts aren't the facts, experts are everywhere, and the smartest person in the room is the room.* Basic Books.

Whittaker, S., & Sidner, C. (1996). Email overload: Exploring personal information management of email. In *Conference on human factors in computing systems—proceedings* (pp. 276–283). doi:10.1145/238386.238530.

Wurman, R. S. (2000). *Information anxiety 2.* Que.

Zeldes, N., Sward, D., & Louchheim, S. (2007). Infomania: Why we can't afford to ignore it any longer. *First Monday, 12*(8). Retrieved from http://www.firstmonday.org/issues/issue12_8/zeldes/#author.

PART II

5

TO SEE OURSELVES AS OTHERS SEE US

How Perceptions of Generational Diversity Affect the Workplace

Rhetta L. Standifer

ESC RENNES SCHOOL OF BUSINESS, RENNES, FRANCE

Scott W. Lester

UNIVERSITY OF WISCONSIN–EAU CLAIRE

The U.S. workplace is increasingly diverse, and one of the ways in which diversity is evident is in the age range and generational composition of its workforce. Employees of different generations often share similar views about work; however, there is also evidence of diversity across generations with respect to workplace norms and varying expectations about such things as leadership, communication, and "correct" employee interaction. Given that there are now four generations simultaneously in the U.S. workforce, people often find themselves in situations with coworkers, supervisors, and customers of various ages who have contrasting (and at times, conflicting) viewpoints. When diverse perspectives about work emerge, they heighten the saliency of age/generational differences and influence individuals' perceptions of workplace outcomes and relationships. Key research questions emerge from this phenomenon. Such as: to what extent do *real* differences among the generations exist and how do these compare to the differences we *perceive* to exist?

This chapter presents an overview of current thought regarding generational diversity (including brief descriptions of each of the generations currently in the workforce). There is also an overview of the differences between generations that have been demonstrated in past organizational studies. In addition, the related but separate issue of age-related diversity and perceptions at work is discussed. The focus then turns to a description of a study conducted by the authors that compares *perceived* differences among the generations to *actual* differences found among workers. Finally, the authors discuss the implications these ideas have for twenty-first-century U.S. managers and employees.

Generational and Age-Related Diversity at Work

A *generation* is defined as individuals who can be identified as a group born during a set range of years and who have experienced specific, significant life events at critical and developmental stages in their lives (Kupperschmidt, 2000). These life events are typically historical and sociological in nature and influence the attitudes and values of that generation (Benson & Brown, 2011; Smola & Sutton, 2002). Researchers have found that generational differences related to work attitudes and values are particularly prevalent (Cennamo & Gardner, 2008; Jurkiewicz & Brown, 1998). In the U.S., there are currently four distinct generations (also known in the literature as *cohorts*) simultaneously represented in the workforce. This is a fairly new phenomenon and one that is not likely to change for the foreseeable future, given the socioeconomic environment and the fact that individuals are opting to (and are physically capable of) extending the time in which they remain active in the workforce. Below is a brief description of the four working generations, compiled through both culturally accepted anecdotal views and research-based observations.

Traditionalists. Born prior to 1946, the Traditionalists are the oldest individuals in the workforce; however, the youngest Traditionalists are at an age commonly viewed as a benchmark for retirement (at least for now). As such, they represent a smaller cohort in the workplace relative to the other three generations. The life events most often associated with this generation are the Great Depression and World War II, and this cohort's adherence to authority and their traditional views of leadership (top-down and based on seniority and rank) demonstrate the influence of these events. This cohort is company-loyal and is motivated primarily by recognition, awards, and public acknowledgement (Patterson, 2007).

Boomers. Born between 1946 and 1964, the Boomers have wielded tremendous influence in the U.S. workplace, both in terms of their cohort's size and in their views about work (Westerman & Yamamura, 2007). Boomers currently occupy more senior positions due to their tenure in the workforce and the knowledge they have obtained over the years (Benson & Brown, 2011). The children of postwar America, they have been noted as the generation who grew up with the psychology of entitlement and optimism (Kupperschmidt, 2000; Patterson, 2007; Smola & Sutton, 2002). Coming of age in the sixties, they were influenced by the Vietnam War, the Civil Rights Movement, and the Kennedy and King assassinations (Adams, 2000). Boomers are generally considered materialistic, with a strong work ethic. This cohort is credited with an increased emphasis on team-oriented work, consensus building, and social networking in the workplace (Kupperschmidt, 2000; O'Bannon, 2001).

Gen X. In contrast to the Boomers, the developmental period in which Gen-Xers (born between 1965 and 1979) came of age was characterized by instability and rapid change. The first "techno" generation, Gen X grew up during

Watergate, an increase in divorce and single-parent households, large-scale organizational layoffs, and economic downfalls. The "latchkey" generation became known for its individualism, cynicism, and strong skepticism of authority and organizational hierarchy (Jurkiewicz & Brown, 1998; Kupperschmidt, 2000). They are also credited as the first generation to push for work–life balance (Cennamo & Gardner, 2008). They are career (versus firm) loyal, techno-competent, and comfortable with multitasking and diversity (as the most diverse generation up to that point in American work history) (Kupperschmidt, 2000; O'Bannon, 2001).

Millennials. The youngest generational cohort currently in the U.S. workforce, Millennials were born between 1980 and 1999. This cohort is the first generation born into a "wired" world and is used to being "connected" twenty-four hours a day (Ryan, 2000). The children of the Boomers, they are similar to that older cohort in their comfortable approach to teamwork and in their optimism, but also echo the desire for work–life balance and involvement in decision-making at work indicative of Gen-Xers (Smola & Sutton 2002; Stevens, 2010).

Views on generational designation. The notion that people vary in their views because of their generational designation is not a new one. In 1952, Mannheim suggested that a bond is created among individuals of the same generation by the fact that they experience similar social phenomena at roughly the same time developmentally. More recently, McMullin, Comeau, and Jovic (2007) argued that a generation "represents a unique type of social location based on the dynamic interplay between being born in a particular year and the socio-political events that occur throughout the life course of the birth cohort" (p. 299–300). Still, the debate about generational differences is far from concluded. Some researchers have voiced doubts as to the voracity of differences between the generations, arguing that perceived differences are more the result of age (and stages of life) than of generation or are simply nonexistent or overly emphasized (Giancola, 2006; Jorgensen, 2003; Schamm, 2004; Smola & Sutton, 2002). Despite a lack of agreement, some evidence in support of the generational differences perspective exists. For example, Schuman and Scott (1989) demonstrated collective memories among those of a similar generation, while other researchers found evidence of lifelong, consistent attitudinal effects within generations (Zaslow, 2002). In addition, generational researchers have produced data that support generational differences in commitment, trust, and the need for authenticity and balance (Daboval, 1998; Robinson & Jackson, 2001; Sullivan, Forret, Carraher, & Mainiero, 2009).

Age-based differences. As pointed out by past researchers, however, it is important to distinguish between "generation-based" and "age-based" differences. Consider an interaction between a sixty-year-old manager and a twenty-eight-year-old assistant manager. If they prefer different communication styles, is it due to the influence of social and developmental events they have experienced (generational), or is it because one is sixty and one is twenty-eight (age-based)? If a difference can be attributed to the life stage of the individual, then it is likely the difference is age-based; for example, it might be that a young, single employee is primarily interested in salary and bonuses whereas another (older) employee is more concerned with health care benefits. In this case, differences in viewpoint stem from each employee's age and stage of life. In contrast, if the difference stems from viewpoints evolved through experience and social development, it is likely to be generationally based. For example, a Boomer is more likely to emphasize tenure and the importance of team-based work due to perspectives developed through their experiences. In contrast, a Gen-Xer is more likely to emphasize competence rather than tenure in determining leadership, and to wish for autonomy which is also indicative of preferences developed through their experiences.

Our workforce is aging, not just in the U.S. but globally. By 2015, the number of workers age fifty-five or older is expected to rise to roughly 20 percent of the working population (U.S. General Accounting Office, 2001). In the U.K., 30 percent of workers are already over fifty (Dixon, 2003). The aging of the workforce means age diversity is increasing as well. Subsequently, greater age diversity increases the chance of age dissimilarity among coworkers (Avery, McKay, & Wilson, 2007, p.1542).

Past research has demonstrated connections between age dissimilarity and outcomes such as organizational commitment and intent to stay (Riordan, 2000). Social identity theory describes the preference we feel in general to those we perceive as similar to ourselves. Such in-group bias predisposes us to respond favorably to those we view as similar and to respond negatively to those we view as "other" or dissimilar (Ashforth & Mael, 1989; Tajfel & Turner, 1986; Turner, 1987). In particular, research has shown such in-group bias on race, gender, and age (Tsui & Gutek, 1999). As such, employee–coworker age similarity has been shown to improve technical communication in work groups (Zenger & Lawrence, 1989) and to decrease conflict (Jehn, Chadwick, & Thatcher, 1997; Pelled, Xin, & Weiss, 2001). The mere perception that a coworker is dissimilar makes age more distinctive and salient (Avery et al., 2007, p. 1544; Randel, 2002).

The term *age similarity preference* describes whether or not a person prefers to work with others of their own age. Does the person like (or dislike) to interact with people of different age groups in the course of performing their job? To date, there has not been extensive research that explicitly examines such a preference or the implications of such a preference. One exception is the study conducted by Avery, McKay, and Wilson (2007) which revealed that perceptions of coworker engagement and dedication in the workplace were age-related. Their findings indicated that perceived age similarity was linked to higher levels of engagement among older workers when those workers were satisfied, but lower levels of engagement when they were dissatisfied (Avery et al., 2007).

In the next section, we present the results of a study conducted that examines real versus perceived differences among the generations.

Generational Differences Study

One of the biggest challenges facing managers today is learning how to effectively lead a multigenerational workforce. As the research above demonstrates, employees from different generations may vary in what they value or consider important in the workplace; they may differ in what motivates them, how they approach work, and what they consider to be "appropriate" workplace norms. The increasingly diverse nature of the workforce has prompted scholars to offer both anecdotal as well as some empirical evidence addressing generational differences. Despite the increased attention being placed on generational diversity, however, there are still questions that remain. For instance: do generational cohorts *actually* demonstrate a difference of values and do they truly require different things in a work context, or do these differences reside solely in the myths and stereotypes we hold about perceived differences across generations? In Lester, Standifer, Schultz, and Windsor (2012), we wished to provide meaningful contributions to this debate by comparing actual and perceived workplace preferences within a multigenerational organization.

To achieve this, we first asked subjects to answer questions about what they desire in the workplace. Then, we asked them to respond to questions about what they believe other generations desire in the same context. With these data, we could compare the actual preferences reported to the perceptions subjects held about the various generations. Subjects were placed into generational categories by age, using established age ranges associated with each generation in previous research. For this study, we included three generational categories: (1) Boomers, (2) Gen-Xers, and (3) Millennials.

Subjects were asked to rate the extent to which they personally valued fifteen specific aspects of the work environment including: (a) teamwork, (b) autonomy, (c) security, (d) professionalism, (e) flexibility, (f) formal authority, (g) technology, (h) face-to-face communication, (i) e-mail communication, (j) social media, (k) structure at work, (l) involvement, (m) continuous learning, (n) fun at work, and (o) recognition. These work aspects were culled from the extant literature (e.g., Anetzberger & Teaster, 2010; Bright, 2010; Giancola, 2008; Simons, 2010). We should note that our use of the term *value* denotes what individuals desire or appreciate in terms of characteristics of their work context, not as a desired personal principle (e.g., honesty, fairness). After this was completed, subjects were asked to rate the extent they believed each generation (Boomer, Gen X, Millennials) valued these fifteen work aspects.

The next step was to identify the items in which we expected to find differences across the generations. Popular culture and academic literature suggest that each generational cohort possesses a unique set of characteristics and preferences that distinguish their workplace tendencies (Hill, 2002; Martin, 2005). We proposed that there would be *actual* disparity in six of the generational preferences including: (a) technology, (b) face-to-face communication, (c) e-mail communication,

(d) social media, (e) formal authority, and (f) fun at work. We based this hypothesis on generational cohort theory which outlines how the core values of adults are shaped by the historic and social aspects of society they experience at critical developmental stages throughout childhood (Kupperschmidt, 2000).

The degree to which individuals value technology would depend on the extent to which technology was available, reliable, and understood as they were growing up. Boomers grew up in a world where technology was not as common place as today. While Gen-Xers enjoyed more exposure to technological advances during their formative years, certain aspects of technology (especially those associated with social media) emerged after Generation Xers entered the workforce. In contrast, Millennials have existed within a digital world their entire lives. Given this, we expected Millennials to place the highest value on technology.

Technology and communication are intricately connected. Indeed, one primary way in which technology has affected the world is through the way we communicate with one another. When Boomers joined the ranks of the employed, communication was predominantly conducted face-to-face, by phone, or through traditional mail. When Gen-Xers entered the workforce, electronic mail (e-mail) and early use of the Internet had arrived. As Millennials begin their work experiences, social media mechanisms, such as Twitter and Facebook, have radically changed the ways in which individuals communicate with each other. As such, we would expect face-to-face communication to be most valued by Boomers and e-mail to be valued by Gen-Xers more than their predecessors. Furthermore, we predicted a significant difference in the extent to which Millennials value technologically oriented communication forms (e.g., social media) compared with the other two generations.

Another actual difference we predicted related to views of formal authority and how one feels work "ought" to be conducted. Again, these differences are believed to arise from the historic events that defined different generations. Boomers entered the workforce when leadership and formal authority were considered to be synonymous. The boss was usually an older worker with seniority in terms of organizational tenure (Crampton & Hodge, 2007). They came of age in the postwar mindset of growth and hard work. Boomers believed that work was a priority and that through loyalty and paying one's dues came reward and seniority (Crumpacker & Crumpacker, 2007; Elsdon & Lyer, 1999; Fogg, 2009). Work, in other words, was work, and "life" (e.g., fun, enjoyment) was separate. In direct contrast to the Boomers' experiences, Generation X was a "latchkey" generation, taught to be self-reliant and independent (Crampton & Hodge, 2007). For this generation who viewed formal authority skeptically, leadership was equated to competency, not tenure. In other words, seniority was not as valued as proving one's ability to lead. This generation also resisted the workaholic mindset of their predecessors, preferring less formality in the workplace, more autonomy in their work, and a greater work–life balance (Crampton & Hodge, 2007; Reynolds, Bush, & Geist, 2008; Twenge, 2010). Millennials represent yet another contrast to previous generations. These individuals have been referred to as the "Nintendo Generation," meaning they prefer a work environment with frequent, high levels of feedback, instant access to information, and clearly defined expectations (Herman & Eckel, 2002; Westerman & Yamamura, 2007). Leadership is shared, and collaboration and involvement in decision-making are valued by this generation.

While we expected that actual differences among the work characteristics would be few, we expected a far greater number of *perceived* differences between generational cohorts in terms of what they desire in their work context. This reasoning is based on previous research that illustrates the discriminating views that arise from generational stereotyping. For example, younger generations persistently hold negative stereotypes of their elders, despite the fact that older generations are living longer, healthier, more productive lives (Yoon & Kolomer, 2007). Kornadt and Rothermund (2011) found that younger generations consistently evaluated older workers as less flexible. For their part, older generations were shown to portray younger generations negatively and to view them as selfish (Arnett, 2010). In particular, Boomers were likely to perceive Millennials as unwilling to pay their dues (Arnett, 2004).

Another reason for our expectation of more perceived differences is the actor–observer effect (Jones & Nisbett, 1972) related to attribution theory. This theory posits that individuals are always searching for explanations for other people's behavior (Heider, 1958). There is a tendency to attribute others' behaviors to internal causes (i.e., something inherent in them) while attributing one's own behavior to external causes (i.e., something inherent in the situation). Thus, we expect to see generations who are observing actors from other generations to make inaccurate attributions.

To test these hypotheses, we surveyed 263 employees at an organization that had demonstrated reasonable representation of the three generations being studied. In addition to generational views and personal preferences, we also collected demographic data such as age and gender in order to control for their effect. Every effort was made to obtain data from as wide a sample of employees as possible; as a result, employee job positions at all levels of the organization were represented, from frontline employees to the CEO.

Analyses of our data revealed significant actual differences for three of the six work aspects we had predicted. Millennials indicated a higher value score than Boomers regarding the use of e-mail. Millennials also indicated a higher value score with regard to social media than either Generation X or Boomers. A similar finding occurred with regard to fun at work; the Millennials' valuation score was significantly higher for this item than for Gen-Xers or Boomers.

In addition to these three actual differences, we found a significant difference in valuation scores for two other work characteristics not hypothesized. Specifically, Millennials appeared to value continuous learning more than Generation X, and Boomers reported a higher value score than their Generation X counterparts for "professionalism." It should be noted that this finding represented the only real significant difference found between Generation X and Boomers.

A series of multivariate analyses were conducted to examine how each generation perceived the other generations with regard to the fifteen work characteristic items. One analysis focused on the degree to which the generations believed the Boomers valued the fifteen work characteristics. A second analysis focused on the degree to which the generations believed Generation X valued the fifteen items. And a third analysis focused on the degree to which the generations believed *Millennials* valued the fifteen items.

Our results indicated significant perceived Boomer generational differences for eight of the fifteen items. Boomers indicated they valued teamwork, flexibility, technology, and fun at work more than Gen-Xers believed Boomers would. We also found that Boomers valued flexibility and technology more than Millennials believed they would. Millennials also believed Boomers would value formal authority and structure more than Boomers actually did. Interestingly, the generations appeared to disagree in their misperceptions at times. For four items (formal authority, face-to-face communication, structure, and recognition), Millennials indicated a higher Boomer value than Gen-Xers indicated—both generations overestimated the actual value placed on these items by Boomers.

In terms of Generation X, results indicated perceived generational differences for five of the fifteen work characteristic items. The only perceived difference between Gen-Xers and Millennials concerned professionalism; Millennials believed Gen-Xers would value it more than that generation actually indicated. For their part, Boomers believed Gen-Xers valued security more than they actually did. In addition, Boomers expected Gen-Xers to value technology in general and social media specifically more than Xers actually did. Millennials and Boomers appeared to differ in their perceptions about what Generation X valued across three items: security, professionalism, and formal authority. In each case, Millennials attributed a higher value score to Gen-Xers than Boomers did (and both were inaccurate).

However, it was the generations' perception of what Millennials valued that revealed the most perceptual differences of all the analyses; in fact, technology was the *only* value item in which there was *not* any statistically significant perceptual difference among the three generations. For eight of the items (teamwork, security, professionalism, flexibility, involvement, continuous learning, fun at work, and recognition), Generation X overestimated the value Millennials would provide. With the exception of technology, face-to-face communication, and e-mail communication, Boomers did not believe Millennials to value these work aspects as much as Millennial participants actually reported. For security, e-mail, social media, and fun at work, Boomers and Gen-Xers differed in their perceptions of Millennials.

Across all analyses, our hypothesis that perceived differences would outnumber actual generational differences held strongly. As noted, we found eight *actual* value differences across generations relating to five of the value items (because Millennials were different from both Generation X and Boomers on three of the five items). In contrast, we found twenty-seven out of the forty-five *perceived* value difference comparisons to be statistically significant. Furthermore, these perceived differences pertained to all fifteen work characteristic items studied.

In summary, our findings would appear to strongly suggest that Boomers, Gen-Xers, and Millennials believe there are far more differences between the generations than actually exist. Our findings demonstrate the importance of perception in the course of interactions with others.

Implications

Diversity requires greater effort on the part of today's managers, as they attempt to communicate with and motivate individuals with varied perspectives, experiences, and needs. To be sure, the differences between those of various generations and ages cannot be ignored. Our research, and that of our colleagues, demonstrates the need for awareness and mindful interaction with regard to these differences. When managers try to manage using a "cookie cutter" approach (one approach applied to all), the results are often less effective than when they recognize and acknowledge such diversity in their workplace interactions. However, we have also demonstrated that often these "differences" exist more in our minds and our perceived notions than in reality. As such, today's managers (and researchers) are encouraged to look for opportunities to shed light on commonalities as often as they look for diversity.

Our study on generational differences revealed that differences people believe to be there far outnumber the differences that actually exist between generational cohorts in work contexts. Two of the actual differences (views on e-mail and social media) demonstrate how generations value technological communication. It should be noted that no significant difference was found in the extent to which the generations valued technology in general. Contrary to the often-stated notion that older generations are resistant to technology, our results suggest that all generations currently active in the workforce understand the value of technology when it comes to competing successfully in today's business environment (Lester, Standifer, Schultz, & Windsor, 2012). Boomers and Gen-Xers appeared to value technologically oriented communication significantly less than their younger counterparts; however, more traditional forms of communication (e.g., face-to-face) did not reveal a significant actual difference, as originally hypothesized. Whereas Boomers tend to rely on face-to-face communication, Millennials may value face-to-face communication more as a necessary means of interaction with older generations.

Two unexpected actual differences with regard to work culture also emerged in our findings related to professionalism and continuous learning. First, Boomers indicated a higher value on professionalism than did Gen-Xers; in fact, Gen X had the lowest mean on this value item of all three generations surveyed. Second, Millennials rated continuous learning significantly higher in value than their older cohorts. In retrospect, this is understandable, given the current emphasis on education and the desire among those just entering the workforce to build and retain marketable skills.

But it is the perceived differences that emerged in our study that are the most revealing, as they highlight mistaken beliefs that seem to align to stereotypical profiles often perpetuated in our culture. For their part, Millennials were more likely to believe that older generations downplay work-related issues, such as flexibility, technology, and fun, more than their older cohorts actually do. Millennials also attributed significantly higher value to professionalism to Gen X and the importance of formal authority to Boomers than was the case in reality. However, it was not only the younger subjects who held misconceptions. Older generations significantly underestimated the extent to which Millennials actually professed to value work involvement, formal authority, face-to-face communication, professionalism, and continuous learning. And Boomers believed Gen-Xers valued technology and social media more than was actually reported.

In addition to generational diversity, it is also important that managers acknowledge the impact of age-related perceptions and preferences on workplace outcomes. Previous research establishes the ways in which workers create in-group and out-group social categorizations based on salient demographic characteristics such as age. The social categorization literature also delineates how such categorizations may affect the success of work interactions. Research that examines perceptions about age is needed. For example, how do the beliefs and preferences an individual might hold with regard to those of differing age influence interactions when age diversity exists in the group? And how might an age-similarity preference interact with other constructs such as uncertainty?

What implications do our findings and previous work on generation and age-oriented diversity have for today's managers? We first suggest that both researchers and managers could benefit from lessons provided by diversity researchers; namely, the need for a work climate that fosters nonjudgmental attitudes, tolerance, and an open exchange of information (Lester et al., 2012). It is also useful to understand that actual and perceived differences both affect how coworkers interact with one another. Managers must be aware of the real differences that exist among their employees and be prepared to help guide interactions mindful of these differences. But managers should also make workers aware of how similar they are to one another and build positive interactions on that common ground.

The power of perception cannot be underestimated. Make workers aware that their perceptions, while perfectly human, can set the stage for problems with their coworkers. Opportunities such as cross-generational mentoring in which younger and older participants educate and share their strengths with each other provide the kind of positive interactions that over time can help break down inaccurate perspectives. Managers should also realize the frustration some feel in age-diverse situations and assist employees in working through these issues in a constructive manner. Prior research demonstrates the benefits of reducing uncertainty whenever possible for employees through effective communication, employee involvement, and empowerment. Specific to age-related perceptions, managers might work with employees to become aware of potentially negative (and often inaccurate) perceptions of workers from different generations and age groups. In addition, managers can monitor employee attitudes about workplace conditions and try to ensure that challenges perceived by workers are validated, but not mistakenly attributed to others.

In conclusion, this research illustrates the need for managers to acknowledge the reality of generational and age-based diversity in their workforce. However, it also demonstrates the problems of perception; namely, that perceptions matter even when they do not accurately represent reality. Awareness, training, communication, and understanding are the keys to making this diversity into an opportunity and competitive strength, rather than a liability. Managers who overcome negative perceptions and the challenges of working in an age-diverse environment will enable their organizations and their workforce to thrive in the twenty-first century.

References

Adams, S. J. (2000). Generation X: How understanding this population leads to better safety programs. *Professional Safety, 45*: 26–29.

Anetzberger, G. J., & Teaster, P. B. (2010). Future directions for social policy and elder abuse: Through the looking glass of generational characteristics. *Journal of Elder Abuse & Neglect, 22*, 207–215.

Arnett, J. J. (2004). *Emerging adulthood: The winding road from the late teens through the twenties.* New York, NY: Oxford University Press.

Arnett, J. J. (2010). Oh, grow up! Generational grumbling and the new life stage of emerging adulthood—Commentary on Trzesniewski and Donnellan (2010). *Perspectives on Psychological Science, 5*, 88–92.

Ashforth, B. E. & Mael, F. (1989). Social identity theory and the organization. *Academy of Management Review, 14*: 20–39.

Avery, D. R., McKay, P. F., & Wilson, D. C. (2007). Engaging the aging workforce: The relationship between perceived age similarity, satisfaction with coworkers, and employee engagement. *Journal of Applied Psychology, 92*: 1542–1556.

Benson, J. & Brown, M. (2011). Generations at work: Are there differences and do they matter? *The International Journal of Human Resource Management, 22*: 1843–1865.

Bright, L. (2010). Why age matters in the work preferences of public employees: A comparison of three age-related explanations. *Public Personnel Management, 39*, 1–14.

Cennamo, L. & Gardner, D. (2008). Generational differences in work values, outcomes and person–organization value fit. *Emerald Group Publishing Limited, 23.*

Crampton, S. M., & Hodge, J. W. (2007). Generations in the workplace: Understanding age diversity. *The Business Review, 9*, 16–22.

Crumpacker, M., & Crumpacker, J. M. (2007). Succession planning and generational stereotypes: Should HR consider age-based values and attitudes a relevant factor or a passing fad? *Public Personnel Management, 36*: 349–369.

Daboval, J. (1998). A comparison between Baby Boomers and Generation X employees' bases and foci of commitment. Unpublished doctoral dissertation, Nova South Eastern University, Fort Lauderdale, FL.

Dixon, S. (2003). Implications of population aging for the labor market. *Labour Market Trends, February*: 67–76.

Elsdon, R., & Lyer, S. (1999). Creating value and enhancing retention through employee development: The Sun Microsystems experience. *Human Resource Planning, 22*, 39–48.

Fogg, P. (2009). When generations collide. *Education Digest*, 74: 25–30.

Giancola, F. (2006). The generational gap: More a myth than reality. *Human Resource Planning, 29*, 32–37.

Giancola, F. (2008). Should generation profiles influence rewards strategy? *Employee Relations Law Journal, 34*, 56–68.

Herman, A., & Eckel, R. (2002). The new American worker: What Generation 'Y' brings to the workplace. *Work Matters, May*, 1–2.

Heider, F. (1958). *The psychology of interpersonal relations*. New York, NY: Wiley.

Hill, R. P. (2002). Managing across generations in the 21st century: Important lessons from the ivory trenches. *Journal of Management Inquiry, 11*, 60–66.

Jehn, K. A., Chadwick, C., & Thatcher, S. M. B. (1997). To agree or not to agree: The effects of value congruence, individual demographic dissimilarity, and conflict on workgroup outcomes. *International Journal of Conflict Management, 8*: 287–305.

Jones, E. E., & Nisbett, R. E. (1972). *The actor and the observer: Divergent perceptions of the causes of behavior*. In E. E. Jones, D. E. Kanouse, H. H. Kelley, R. E. Nisbett, S. Valins, & B. Weiner (Eds.), *Attribution: Perceiving the causes of behavior* (pp. 79–94). Morristown, NJ: General Learning Press.

Jorgensen, B. (2003). Baby Boomers, Generation X, and Generation Y: Policy implications for defense forces in the modern era. *Foresight, 5*: 41–49.

Jurkiewicz, C. L., & Brown, R. G. (1998). GenXers vs. Boomers vs. Matures: Generational comparisons of public employee motivation. *Review of Public Personnel Administration, 18*, 18–37.

Kornadt, A. E., & Rothermund, K. (2011). Contexts of aging: Assessing evaluative age stereotypes in different life domains. *Journal of Gerontology, 66*(B), 547–556.

Kupperschmidt, B. R. (2000). Multigenerational employees: Strategies for effective management. *The Health Care Manager, 19*, 65–76.

Lester, S. W., Standifer, R. L., Schultz, N. J., & Windsor, J. M., (2012). Actual versus perceived generational differences at work: An empirical examination. *Journal of Leadership and Organizational Studies, 19*: 341–354.

Martin, C. A. (2005). From high maintenance to high productivity. *Industrial and Commercial Training*, 37: 39–44.

McMullin, J., Comeau, T., & Jovic, W. (2007). Generational affinities and discourses of difference: A case study of highly skilled information technology workers. *British Journal of Sociology, 58*: 297–316.

O'Bannon, G. (2001). Managing our future: The Generation X factor. *Public Personnel Management, 29*: 55–74.

Patterson, C. K. (2007). The impact of generational diversity in the workplace. *The Diversity Factor, 15*: 17–22.

Pelled, L. H., Xin, K. R., & Weiss, A. M. (2001). No es como mi: Relationship demography and conflict in a Mexican production facility. *Journal of Occupational and Organizational Psychology, 74*: 63–84.

Randel, A. E. (2002). Identity salience: A moderator of the relationship between group gender composition and work group conflict. *Journal of Organizational Behavior, 23*: 749–766.

Reynolds, L., Bush, E. C., & Geist, R. (2008). The Gen Y imperative. *Communication World, 25*, 19–22.

Riordan, C. M. (2000). Relational demography within groups: Past developments, contradictions, and new directions. *Research in Personnel and Human Resources Management, 19*: 131–173.

Robinson, R. V., & Jackson, E. F. (2001). Is trust in others declining in America? An age-period-cohort-analysis. *Social Science Research, 30*: 117–145.

Ryan, M. (2000). Gerald Celente: He reveals what lies ahead. *Parade Magazine*, Sept. 10: 22–23.

Schamm, J. (2004). Age groups mostly in accord. *HR Magazine, 49*: 208.

Schuman, H., & Scott, J. (1989). Generations and collective memories. *American Sociological Review, 54*: 359–381.

Simons, G. (2010). Leveraging generational work styles to meet business objectives. *Information Management, 44*, 28–33.

Smola, K. W., & Sutton, C. D. (2002). Generational differences: Revisiting generational work values for the new millennium. *Journal of Organizational Behavior, 23*: 363–382.

Stevens, R. H. (2010). Managing human capital: How to use knowledge management to transfer knowledge in today's multi-generational workforce. *International Business Research, 3*: 77–82.

Sullivan, S. E., Forret, M. L., Carraher, S. M., & Mainiero, L. A. (2009). Using the kaleidoscope career model to examine generational differences in work attitudes. *Career Development International, 14*: 284–302.

Tajfel, H., & Turner, J. C. (1986). The social identity theory of intergroup behavior. In S. Worchel & W. G. Austin (Eds.), *Psychology of intergroup relations* (2nd ed.) (pp. 7–24). Chicago: Nelson-Hall.

Tsui, A. S., & Gutek, B. A. (1999). *Demographic differences in organizations: Current research and future directions.* Lanham, MD: Lexington Books.

Turner, J. C. (1987). *Rediscovering the social group: A self-categorization theory.* Oxford, England: Blackwell Publishing.

Twenge, J. M. (2010). A review of empirical evidence on generational differences in work attitudes. *Journal of Business Psychology, 25*: 201–210.

U.S. General Accounting Office, (2001). Older workers: Demographic trends pose challenges for employers and workers. Washington D.C.

Westerman, J. W., & Yamamura, J. H. (2007). Generational preferences for work environment fit: Effects on employee outcomes. *Career Development International Journal, 12*, 150–161.

Yoon, E., & Kolomer, S. R. (2007). Refining the measure and dimensions of social values of older people (SVOP). *Educational Gerontology, 33*, 649–663.

Zaslow, J. (2002). *Janis who? Selling yesterday's stars to today's teenagers is a challenge.* Wall Street Journal, May.

Zenger, T. R., & Lawrence, B. S. (1989). Organizational demography: The differential effects of age and tenure distributions on technical communication. *Academy of Management Journal, 32*: 353–376.

6

MANAGING TENSIONS IN VIRTUAL WORK ARRANGEMENTS

Jennifer L. Gibbs

RUTGERS UNIVERSITY

Introduction

Modern work settings such as virtual work arrangements—which are geographically distributed and in which workers rely heavily on information and communication technologies (ICTs)—allow for work to be conducted in new ways, but they also give rise to new types of work pressures that differ from those faced by workers in traditional organizations. This chapter will consider tensions arising from global, geographically distributed, and technologically mediated work arrangements and the ways in which these tensions are communicatively managed by organizational members. When people hear the word "tension," they typically think of something negative, like stress or interpersonal conflict. While the modern workplace is often fraught with work pressures and stress due to information overload from email and other sources (e.g., Barley, Meyerson, & Grodal, 2011), we will be discussing a different sort of tensions. The tensions that will be discussed here can both alleviate and add to work pressures involving virtual work arrangements and increased use of new communication technologies. In this chapter, we will consider tensions as normal features of organizing that can be productive for organizations, depending on how they are managed. We do so by highlighting several virtual work contexts in which tensions are likely to arise: global team collaboration, telework policies, and technology use in distributed work. Drawing on examples from my own and other related research, this chapter will illustrate the ways in which dialectical tensions arise and are discursively managed through communication practices in ways that are productive for virtual workers. This has important implications for anyone who works in or manages a virtual organization.

Dialectical Tensions in the Workplace

The notion of dialectical tensions originates with Bakhtin's work on dialogism (1981). In Bakhtin's theory, "dialogue is the concept that brings coherence to the whole" (Baxter, 2004, p. 2). Bakhtin regarded social life as an open dialogue that was indeterminate and multivocal, comprised of multiple voices, rather than fixed and totalizing (Baxter, 2004). His notion was of dialogue as a constitutive process in which relationships are constituted in communication practices, in the interaction of self and other. This process is one of dialectical flux—it is dynamic, emergent, and messy. Relating and dialogue are as much about differences as similarities, positioned as a dialectical or contradictory interplay between centripetal forces of unity and centrifugal forces of difference (Bakhtin, 1981). Bakhtin's work differs from other theorists such as Marx and Hegel whose notion of dialectics is more linear and deterministic, in which a contradiction between thesis and antithesis is subsequently neatly resolved through synthesis. Another key difference is that while Marxist–Hegelian dialectics characterize social life on a more macro level, Bakhtin's work is situated at more of an interpersonal level, as forces pulling individuals in opposing directions. As such, his theory highlights the individual agency involved in the actions and choices of individuals—and their multiple voices—as they act and respond to pressures in the environment around them to accomplish complex goals.

Communication scholars of relationships have adapted Bakhtin's theory to explain the tug of war individuals routinely face in their interpersonal relationships through relational dialectics theory (Baxter & Montgomery, 1996). For instance, relational partners often swing back and forth between poles of autonomy and connectedness, as they want to feel connected to their partner without losing themselves or their independence in the process. At times the relationship may become strained when one partner desires more connectedness while the other partner desires more autonomy; at other times the emphasis on one pole or the other may change over time or in different situations as the relationship evolves. Nevertheless, the necessity to attend to both opposing poles creates tensions in the relationship that require management through communication. And finding a way to attend to both needs without contradiction helps maintain a healthy balance in the relationship, although it never reaches equilibrium but is always in flux.

Organizational members also face tensions in the workplace that pull them in different directions. They may find their own needs or goals at odds with those of the organization, or of other coworkers, or even be pulled apart by competing goals of their own (e.g., being a committed worker versus being a committed spouse or parent). Sometimes these competing goals and interests are both important and necessary to attend to, requiring creative solutions to do seemingly opposite things. To address this "dilemmatic" nature of organizing (Trethewey & Ashcraft, 2004) in which organizations are seen as conflicted sites of activity rather than sites of stability and determinacy, scholars have applied dialectical theory to examine organizational tensions (e.g., Putnam, 1986; Trethewey & Ashcraft, 2004). A tension is defined as an opposition between two conflicting poles, which can be goals or interests of an individual or group, or set of "unified opposites" (Baxter & Montgomery, 1996). Rather than being a simple either-or choice, however, it involves pressures to attend to seemingly contradictory needs. Tensions are regarded as normal, ubiquitous features of organizing (Pepper & Larson, 2006; Seo, Putnam, & Bartunek, 2004; Trethewey & Ashcraft, 2004) rather than anomalies or problems to be resolved or minimized. The existence of tensions is not inherently productive or destructive, but depends on how such tensions are discursively managed (Tracy, 2004). While simple contradictions (involving an either-or choice between two competing alternatives) and pragmatic paradoxes (that demand impossible choices between mutually exclusive options, as in the saying "be spontaneous") have been found to produce negative responses as they paralyze action and limit possibilities for response, dialectical tensions have been found to be productive as they allow for the merging of opposites through "both-and" options (Putnam & Boys, 2006).

Communication plays an important role in the management of organizational contradictions. The range of responses has been categorized into several types: selection (selecting one pole and ignoring the other), separation (vacillating back and forth between the two poles), integration (attending to both poles through a "forced merger" or neutralization, which does not allow for either to be fully realized), transcendence (creatively transforming dualities through reframing or synthesis so that the opposition no longer exists), and connection (treating tensions as mutually reinforcing in order to attend to both poles) (Seo et al., 2004). In this chapter we are particularly interested in the productive functions of tensions in terms of the ways in which they enable rather than constrain behavior and the ways they provide balance by enabling the accomplishment of multiple goals.

A dialectical approach also situates ambiguity as a central feature of organizing (Eisenberg, 1984; Weick, 1979), in contrast to traditional assumptions of communication and organizations that privilege openness, clarity, and consensus and regard communication as a process of uncertainty reduction. It acknowledges that organizational members are strategic, symbolic actors (Eisenberg, 2007) who often engage in "strategic ambiguity" (Eisenberg, 1984) in which they deliberately engage in ambiguous communication to foster multiple meanings of messages or communicative events—such as organizational mission and vision statements—in order to accomplish particular goals or appeal to a variety of stakeholders with diverse values. While clear and open communication is often taken for granted as the ideal and most effective form, this "ideology of openness" has been critiqued on the grounds that open communication is not always desirable, and in fact, can be risky as too much disclosure may surface differences and jeopardize relationships, as well as damage organizational reputation or employee morale (Eisenberg & Witten, 1987). Covert or ambiguous communication often plays a strategic role in organizations by allowing for political behavior or face-saving that is not just self-interested but concerned with preserving good relationships and face of others.

This perspective is also grounded in a constitutive view of virtual organizing (and other organizing processes) as constituted through communication (Gibbs, Nekrassova, Grushina, & Abdul Wahab, 2008) that recognizes that such processes are not fixed or determinate but are continually recreated and reproduced in interaction among organizational members. This chapter addresses research questions such as: What dialectical tensions emerge in virtual work settings? How do virtual workers manage and negotiate these tensions? How do responses to these dialectics constrain or enable processes of organizing? To illustrate how a tensional view may apply in the modern workplace and work to manage a variety of work pressures, this chapter will address these questions in the context of several types of virtual work environments.

Tensions in Virtual Work Settings

Due to the rise of global competition and pressure to compete in a global workplace, along with the convergence of new communication technologies that enable interaction across time and space, new nonstandard work arrangements such as global teams, telework, and temporary or part-time work are on the rise (Ballard & Gossett, 2007). The infusion of new communication technologies in the workplace means that coworkers are no longer confined to a single physical space such as an office building to conduct their work. Rather, they may work from home or conduct work across geographically dispersed sites, within the same country or internationally. This poses challenges such as scheduling real-time meetings, when members are located in different time zones and may not be working during the same time intervals, and sharing knowledge across geographical or cultural contexts (Gibson & Gibbs, 2006). Virtual work settings require more complexity in management and coordination, and are full of tensions. We will now discuss three different virtual work contexts to provide examples of the sorts of tensions that arise and how they may be communicatively managed.

Global Team Collaboration

Tensions play a critical role in global organizing. Prior research has found that global teams are more loosely coupled (Gibbs, 2006) and global collaboration is characterized by ambiguity and contradiction rather than by clarity and consensus (Gibbs, 2009b). Global teams face more complexity in many ways (Gluesing & Gibson, 2004) because they are embedded in multiple geographical, temporal, organizational, and cultural contexts. Global organizations may even face differences in organizational culture from region to region, creating tensions between standardization and differentiation in corporate culture (Gibbs, 2009a). Differences in cultural norms, values, structure, and policies are likely to lead to conflicting goals, priorities, and processes that create irresolvable tensions among global team members. It may be impossible to create standardized policies regarding salary, bonuses, and other benefits because team members come from units with different structures. For instance, global software teams involved in offshore outsourcing face tensions in evaluating performance of temporary contractors whose project managers may not be subject to the same metrics or procedures for performance appraisals as their permanent managers in other country locations, resulting in their career development being in limbo during their assignments while meanwhile other employees are promoted back home (Gibbs, 2006). Further, it can be difficult to determine what is fair in terms of bonuses or financial rewards due to different pay structures in different country locations (Gibbs, 2009b; Gibbs & Boyraz, 2015).

In an ethnographic study of a global software team in a high-tech organization, Gibbs (2009b) identified several irresolvable tensions arising in global team inter-action: autonomy versus connectedness, inclusion versus exclusion, and empow-erment versus disempowerment. Global team managers faced a tension between maintaining autonomy in their work while preserving team connectedness, caused in part by the unclear dual reporting structure and amorphous team pro-cesses. While they worked to preserve unpredictability and detachment in their relationships with foreign assignees, these assignees often pushed for predictability and involvement. Customers faced a dilemma in negotiating work relationships with assignees who were temporary employees in their teams in terms of including or excluding them. While there were benefits to integrating them into the team and giving them more responsibility, there were also costs to investing too much time and resources into them, since they were eventually going to leave. Finally, tensions arose around perceptions of the foreign assignees as empowered or disempowered, due to pressures to treat them equitably compared to, on one hand, their colleagues back in their home center and, on the other hand, their temporary teammates. The uncertainty and lack of career path they faced while on assignment led to perceptions of marginalization, which clashed with the managers' perceptions of their assignments as a privilege since they offered career growth and additional benefits. Team members responded to these tensions through several discursive responses, some of which (transcendence) enabled creative attendance to both poles and were thus more productive than others (selection and withdrawal) which constrained team members' actions. Managers were more likely to draw on productive strategies that enabled them to transcend oppositions and embrace ambiguity, while lower-level assignees were less able to cope with tensions and more constrained by them.

As the above findings indicate, dialectical tensions may be productive in global teams by allowing for irresolvable differences to coexist. Preserving ambiguity in organizing processes rather than pushing for clarity and uncertainty reduction can be beneficial in allowing for "unified diversity" in which diverse perspectives and interpretations coexist while members believe they are all in agreement

(Eisenberg, 1984). Taking a dialectical view may also present a useful way of managing cultural differences in global or multicultural teams. Gibbs (2009a) proposed a dialectical framework employing the metaphor of "culture as kaleidoscope" to better conceptualize the complexity of culture in global teams in which cultural differences may cohere around national, organizational, functional, or other fault lines. Regarding culture as kaleidoscope is a more fluid, dynamic view that regards culture as multifaceted and constituted through communication. This goes against more traditional "corporate culture" views of culture as unified, strong, integrated, and subject to managerial control (e.g., Schein, 1992). This view reframes cultural differences as dynamic cultural tensions, rather than static polar oppositions. As Gibbs (2009a) writes, "By reframing cultural differences as dynamic tensions, rather than static oppositions, as they are often regarded in the literature (e.g., Hofstede, 2001, 2005), these differences can be managed more productively and generate creative new solutions rather than leading to conflict and deadlock. Rather than suggesting that cultural differences be minimized or homogenized, this view proposes that they may generate productive intercultural collaboration when different views are in healthy tension with one another" (p. 2). This framework is helpful in explaining tensions in national culture, regional differences in organizational culture, and tensions among various micro-organizational identities (e.g., home software center versus temporary project team) that bifurcate employee allegiances in global work arrangements.

Telework Policies

Another form of virtual work that has been found to be characterized by tensions is telework. Participatory and democratic work structures and practices more broadly have been characterized as fraught with paradoxes and contradictions as they purport to give workers more freedom and voice but often become co-opted as forms of managerial control (Stohl & Cheney, 2001). Similarly, with telework, there is often a disconnect between the utopian discourse that emphasizes its personal benefits such as increased flexibility and work–life balance as well as organizational benefits such as cost savings, greater productivity, and environmental impacts, and the realities of telework experiences that do not achieve these benefits. For instance, Hylmo and Buzzanell's (2002) qualitative study of telecommuters reveals that telework is a paradoxical process as teleworkers routinely worked longer hours than in-house employees while being marginalized for their lack of physical presence; in this and other ways, the very systems designed to provide greater autonomy limited their freedom and flexibility.

Even formal policies and guidelines surrounding virtual work, such as telework policies, have been found to be more ambiguous and less clear-cut than might be expected. A qualitative content analysis of a set of thirty-five U.S. state governments' formal telework policies revealed regular contradictions that provided challenges to virtual workers and their employing organizations (Gibbs, Scott,

Kim, & Lee, 2010). This study found two key tensions: autonomy versus control, and flexibility versus rigidity. The first tension between employee autonomy and employer control was manifested in the framing of telework as a management option rather than an employee choice, the extent to which teleworkers were monitored by the agency versus self-managed, and slippage in whether agencies or individual teleworkers were responsible for provision of equipment and data and physical safety. The tension between flexibility and rigidity was evident through standardized versus ad hoc eligibility criteria and stated guidelines for teleworkers, clear versus ambiguous statement of rules, and the degree to which work and family commitments were explicitly separated versus allowed to blend. While some policies were quite vague about rules and requirements for teleworkers, other policies attempted to regulate teleworkers' home and personal lives (by specifying required levels of home maintenance, explicitly prohibiting non-work activities or visitors, and setting requirements for how often to check email) in ways that were more restrictive and controlling than typical traditional work arrangements. Although explicit contradictions between telework benefits and realities may be problematic, most of the policies were found to employ ambiguity productively to allow for individual and organizational interests to coexist.

Technology Use

Virtual workers typically rely heavily on new communication technologies such as email, instant messaging, video conferencing, smart phones, and social media applications to communicate and collaborate. The use of such technologies has also been associated with work pressures such as increased communication load (or overload) and stress (Barley et al., 2011). Jian (2007) adopts a tensional perspective to explain organizational resistance to ICT implementation, finding that adoption of a new software system brought a variety of organizational tensions into play, which contributed to competing interpretations of the technology, and the reactions to these tensions and interpretations in turn produced resistance behaviors.

Other research on multiple media use among managers and subordinates regards media use as a contested site of struggle in which conflicting role-based goals play out (Erhardt & Gibbs, 2014). Drawing on rich qualitative data from ninety-one semi-structured interviews and observations with six project teams in Sweden and the U.S., the authors found that managers and employees engaged in impression management tactics that were often in dialectical tension with one another as managers and subordinates pursued individual role-related goals while attempting to maintain cooperative working relationships with one another, and that each group drew on different technological affordances to accomplish these often conflicting goals. This work portrays impression management as a dialectical process in which actions by managers often provoked counteractions by subordinates and vice versa, as the actions of each were recursively shaped by one another in dialectical tension. Further, the actor–audience relationship was constantly shifting as was the stage on which impression management tactics took place, which took the form of a variety of media including face-to-face.

Specifically, Erhardt and Gibbs (2014) identified three sets of interrelated tactics: dodging response versus exerting social pressure, multicommunicating versus singular communicating, and promoting oneself versus giving credit to all. For instance, managers would often strategically ignore or selectively respond to email (by not responding in a timely fashion or avoiding difficult questions) so as to protect their time and face while attending to the needs of their subordinates. This strategic nonresponse was met by efforts to exert pressure on them to respond to requests by subordinates through mobilizing multiple media and multiple coworkers to indirectly reinforce the message without being perceived as pushy. At other times, the situation was reversed and subordinates were motivated to protect their time and attend to individual tasks (often in an attempt to maintain work–life balance) while managers pushed them to engage in collaborative work. In the single versus multi-communicating set of tactics, employees would leverage the invisibility of cues provided by unobtrusive devices such as smart phones and laptops to "multi-communicate" (Stephens, 2012) or attend to multiple communicative activities during meetings by muting the phone while calling in from a child's soccer game, or reading and drafting emails and text messages while appearing present in the conversation. Managers responded by exerting subtle indirect tactics to secure employees' full engagement and focus in face-to-face meetings.

In the third set of tactics related to demonstrating competence, a tug of war over media use was evident as managers preferred the non-traceability and nonverbal cues in face-to-face communication to demonstrate competence to their employees by exerting control over the task at hand and guarding against unanticipated, documented responses that could undermine their credibility. By contrast, subordinates preferred editable and persistent ICTs such as email to strategically demonstrate competence and make themselves more visible to their managers. Other research has also found that ICTs can be used to strategically alter perceptions of expertise; Leonardi and Treem (2012) found that distributed workers often used knowledge-sharing technologies strategically to enhance perceived rather than actual expertise. These counter tactics were productive in enabling both parties to meet conflicting needs while maintaining face with one another. Although managers and subordinates were driven by conflicting goals that created tensions between them, their communicative management of these tensions ultimately served to keep team interaction in balance by allowing for the accomplishment of both groups' goals.

In another recent study, Gibbs et al. (2013) found that the use of social media by engineers in a distributed high-technology organization was characterized by tensions created by unique affordances that led to strategic use of social media to communicatively manage these tensions. While emerging research on social media use is often characterized by an "ideology of openness" that assumes that social media will increase open communication and knowledge sharing in organizations (and that this is always desirable), Gibbs et al. (2013) find that the unique affordances of social media such as visibility, association, persistence, and editability (Treem & Leonardi, 2012) lead to a dialectic of openness versus closedness, as distributed workers use social media to both increase and limit knowledge sharing, requiring strategic communication practices designed to preserve both openness and ambiguity. They identified three tensions: visibility versus invisibility, engagement versus disengagement, and sharing versus control.

First, employees relied heavily on Skype chat as a collaborative group-based instant messaging tool to enable remote coworkers to be more available or visible to one another, but also to become more invisible in order to avoid being disturbed. For example, one strategy was for East Coast engineers to "go invisible" on Skype at the end of their work day when they would typically get barraged by questions from the West Coast (where it was still afternoon) in order to limit their availability to others and work undisturbed while still being able to respond to urgent requests at their discretion. This use of ambiguity to maintain good impressions and relationships was also evident in research finding that organizational members engaged in strategic behavior that exploited ambiguities afforded by media use, such as using shared calendars to indicate availability but not necessarily attendance of meetings, and avoiding use of the "return receipt" feature in email in order to retain ambiguity regarding whether the email was read and being ignored or just had not been read yet (Birnholtz, Dixon, & Hancock, 2012).

Second, managers and other engineers would limit their engagement in the many Skype chat windows they used as news feeds or media streams (Ellison & boyd, 2013) to manage the tension between engagement versus disengagement. Their use of Skype groups allowed them to easily traverse information by scrolling through status updates to see what required their attention. While this provided more immediacy and interactivity than email, attending to the constant updates popping up in open chat windows could be quite time consuming and disruptive to work. To combat this tension, managers and other employees found ways to simultaneously engage yet disengage, such as quickly scanning conversation threads to monitor project status but limiting their engagement only to issues that required their attention, akin to the "triggered attending" affordance in which notifications provided by social media tools allow participants to monitor discussions and participate only when relevant (Majchrzak, Faraj, Kane, & Azad, 2013). This use of technologies to disengage was also illustrated by Leonardi, Treem, and Jackson (2010), who found that teleworkers engaged in strategic use of technologies to increase (rather than decrease) perceptions of distance in order to counteract the expectation that they would be constantly connected.

Finally, employees faced pressures to both share and control knowledge through social media. While most were quite open to sharing information with their colleagues as needed, they tended to limit what was shared by restricting permission settings to particular audiences or "selective sharing" of expertise, out of concern for job security as well as confidentiality of data. These findings also illustrate the productive role of dialectical tensions in enabling organizational members to attend to multiple goals.

Conclusion: Navigating Communicative Tensions in the Modern Workplace

As this chapter has shown, tensions play a critical role in virtual work contexts in enabling workers to attend to multiple, conflicting goals. The research discussed above highlights the role of tensions between standardization and flexibility and between autonomy and connectedness in virtual work arrangements such as global teams and telework, as well as in management of time, attention, and information load in technology-mediated work settings. These findings highlight the fact that virtual workers (as well as organizational members more broadly) often struggle with workplace pressures/tensions due to the need to manage multiple, sometimes conflicting goals. There may be tensions between various role-based members (e.g., managers versus subordinates) as well as tensions among individual goals (e.g., autonomy versus connectedness). Communication practices play a significant role in managing tensions, as members make strategic choices about how to respond to them. While tensions may be productive or detrimental, this chapter has focused particularly on the productive role of tensions in enabling organizing processes, as they hold together "necessary incompatibles" (Trethewey & Ashcraft, 2004) and maintain flexibility and balance among opposing goals that do not force a resolution of oppositions. These findings also call attention to the ways in which ambiguity plays a positive role in organizing processes, by allowing for conflicting goals and interests to coexist and maintaining positive impressions and relationships.

Virtual work contexts are a key feature of the modern workplace. Under-standing their tensional nature and the communicative responses to such tensions has practical implications for managers and other organizational members who face work pressures, such as information overload, stress and burnout, the struggle to maintain work–life balance, and pressures for constant connectivity through smartphones and other mobile technologies (e.g., Mazmanian, Orlikowski, & Yates, 2013), and can help them cope with such pressures. While it may be impossible to resolve or eliminate such tensions, employees do engage in strategic behavior to respond to such tensions in a way that enables them to meet complex and competing needs and maintain balance among them. As work arrangements become more distributed and new technologies such as social media become more prevalent in organizations, it will become more important to learn to manage these tensions in productive ways.

References

Bakhtin, M. M. (1981). *The dialogic imagination: Four essays*. (M. Holquist, Ed., C. Emerson & M. Holquist, Trans.). Austin, TX: University of Texas Press.

Ballard, D. I., & Gossett, L. M. (2007). Alternative times: Communicating the non-standard work arrangement. In C. S. Beck (Ed.), *Communication yearbook 31* (pp. 274–321). Mahwah, NJ: Erlbaum.

Barley, S. R., Meyerson, D. E., & Grodal, S. (2011). E-mail as a source and symbol of stress. *Organization Science, 22*, 887–906.

Baxter, L. A. (2004). Relationships as dialogues. *Personal Relationships, 11*, 1–22.

Baxter, L. A., & Montgomery, B. M. (1996). *Relating: Dialogues & dialectics*. New York: Guilford Press.

Birnholtz, J., Dixon, G., & Hancock, J. (2012). Distance, ambiguity and appropriation: Structures affording impression management in a collocated organization. *Computers in Human Behavior, 28*(3), 1028–1035. doi:10.1016/j.chb.2012.01.005.

Eisenberg, E. M. (1984). Ambiguity as strategy in organizational communication. *Communication Monographs, 51*(3), 227–242. doi:10.1080/03637758409390197.

Eisenberg, E. M. (2007). *Strategic ambiguities: Essays on communication, organization, and identity*. Thousand Oaks, CA: Sage Publications.

Eisenberg, E. M., & Witten, M. G. (1987). Reconsidering openness in organizational communication. *Academy of Management Review, 12*(3), 418–426. doi:10.5465/AMR.1987.4306557.

Ellison, N. B. & boyd, d. m. (2013). Sociality through social network sites. In W. H. Dutton (Ed.), *The Oxford handbook of Internet studies* (pp. 151–172). Oxford: Oxford University Press.

Erhardt, N., & Gibbs, J. L. (2014). The dialectical nature of impression management in knowledge work: Unpacking tensions in media use between managers and subordinates. *Management Communication Quarterly, 28*, 155–186. doi: 10.1177/0893318913520508.

Gibbs, J. L. (2006). Decoupling and coupling in global teams: Implications for human resource management. In G. K. Stahl & I. Bjorkman (Eds.), *Handbook of research in international human resource management* (pp. 347–363). Northampton, MA: Edward Elgar Publishing.

Gibbs, J. L. (2009a). Culture as kaleidoscope: Navigating cultural tensions in global collaboration. In *Proceedings of the ACM international workshop on intercultural collaboration* (IWIC 2009).

Gibbs, J. L. (2009b). Dialectics in a global software team: Negotiating tensions across time, space, and culture. *Human Relations, 62*(6), 905–935.

Gibbs, J. L., & Boyraz, M. (2015). International HRM's role in managing global teams. In Collings, D. G., Wood, G., & Caligiuri, P. (Eds.), *The Routledge companion to international human resource management* (pp. 532–551). New York: Routledge.

Gibbs, J. L., Nekrassova, D., Grushina, Y., & Abdul Wahab, S. (2008). Reconceptualizing virtual teaming from a constitutive perspective: Review, redirection, and research agenda. In C. S. Beck (Ed.), *Communication yearbook 32* (pp. 187–229). New York: Routledge.

Gibbs, J. L., Rozaidi, N. A., & Eisenberg, J. (2013). Overcoming the "ideology of openness": Probing the affordances of social media for organizational knowledge sharing. *Journal of Computer-Mediated Communication, 19*(1), 102–120. doi: 10.1111/jcc4.12034.

Gibbs, J. L., Scott, C. R., Kim, Y. H., & Lee, S. K. (2010). Examining tensions in telework policies. In S. D. Long (Ed.), *Communication, relationships, and practices in virtual work* (pp. 1–25). New York: IGI Global.

Gibson, C. B., & Gibbs, J. L. (2006). Unpacking the concept of virtuality: The effects of geographic dispersion, electronic dependence, dynamic structure, and national diversity on team innovation. *Administrative Science Quarterly, 51,* 451–495.

Gluesing, J. C. & Gibson, C. B. (2004). Designing and forming global teams. In H. W. Lane, M. L. Maznevski, M. E. Mendenhall & J. McNett (Eds.), *Handbook of global management* (pp. 199–226). Malden, MA: Blackwell.

Hofstede, G. (2001). *Culture's consequences: International differences in work-related values* (2nd Ed.). Thousand Oaks, CA: Sage.

Hofstede, G. (2005). *Cultures and organizations: Software of the mind* (2nd Ed.). New York: McGraw Hill.

Hylmo, A., & Buzzanell, P. (2002). Telecommuting as viewed through cultural lenses: An empirical investigation of the discourses of utopia, identity and mystery. *Communication Monographs, 69,* 329–356.

Jian, G. (2007). "Omega is a four-letter word": Toward a tension-centered model of resistance to information and communication technologies. *Communication Monographs, 74,* 517–540.

Leonardi, P. M., & Treem, J. W. (2012). Knowledge management technology as a stage for strategic self-presentation: Implications for knowledge sharing in organizations. *Information and Organization, 22*(1), 37–59. doi:10.1016/j.infoandorg.2011.10.003.

Leonardi, P. M., Treem, J. W., & Jackson, M. H. (2010). The connectivity paradox: Using technology to both decrease and increase perceptions of distance in distributed work arrangements. *Journal of Applied Communication Research, 38*(1), 85–105. doi:10.1080/00909880903483599.

Majchrzak, A., Faraj, S., Kane, G. C., & Azad, B. (2013). The contradictory influence of social media affordances on online knowledge sharing. *Journal of Computer-Mediated Communication, 19,* 38–55. doi:10.1111/jcc4.12030.

Mazmanian, M., Orlikowski, W. J., & Yates, J. (2013). The autonomy paradox: The implications of mobile email devices for knowledge professionals. *Organization Science, 24*(5), 1337–1357. http://dx.doi.org/10.1287/orsc.1120.0806.

Pepper, G. L., & Larson, G. S. (2006). Cultural identity tensions in a post-acquisition organization. *Journal of Applied Communication Research, 34,* 49–71.

Putnam, L. L. (1986). Contradictions and paradoxes in organizations. In L. Thayer (Ed.), *Organization-communication: Emerging perspectives I* (pp. 151–167). Norwood, NJ: Ablex.

Putnam, L. L., & Boys, S. (2006). Revisiting metaphors of organizational communication. In S. Clegg, C. Hardy, & W. Nord (Eds.), *Handbook of organizational studies* (2nd ed., pp. 541–576). London: Sage.

Schein, E. H. (1992). *Organizational culture and leadership* (2nd ed.). San Francisco: Jossey-Bass Publishers.

Seo, M., Putnam, L. L., & Bartunek, J. M. (2004). Dualities and tensions of planned organizational change. In M. S. Poole & A. H. van de Ven (Eds.), *Handbook of organizational change and innovation* (pp. 73–107). New York: Oxford University Press.

Stephens, K. K. (2012). Multiple conversations during organizational meetings: Development of the multicommunicating scale. *Management Communication Quarterly, 26,* 195–223.

Stohl, C., & Cheney, G. (2001). Participatory processes/paradoxical practices: Communication and the dilemmas of organizational democracy. *Management Communication Quarterly, 14,* 349–407.

Tracy, S. J. (2004). Dialectic, contradiction, or double bind? Analyzing and theorizing employee reactions to organizational tension. *Journal of Applied Communication Research*, *32*, 119–146. doi:10.1080/0090988042000210025.

Treem, J. W., & Leonardi, P. M. (2012). Social media use in organizations: Exploring the affordances of visibility, editability, persistence, and association. *Communication Yearbook 36*, 143–189.

Trethewey, A., & Ashcraft, K. L. (2004). Practicing disorganization: The development of applied perspectives on living with tension. *Journal of Applied Communication Research*, *32*(2), 81–88. doi:10.1080/0090988042000210007.

Weick, K. E. (1979). *The social psychology of organizing* (2nd ed.). New York: McGraw-Hill, Inc.

7

MODERN TIMES, MODERN SPACES

Interaction Genres and Multiminding in Network-Based Work

Dawna I. Ballard

UNIVERSITY OF TEXAS AT AUSTIN

Dina Inman Ramgolam

UNIVERSITY OF TEXAS AT AUSTIN

Estee Solomon Gray

MMINDD LABS

A few decades into the twentieth century, famed American historian and sociologist Lewis Mumford (1934) declared in *Technics and Civilization* that: "The clock, not the steam engine, is the key-machine of the modern industrial age. For every phase of its development the clock is both the outstanding fact and the typical symbol of the machine: even today no other machine is so ubiquitous" (p. 14). This declaration came on the heels of Charlie Chaplin's *Modern Times*, which depicted the centrality of clock-based timekeeping in fueling modern industrialization. More than a decade into the twenty-first century, communication, connection, and connectivity have joined time clocks and conveyor belts as the *zeitgebers*, or "time givers," that fuel global commerce. Today, in postindustrial work, the communication network has joined the clock for a large segment of the global workforce, as new forms of time and space have emerged (Castells, 2000). Consequently, the nature of work is being redefined.

While industrial work centers largely on sequential *individual* contributions, network-based (or postindustrial) work centers on concurrent *collective* contributions. As a result, both those who manage and those who perform network-based work are struggling to shift from a focus on *the time needed to complete a well-defined task* in industrial work to a focus on the *organizational and individual capabilities required to reliably achieve the more complex, interlocking outcomes* characteristic of postindustrial work. According to a recent report by the McKinsey Global Institute, the fastest-growing segment of the workforce in advanced economies is the interaction worker (McKinsey, 2012). This suggests that scholars must consider the utility and relevance of extant theory and models to account for the experience of this new front line of the network-based economy. Indeed, because interaction work relies upon complex communication and coordination with others yet requires independent judgment, the study of communication is critical to consider the implications of this shift for organizations and their members.

All of the above shifts—in the key-machine that drives work, in the practices needed to accomplish it, and in the relationships among the people who perform it—translate to equally profound shifts in how organizational members come to apprehend time and space, or spatiotemporality. Particularly, Castells and colleagues (2000; Castells, Fernandez-Ardevol, Qui, & Sey, 2007) theorize about how societal shifts associated with new communication technologies find us collectively experiencing "space" that is not defined by place but by a given network of relationships, and "time" that is not defined by a clock but through constant interaction that saturates all moments with activity. Indeed, Castells and colleagues argue that these new communication processes associated with space and time are key to the emergence of the network society, owed to the fact that: "Time and space are the fundamental, material dimensions of human existence. Thus, they are the most direct expression of social structure and structural change." (Castells et al., 2007, p. 171).

Therefore, the growth of interaction work means that these organizational members have experienced profound spatiotemporal change in a remarkably short period of time. Not surprisingly, this has led to intense work pressures as organizations and their members seek to develop effective organizational communication practices to manage this shift. Therefore, our focus in this paper is to explore the various spatiotemporal interaction genres—*coworking, commuting, choosing, contemplating*—and the broader repertoire—*multiminding*—that emerges from an oscillation within and among the various genres.

We begin our discussion by exploring the temporal dimension, *separation*, described by Ballard and Seibold (2003) in their meso-level model of organizational temporality. It is conceived as a measure of (spatiotemporal) connection or availability among organizational members; therefore, it is an excellent starting point to consider contemporary enactments of spatiotemporality (Ballard & Seibold, 2003). We then explore Orlikowski and Yates' (1994) concept of an *interaction*, or *communicative genre*, and describe four genres—*contemplating, choosing, coworking, commuting*—used to manage spatiotemporal connection in various ways (Ballard & Seibold, 2003; Ballard, 2007; Ballard & Gossett, 2007). Finally, we define a larger genre repertoire, *multiminding*, that includes each of these genres yet extends our understanding of contemporary enactments of time and space at work.

Separating and Connecting in Time

Chronemics at Work

Based on any number of mainstream business outlets, the sense that time matters to work is abundantly clear (Bluedorn, 2002). However, the "time" referenced in these popular contexts is typically drawn with a broad stroke: People are worried about "wasting time," reminded that "time is money," driven by "deadlines," concerned about reaching "daily quotas," finishing "quarterly reports," receiving "annual evaluations," and lobbying for more "vacation time," "time off," or family "leave." Yet, with all of this emphasis on time in organizational life, time is still considered—by organizational members, practitioners, and scholars—merely the backdrop against which substantive issues unfold. This incomplete understanding of time in work is embodied in many popular approaches, including Taylorism, Fordism, and Six Sigma to name a few. Time is considered a simple, linear fact of nature, an objective and independent factor in work life. It is a commodity subject to ownership, usage, and the like.

Our interest here, however, is on the study of time as it is bound to human communication, or *chronemics*. Bourdieu (1977) argued that the human experience of time only comes into being through our interaction with others. For example, prior to clocks and formal timekeeping devices, persons were able to notice particular temporal, or time-based, patterns—e.g., the frequency, pace, duration, and regularity—based solely on their occurrence vis-à-vis communication episodes. Imagining our early forebears, this seems quite rudimentary and, perhaps, irrelevant for comparisons to contemporary life. Yet this same quality of time abounds in our current daily lives. For example, in skilled nursing facilities around the world, persons without access (visually, cognitively, or logistically) to mechanized timepieces experience time through group activities and one-on-one interaction (including long visits and regular phone calls from loved ones). As well, in organizations everywhere, the pace, regularity, duration, and frequency of communication—from meetings to email—signals clearly when a deadline is approaching, the fiscal year is ending, or the day is almost over (Flaherty & Seipp-Williams, 2005). Likewise, these same meetings and email requests are noticed or overlooked, celebrated or dreaded, and prioritized or avoided based upon their relationship to the fiscal year, the time of day, or their relationship to a deadline. Thus, our communication patterns and practices are vitally important in signaling time, and our temporal experience is also important in shaping the communication patterns and practices of a given group (Ballard & Seibold, 2003).

The importance of this chronemic, or interaction-based, focus on human temporality—over a solely task-based focus—is that it allows organizational members, practitioners, and scholars to understand (and to, potentially, shape) the bigger relational picture within which our temporal experience unfolds (Ballard & McVey, 2014). Under ordinary conditions, the socially constructed nature of time is obscured. Instead, temporal behavior becomes guided by a set of rules that are "known to all, obeyed by all, but seldom if ever stated ... implicit, taken for granted, almost impossible for the average person to state as a system, and generally out of awareness" (Hall, 1983, p. 211). Thus, implicit norms necessarily preclude strategic, proactive change. Nonetheless, critical aspects of our organizational and individual performance are shaped by our temporal behaviors and construals, described next.

Interpreting and Performing Time: Dimensions of Organizational Temporality

In their research on time and work, or *organizational temporality*, Ballard and colleagues (Ballard & Seibold, 2006; Ballard & Gomez, 2006) report that organizational members experience time across at least twelve distinct dimensions: *flexibility, linearity, pace, punctuality, delay, scheduling, separating,*[1] *scarcity, urgency,* and *present, past,* and *future time foci.* These twelve dimensions, divided into temporal construals and temporal enactments, highlight the numerous and dynamic ways in which organizational temporality shapes and is shaped by organizational members' quality of life and work.

First, temporal *construals* represent the way organizational members "interpret" or "orient" to time. This includes construals of: *scarcity,* a focus on time as a limited and exhaustible resource (Karau & Kelly, 1992); *urgency,* a preoccupation with deadlines and task completion (Waller, Conte, Gibson, & Carpenter, 2001); and *present, past,* and *future time foci,* characterized by intentions oriented toward immediate action or long-term planning, respectively (Bluedorn, 2002; Jones, 1988). To construe something means "to interpret, give a meaning to, put a construction on (actions, things, or persons)" (Simpson et al., 2005). While perceptions are typically associated with personal, even neurological, processes, the notion of *construals* emphasizes the social process of deriving meaning and opens up the possibility of shared interpretations as well.

Next, temporal *enactments* refer to the way work group members "perform" time. Enactment encompasses more than behavior. Enactments are both the medium and the outcome of human interaction with the environment. As such, they highlight the ways in which temporality is communicatively constituted. As Weick (1979) describes, "the external environment literally bends around the enactments of people" (p. 130). Enactments impact and are impacted by the interaction of organizational members with a variety of environmental factors, including colleagues, clients, family members as well as task timelines, project deadlines, and the like. They include *pace,* tempo or rate of activity (Levine, 1988); *flexibility,* the degree of rigidity in time structuring and task completion plans (Starkey, 1989); *linearity,* the degree to which tasks are completed one at a time (Graham, 1981); *punctuality,* the exacting nature of timing and deadlines (Schriber & Gutek, 1987); *delay,* working behind schedule—orthogonal with punctuality; *scheduling*, the extent to which the sequencing and duration of plans, activities, and events are formalized (Zerubavel, 1981); and *separation*, the degree to which a given use of time and/or space signals an intent to include or exclude interaction with others in the process of accomplishing work[2] (Perlow, 1997). The role of separation behaviors in managing interaction work is the focus of this paper, and is developed and described in detail below.

Separation and Spatiotemporality

The spatiotemporal experience of *separation* is evidenced in the extent to which individuals are available for interaction in time and space. If activities without apparent connection to the focal activity are seen as unwelcome "interruptions,"[3] a high level of separating is being enacted. Screening behaviors, including closing the door or not answering the phone, are common in these contexts. In contrast, low levels of separation—i.e., high connection—are evident in practices like the open door, discursively or literally used to communicate less restricted spatiotemporal norms.

Separation is signaled in spatial and temporal barriers to interaction, whereas connection has been signaled in the removal of these same barriers in order to facilitate interaction. For example, leave-taking behaviors like standing up, gathering one's belongings, physically orienting one's body away from another, and/or checking one's watch are all ways that individuals signal the intent to separate from the stream of communication. Similarly, sitting down, taking off one's coat, and moving closer to another are ways that—for many generations—individuals have expressed that they have time for face-to-face interaction (Hall, 1983). However, the emergent forms of spatiotemporality afforded by new mobile communication technologies such as laptops, smartphones, netbooks, and tablets shed new light on ways in which separation may be enacted. As such, literature on mobile communication (elaborated below) offers a rich exemplar base to consider how separation has varied across time and across cultural groups based upon the unique interaction goals that persons seek to accomplish.

As Castells and colleagues (2007) assert, technology adoption is shaped by the value that users perceive it offers. While certain features and usage patterns are now shared universally, differences across group values still account for major differences in use (Yu & Tng, 2003). While the cultural comparisons across national boundaries (with regard to mobile communication technologies) are growing slowly, one cultural group understandably absent from the technological adoption literature is the Amish. While this absence is logical—given their reputation for rejecting even the most basic of technologies (including the convenience of outside pockets on their clothes)—examining Amish discourse and practices concerning communication technology, in general, and mobile communication technology, in particular, highlights the centrality of spatiotemporal values in separation norms and practices (Kraybill, 2001; Kraybill & Hurd, 2006).

Kraybill (2001) describes the communicative, especially the relational, aspects of separation and spatiotemporality:

> The telephone line was the first visible link to the larger industrial world—a real and symbolic tie that mocked Amish belief in separation from the world. Phones literally tied a house to the outside world and permitted strangers to enter the house at the sound of a ring.
>
> *(p. 192)*

Concern with interruptions during business hours and disruptions in the natural flow of family rhythms was among the reasons given for the initial ban on landline phones in Amish communities. Nonetheless, a compromise was eventually made due to church members' concerns about issues of safety (e.g., the ability to call a doctor or fire department). Thus, after 1940, telephone shanties (resembling an outhouse) began to appear in order to house a "community phone." While separation from the outside world is a classic value of their culture, separation within families and communities is the antithesis of Amish tradition, thus the community phone, located outside of the home, was palatable. Kraybill (2001) observes, "The Amish believe that a home phone separates but that a community phone integrates" (p. 196). Not surprisingly, then, in many Amish communities, mobile telephones are strictly forbidden due to their ability to invade home space. At their fall 2003 conference, mobile phones were expressly forbidden from invading the communal space because, as one member notes, "When it's connected to a line it controls mobility" (Kraybill & Hurd, 2006, p. 217).

The references to connection and separation throughout the studies of mobile communication highlight the importance of time and space in groups' communication technology use patterns and the underlying interaction genres they seek to accomplish. Below, we explicate a typology of spatiotemporal enactments through offering examples from a variety of technologies-in-use relevant to managing interaction work.

The Spatiotemporality of Interaction Work: Contemplating, Choosing, Commuting, Coworking, and Multiminding

There are a variety of communication, or interaction, genres (Orlikowski & Yates, 1994) signaled in members' spatiotemporal enactments associated with work. Interaction genres are "socially recognized types of communicative actions—such as memos, meetings, expense forms, training seminars—that are habitually enacted by members of a community to realize particular social purposes. A genre established within a particular community serves as an institutionalized template for social action—an organizing structure—that shapes the ongoing communicative actions of community members through their use of it" (Orlikowski &

Yates, 1994, p. 542). They go on: "Members of a community rarely depend on a single genre for their communication. Rather, they tend to use multiple, different, and interacting genres over time. Thus to understand a community's communicative practices, we must examine the set of genres that are routinely enacted by members of the community. We designate such a set of genres a community's 'genre repertoire'" (p. 542). We are interested in four different spatiotemporal communication genres—contemplating, choosing, commuting, and coworking—that characterize how organizational members appropriate communication technologies-in-use as well as a broader genre repertoire—multiminding—that reflects a higher order strategy wherein members move across these interrelated genres to sustain multiple ongoing flows of interaction work.

We develop a spatiotemporal typology that utilizes the two elements of separation—both temporal and spatial qualities of communication—to arrive at various communication genres. Temporality and spatiality are described along a conventional dichotomy of states—*synchronous* versus *asynchronous* interaction across time, and *face-to-face* versus *remote* interaction across space—each of which is being complicated and reshaped by the rise of interaction work. Due to the affordances of networked technologies, these dichotomies (while familiar) are no longer sufficient on their own: They are being reshaped, punctuated by new intermediate spatiotemporal states that are rapidly becoming predominant: *continuous* (temporality) and *together* (spatiality). Together, the grounded ends of the continuum along with these fluid intermediate states reflect the protean shapeshifting that Shockley-Zalabak (2002) describes in her explication of the Protean Places which characterize contemporary work environments.

In terms of chronemics, whereas asynchronous communication is drawn on to signal interaction on "my time," or a "different time" than another, and synchronous communication signals interaction on "our time," or the "same time" as another, there is also a type of *continuous* communication—neither synchronous nor asynchronous, but a constant movement between both. Instead, continuous communication signals the value of interaction "over time" in interaction work—transcending industrial conceptions that time is a commodity to be owned by one or more interactants. Continuous communication operates on Castells's notion of timeless time in network-based society.

Similarly, in terms of proxemics, whereas face-to-face communication signals that one is "here" and remote communication signals that one is "there," communication can also have the quality of occurring *together* with another—which operates differently than either face-to-face or remote. Spatially, together is reflected in Castells's notion of the space of flows, defined by interaction within one's network of relationships. So, rather than communicating from here or there, communicating together occurs "shoulder-to-shoulder" in either virtual or real space. The spatial metaphor of shoulder-to-shoulder conveys an image of working together in a collaborative space—with only a few inches, or a desk, or mere cyberspace separating and connecting another. For example, a "shared folder" on

Dropbox is the network-based equivalent of a shared, locked, filing cabinet that a group of office mates share where anyone who needs access has the key. The space of flows literally enables us to work shoulder-to-shoulder, or together.

The *contemplating, choosing, coworking,* and *commuting* genres anchor the ends of the continuum. At the center, driven by a shapeshifting intersection of the other qualities of communication, the intermediate states give rise to the broader genre repertoire of *multiminding*—a higher order strategy—that undergirds sustainable, networked work, workers, and workplaces. Thus, throughout we note where the neatly defined boundaries—*asynchronous versus synchronous* and *face-to-face versus remote*—routinely fall apart and then come together as *continuous* and *together.*

Note that this is not a typology of technologies, but of types of interaction accomplished using a range of communication technologies in multiple ways. Indeed, in the course of becoming mainstream, it is almost required that a given practice be appropriated in more than one way to signal various genres. Below, we describe each genre in turn and offer examples of typical spatiotemporal enactments for each. We then end this section with a discussion of multiminding.

The Contemplating Interaction Genre

The *contemplating* interaction genre is drawn upon in settings where individuals are spatially co-located in a face-to-face setting with others but interacting with them in an asynchronous fashion as a means of momentarily offering more focused attention to other people and activities.

The classic contemplative strategy is simply closing one's door at the office (Ballard & Seibold, 2000; Hall, 1983). The history of this practice reflects the power relations associated with organizational spatiotemporality, since higher-ranking organizational members are often the only persons with an office door to close. More typically, the majority of organizational members work in cubicles that prohibit this privileged door closing practice. In contemporary settings, the strategy is often appropriated by persons who may be expected to interact continuously with others (either by role or by group norm) by simply wearing ear buds or headphones that signal their attention is devoted to another task or interaction. Enacting this genre requires an interlocutor to "ask" for another's attention, rather than to assume ownership of it.

Recently, some organizations have instituted "No Email Fridays" as a way to decrease the flow of messages and resultant problem of communication overload. This policy exists for co-located and teleworking colleagues the same. As well, smartphone makers recently have built-in systems to allow users to enact the contemplating genre. Apple calls this function on the iPhone "Do Not Disturb." "Do Not Disturb" is exemplary of the discursive construction of contemplating long used by bank tellers, cashiers, etc., to convey the need to concentrate their attention on one activity before moving back into interaction with others. Notably, in the absence of formal mechanisms to enact contemplating, many organizational members simply appropriate calendaring systems (such as Outlook or Doodle) in such a way as to decline availability.

The practice of contemplating is appropriated to manage the timing of interaction and offer focused attention on a given set of activities. Notably, this genre is often met with impatience due to the perceived inconvenience to others, reflective of cultural attitudes against contemplation in a network-based economy. As well, the time scale over which contemplating occurs may extend from seconds to hours (Ballard & McVey, 2014).

In interaction work there is frequent movement back and forth between *asynchronous* and *synchronous* communication, resulting in a kind of *continuous* interaction when one zooms out to see a larger time scale (such as across the day). Consider the office administrator described earlier who is continually engaged by others. Between interactions, she resumes her work wearing headphones in order to discourage unnecessary interruptions and regain attention for the report she is preparing (due the following day). From moment to moment, we might see either asynchronous communication or synchronous communication, but—due to the constant movement across the two over the longer day—her interaction with others has a decidedly continuous character. Thus, like the other genres, they are analytically distinct but deeply interwoven in the course of interaction work.

The Choosing Interaction Genre

The potential for more accessibility (compared to the contemplating genre) is reflected in the *choosing* genre wherein individuals located remotely from their colleagues use communication technologies in an asynchronous fashion as a way to offer availability to some activities but not other activities in a given unit of time.

Castells and colleagues (2007) describe how pagers and Caller ID were some of the earliest communication technologies explicitly designed to offer remote users the choice to engage in immediate interaction or to decline availability until a later time of their own choosing. Both were used to selectively choose with whom one wants to interact, deciding in the moment whether or not to be available. In the last century, answering machines were used in the same way. Digital voicemail and "recent call" lists on cellphones now stand in as ways that individuals screen phone calls, choosing interaction on their "own time": Persons can ostensibly capture the intended message or simply the caller's name and return the call at a time of temporal convenience (if at all).

While organizational members frequently appropriate email as an almost synchronous communication media, it was designed as (and can still be used as) an asynchronous media that permits individuals to choose when they are available. Nonetheless, as is the case for each of the contemporary enactments of the choosing genre, the presumption of speed in response means that persons may attempt to keep up in real time (Barley, Meyerson, & Grodal, 2011; Kalman & Rafaeli, 2011). Thus, the line between asynchronous and synchronous communication is again blurred, resulting in interaction patterns that are best characterized as continuous (Fallows, 2013), moving regularly between synchronous and asynchronous interaction. As an example, when required to indicate whether email is a synchronous or asynchronous communication technology (even when the definition of synchronous and asynchronous were provided), respondents indicated that email was synchronous despite the fact that email is described as asynchronous in the literature (Jourdan, 2006).

Additionally, organizational members often face a professional–personal tension that requires a choice between attending to their personal wellness and relationships by regularly taking "time off" and being away from work versus being ever available to coworkers (Perlow, 2012). Perlow developed an arrangement called Predictable Time Off (PTO) where members of the Boston Consulting Group were afforded one night a week where they would leave the office and not be available to coworkers or clients, with the exception of emergencies. This may not seem related to workplace interaction, but it was centered precisely on creating a shift in the temporal expectations of work. Ultimately, it transformed the work environment itself: employee satisfaction rose, recruitment and retention improved, and client satisfaction increased as well. Thus, the choosing genre covers a range of approaches to attention management at various time scales. From in-the-moment decisions about responding to a given caller or messenger (SMS or IM), to waiting to answer email until later, to actually having regular time off each week, to leaving town for several months. At various time scales, organizational members often benefit from being allowed to choose the time and place of interaction, rather than offering continuous availability to all others' work-related requests.

To summarize, the choosing genre is appropriated to help manage the ebb and flow of communication in time and space. Spatiotemporal enactments associated with the commuting interaction genre are described next.

The Commuting Interaction Genre

The *commuting* interaction genre allows individuals to use remote communication practices in a synchronous fashion (or a close approximation of it) in order to signal their temporal availability to others. Often physical absence is desired, as in the case of an arranged teleworking agreement, but this genre applies in a variety of other contemporary settings (Ballard & Gossett, 2007). The term *commuting* does not apply only to those in formal telecommuting situations, but that which is commonly enacted by members throughout the organization (Ramgolam, 2007): This includes working from home at the end of the day (after leaving the office), being on-call over the weekend, and being generally available after hours (despite the day or time). Independent contractors and freelancers often find themselves in this situation as well.

Commuting enactments include phoning into the office from home (and receiving phone calls at home) in order to facilitate availability from a fixed location, as well as utilizing a mobile phone to facilitate availability from any location (including while traveling on business or on a family outing). Video conferencing is a common means to connect virtual teams from around the globe. With the advent of Skype, this technology is widely available to organizations and individuals. The instant messaging features of Skype and its competitors are often used to maintain mutual awareness and intermittent conversation between pairs of people and small groups. Twitter-like workplace microblogging systems like Yammer, along with Skype, add another form of continuous connectivity to the mix. Organizational members also regularly use SMS (short message service) to facilitate availability from any location, and instant messaging has been commonplace among work colleagues for some time (Mamberto, 2007). Finally, in some corporate cultures, email "fire drills" are commonplace as a means of decision-making (Ballard, 2007). A fire drill is used to hold meetings in lieu of face-to-face communication and is characterized by rapid-fire back-and-forth among a group. Being unavailable during such a drill often leads to negative perceptions by others.

Within a commuting genre, organizational members are extended across space but have the goal of connecting with others in real time. Thus, the synchronous nature of communication can be associated with a quality of togetherness as organizational members work "shoulder-to-shoulder" via video conferencing software as well as in using Google Drive, Evernote, or Dropbox. This distinction occurs in interaction work owed to its reliance upon complex communication and coordination.

The Coworking Interaction Genre

The greatest level of spatiotemporal availability is reflected in the *coworking* interaction genre, wherein individuals are co-located with colleagues and interacting synchronously with multiple others. In his original treatment of monochronic and polychronic time, Hall (1983) wrote about office configuration as one of the most visible signs of culture. In polychronic cultures where relationships are afforded priority over task completion, office spaces are huge open rooms where all are welcome to congregate and interact at once. Short of this polychronic ideal, the open door has long been another cultural symbol of availability in many Western organizations. However, in an environment characterized by virtual teams, virtual organizations, independent contractors, and telework, the open door of yore has been replaced by its technological equivalent.

As an example, mobile phoning to micro-coordinate (Ling, 2004) en route to a meeting while on the same corporate campus or in the same vicinity is a familiar occurrence (Geser, 2006). Texting is also being used as a tool to strategize, and subversively change coalition strategies, during face-to-face meetings with co-located colleagues (Stephens & Davis, 2009). Colleagues with adjoining cubicles are instant messaging each other as a means of collaborating among co-located colleagues at work (Schmitz Weiss, 2008). As well, during a SXSW (South by Southwest)

Interactive Festival panel held to discuss the latest innovations in Web 2.0, several co-located members of the audience began Tweeting on their smartphones about how the panel was boring and ineffective (Wallace, 2008). In real time, a moderator informed the panelists of the feedback and the direction of the panel was changed immediately.

The level of openness and connectivity achieved through the use of new communication technologies exceeds that of the open door (unless we plan to stay at the office twenty-four hours a day, seven days a week). The smartphone affords exceptional access to the coworking genre—from phoning, to texting, to emailing, to following received links, to sharing information through social networking sites. It offers an always-on, always-there capability not available in the past (Fortunati, 2002; Katz & Aakhus, 2002; Lee & Whitley, 2002) that extends from our professional into our personal lives (Ballard, 2007). As such, it symbolizes the new open door characterized by a space of flows and timeless time. Castells and colleagues note, "it is this time-based (rather than space-based) organization of activities that defines 'accessibility,' leading to a redefinition of 'public time' and 'private time' into 'on time' and 'off time'" (2007, p. 176). Not the shift from a space-based to a time-based metaphor. As Green (2002) describes, it enables a "boundary rearrangement" (p. 288).

From Coworking to Minding

Scholars have variously described the spatiotemporal enactments associated with the coworking genre as reflecting and enabling *perpetual contact* (Katz & Aakhus, 2002), *presence absence* (Fortunati, 2002) as well as *network time* (Hassan, 2007). Additionally, a prominent practitioner and researcher described the phenomenon of *continuous partial attention* (Stone, 2008) to describe our ability to be always on, but only half present, despite our physical location. These characterizations all point to various spatiotemporal aspects of interaction work. Fortunati (2002) sums them up well, where he describes both their communicative purpose and common form:

> The mobile, much more than the fixed phone, makes it possible to speak and do various actions at the same time as it being used: walking, driving, and so on. Doing more than one thing at a time allows you to live a double or triple life, even if this obviously raises your level of stress. The mind gets used to spreading attention in various directions. Certainly it is less brilliant attention, more opaque, but it enables people to cope with multiple actions.
>
> *(p. 517)*

This characterization of more opaque attention in the coworking genre reflects the research on the cognitive limitations associated with multitasking in contemporary media environments (Ophir, Nass, & Wagner, 2009). However,

Fortunati's (2002) description ignores literature on polychronic cultures whose members have always done more than one thing at a time—in both their professional and personal lives (Hall, 1983). So the spatiotemporal enactments are not new, but the psychological stress associated with multiple task accomplishment is a result of the speed that also characterizes it (Bluedorn, 2002).

Bluedorn (2002), König and Waller (2010), as well as Stephens, Cho, and Ballard (2012), have all tried to clarify that there are important distinctions between multiple task accomplishment in traditionally monochronic cultures (such as the U.S. and much of the Western world)—where time is seen as a scarce commodity to be hoarded and space is seen as private—compared to traditionally polychronic cultures—where time and space are used in more fluid, intangible ways. Hall (1983) explained these differences:

> *Monochronic* cultures are those in which the time base is an outgrowth of the industrial revolution. Monochronic cultures stress a high degree of scheduling, concentration on one thing at a time (hence the name), and an elaborate code of behavior built around promptness in meeting obligations and appointments. *Polychronic* cultures are just the opposite: human relationships and interactions are valued over arbitrary schedules and appointments. Many things may occur at once (since people are involved in everything), and interruptions are frequent.
>
> *(p. 184)*

Multiminding involves qualities of both the monochronic valuation of time in the form of punctuality and appointments but also of a polychronic approach toward relationships and interactions.

Thompson's (1967) classic description of preindustrial cultures also reflects a core aspect of multiminding: minimal "demarcation between 'work' and 'life'" (1967, p. 60) compared to the time (clock) orientation observed in industrial cultures. In the twenty-first century we again find that interaction work is less reliant upon the clock time that dominated the twentieth century. Below, we explore this genre repertoire in more detail—including on the issues of *attention* and leading *multiple lives* that Fortunati (2002) references. Rather than a simple return to preindustrial or an obliteration of the industrial, multiminding emerges in the course of postindustrial shapeshifting between synchronous versus asynchronous (in *continuous* time) and remote versus face-to-face contexts (in space *together*).

The Multiminding Genre Repertoire

Multiminding reflects a genre repertoire typical of the interaction worker engaged in protean shapeshifting within and among the various genres described previously. As Solomon Gray (2014) describes, it is a naturally occurring attention management strategy characterized by five key components: a) maintaining a channel of attention on the activities and well-being of key dependents and interdependents; b) pursuing an outcome or state of being that is more expansive—including in terms of both shared histories and futures—than a discrete task; c) allocating individual and collective effort over time as needed; d) performing an agreed upon role in a dynamic narrative; and e) operating with a sense of sustained responsibility and intentionality. At its root, it is a relationship-based, multithreaded way of attending to personal and professional objectives, in time and over time.

Notably, it centers on a shift from tasking (focused on managing one's time) to minding (focused on managing one's attention). Recall two of our earlier observations about interaction work (McKinsey, 2012): 1) While industrial work centers on sequential individual contributions, interaction work centers on concurrent collective contributions. 2) Interaction work requires a shift from focusing on the time needed to complete a well-defined task to the collective and individual capabilities required to reliably achieve complex, interlocking outcomes. Thus, while industrial constructions of time and space remain, interaction work also occurs in the timeless time and space of flows that Castells (2000) describes as characteristic of network society. Solomon Gray (2014) points out that tasking is the predominant way to manage work in industrial time–space, while minding is a naturally acquired skill we practice from birth but is also now an emergent way of managing work in postindustrial time–space.

The term *multiminding* was originally flung into marketing discourse by the business unit of a leading PR firm (Skoloda, 2009) to dramatize why women (responsible for more than 80 percent of consumer spending across all categories) now needed to be advertised and marketed to differently. They boldly asserted that women aged twenty-five to fifty-four had moved beyond (or above) multi-tasking to "a new level" of busyness and time compression. However, what the founder and early funders of Mmindd Labs discovered at StudioLab in 2007, just as the iPhone was being introduced, was that these women were not simply exhibiting *time and task* management "on steroids" as it were. They were pursuing a different *attention* management strategy—one based on meeting multiple goals at the same time so as to care for and orchestrate not only their own lives, but the lives of those to whom they were most closely connected. This was a stark contrast to the short-term, goal-centered, conical single-point-of-focus attention mode conventionally attributed to the ancient "hunter" and still embodied in most time management tools and methods.

This genre repertoire employed by interaction workers relies upon the *commuting* genre to manage global commerce with virtual teams around the world, the *coworking* genre to appropriate speed and social presence, the *choosing* genre to achieve personal renewal away from work, and the *contemplating* genre to handle distractions while working. Each of these genres is necessary to create a sustainable working environment. Because of the constant attention management required in interaction work, minding occurs in *continuous* time and *together* in space (either virtual or real). Thus it also reflects the Protean Places that Shockley-Zalabak (2002) describe as "simultaneously maintaining core values while supporting continually changing practices" (p. 238).

Conclusion

Our objective in this paper was to consider the importance of spatiotemporality with regard to communication processes, in general, and organizational communication processes, in particular. While the study of time and space are seen as vital to communication scholarship, we have often held limited conceptions of the ways that time and space function in organizational communication processes. As part of extending traditional notions of chronemics and proxemics scholarship, we elaborated Ballard and Seibold's (2003) construct of *separation* through a typology of communicative genres—coworking, commuting, contemplating, and choosing—and a broader genre repertoire—multiminding—employed by inter-action workers. Ultimately, we hope to stimulate theorizing and research on the role of time and space in the twenty-first century, challenging accepted notions of spatiotemporality and communication in work.

Notes

1 In previous publications, this dimension was referred to as separation (as opposed to separating). This dimension was renamed, if slightly, to emphasize its processual nature.
2 The original definition of this dimension was "the degree to which extraneous factors are eliminated or engaged in the completion of a work task." This definition has been modified to reflect the fact that work increasingly is not defined by tasks and that "extraneous factors" are also becoming difficult, or impossible, to identify. Our intent is to modify the definition so that it offers a timeless representation of both enduring and contemporary chronemic patterns.
3 The very concept of interruption or distraction is culturally defined and has very different meanings in clock-based versus event-based cultures (Hall, 1983).

References

Ballard, D. I. (2007). Chronemics at work: Using socio-historical accounts to illuminate contemporary workplace temporality. In R. Rubin (Ed.), *Research in the sociology of work: Vol. 17 Workplace temporalities* (pp. 29–54). Cambridge, MA: Elsevier.

Ballard, D. I., & Gomez, F. (2006). Time to meet: Meetings as sites of organizational memory. In J. Parker, M. Crawford, & P. Harris (Eds.), *Study of time XII: Time and memory* (pp. 301–312). Boston, MA: Brill.

Ballard, D. I., & Gossett, L. M. (2007). Alternative times: The temporal perceptions, processes, and practices defining the non-standard work arrangement. In C. Beck (Ed.), *Communication yearbook, 31* (pp. 269–316). Mahwah, NJ: Lawrence Erlbaum Associates.

Ballard, D. I., & McVey, T. (2014). Measure twice, cut once: The temporality of communication design. *Journal of Applied Communication Research, 42*(2), 190–207. doi: 10.1080/00909882.2013.874571.

Ballard, D. I., & Seibold, D. R. (2000). Time orientation and temporal variation across work groups: Implications for group and organizational communication. *Western Journal of Communication, 64,* 218–242.

Ballard, D. I., & Seibold, D. R. (2003). Communicating and organizing in time: A meso-level model of organizational temporality. *Management Communication Quarterly, 16,* 380–415.

Ballard, D. I., & Seibold, D. R. (2006). The experience of time at work: Relationship to communication load, job satisfaction, and interdepartmental communication. *Communication Studies, 57,* 317–340.

Barley, S., Meyerson, D. E., & Grodal, S. (2011). Email as a symbol and source of stress. *Organization Science, 22,* 887–906.

Bluedorn, A. C. (2002). *The human organization of time: Temporal realities and experience.* Stanford, CA: Stanford Business Books.

Bourdieu, P. (1977). *Outline of a theory of practice.* Cambridge, UK: Cambridge University Press.

Castells, M. (2000). *The rise of the network society.* US: Blackwell Publishing.

Castells, M., Fernandez-Ardevol, M., Qui, J. L., & Sey, A. (2007). *Mobile communication and society: A global perspective.* Cambridge, MA: MIT Press.

Fallows, J. (2013). Linda Stone on maintaining focus in a maddeningly distractive world. Retrieved from http://www.theatlantic.com/national/archive/2013/05/lindastone onmaintainingfocusinamaddeninglydistractiveworld/276201/.

Flaherty, M. G., & Seipp-Williams, L. (2005). Sociotemporal rhythms in e-mail: A case study. *Time & Society, 14*(1), 39–49.

Fortunati, L. (2002). The mobile phone: Towards new categories and social relations. *Information, Communication, and Society, 5,* 513–528.

Geser, H. (2006). Is the cell phone undermining the social order?: Understanding mobile technology from a sociological perspective. *Knowledge, Technology, & Policy, 19,* 8–18.

Graham, R. J. (1981). The role of perception of time in consumer research. *Journal of Consumer Research, 7,* 335–342.

Green, N. (2002). On the move: Technology, mobility, and the mediation of social time and space. *The Information Society, 18,* 281–292.

Hall, E. T. (1983). *The dance of life.* New York: Doubleday.

Hassan, R. (2007). Network time. In R. Hassan & R. E. Purser (Eds.), *24/7: Time and temporality in the network society* (pp. 37–61). Stanford, CA: Stanford Business Books.

Jones, J. M. (1988). Cultural difference in temporal perspectives: Instrumental and expressive behaviors in time. In J. E. McGrath (Ed.), *The social psychology of time: New perspectives* (pp. 21–38). Newbury Park, CA: Sage.

Jourdan, J. S. (2006). *Perceived presence in mediated communication: Antecedents and effects.* Unpublished doctoral dissertation, University of Texas at Austin, Austin, TX.

Kalman, Y. M., & Rafaeli, S. (2011). Online pauses and silence: Chronemic expectancy violations in written computer-mediated communication. *Communication Research, 38*(1), 54–69.

Karau, S. J., & Kelly, J. R. (1992). The effects of time scarcity and time abundance on group performance quality and interaction processes. *Journal of Experimental Social Psychology, 28,* 542–571.

Katz, J. E., Aakhus, M. (Eds.) (2002). *Perpetual contact: Mobile communication, private talk, public performance.* Cambridge, UK: Cambridge University Press.

König, C. J., & Waller, M. J. (2010). Time for reflection: A critical examination of polychronicity. *Human Performance, 23,* 173–190.

Kraybill, D. B. (2001). *The riddle of Amish culture* (Rev. ed.). Baltimore, MD: Johns Hopkins University Press.

Kraybill, D. B., & Hurd, J. P. (2006). *Horse-and-buggy Mennonites: Hoofbeats of humility in a postmodern world.* University Park, PA: University of Pennsylvania Press.

Lee, H., & Whitley, E. A. (2002). Time and information technology: Temporal impacts on individuals, organizations, and society. *The Information Society, 18,* 235–240.

Levine, R. V. (1988). The pace of life across cultures. In J. E. McGrath (Ed.), *The social psychology of time: New perspectives* (pp. 39–60). Newbury Park, CA: Sage.

Ling, R. S. (2004). *The mobile connection: The cell phone's impact on society.* US: Morgan Kaufmann.

Mamberto, C. (2007, July 24). "Instant messaging invades the office." *The Wall Street Journal,* B1.

McKinsey Global Institute. (2012). The social economy: Unlocking value and productivity through social technologies. Washington, DC: M. Chui, J. Manyika, J. Bughin, R. Dobbs, C. Roxburgh, H. Sarrazin, G. Sands, M. Westergren.

Mumford, L. (1934). *Technics and civilization.* New York: Harcourt, Brace & Company.

Ophir, E., Nass, C., & Wagner, A. D. (2009). Cognitive control in media multitaskers. *Proceedings of the National Academy of Sciences, 106,* 15583–15587.

Orlikowski, W. J., & Yates, J. (1994). Genre repertoire: The structuring of communicative practices in organizations. *Administrative Science Quarterly, 39,* 541–574.

Perlow, L. A. (1997). *Finding time: How corporations, individuals, and families can benefit from new work practices.* Ithaca, NY: Cornell University Press.

Perlow, L. A. (2012). Sleeping with your smartphone: How to break the 24/7 habit and change the way you work. Boston, MA: Harvard Business Review Press.

Ramgolam, D. I. (2007). Virtual work practices and the experience of time. Unpublished master's thesis, University of Texas at Austin, Austin, TX.

Schmitz Weiss, A. (2008). The transformation of the newsroom: The collaborative dynamics of journalists' work. Unpublished doctoral dissertation, University of Texas at Austin, Austin, TX.

Schriber, J. B., & Gutek, B. A. (1987). Some time dimensions of work: The measurement of an underlying dimension of organizational culture. *Journal of Applied Psychology, 72,* 642–650.

Shockley-Zalabak, P. (2002). Protean places: Teams across time and space. *Journal of Applied Communication Research, 30,* 231–250.

Simpson, J. et al. (Eds.). (2005). *Oxford English Dictionary (OED) Online.* Oxford: Oxford University Press.

Skoloda, K. M. (2009). *Too busy to shop: Marketing to "multi-minding" women.* Westport, CT: Praeger Publishers.

Solomon Gray, E. (2014). *About Mmindd.* Retrieved from http://www.mminddlabs.com.

Starkey, K. (1989). Time and work: A psychological perspective. In P. Blyton, J. Hassard, S. Hill, & K. Starkey (Eds.), *Time, work, and organization* (pp. 57–78). New York: Routledge.

Stephens, K. K., Cho, J. K., & Ballard, D. I. (2012). Simultaneity, sequentiality, and speed: Organizational messages about multiple task completion. *Human Communication Research, 38*(1), 23–47. doi:10.1111/j.1468–2958.2011.01420.x.

Stephens, K. K., & Davis, J. D. (2009). The social influences on electronic multitasking in organizational meetings. *Management Communication Quarterly, 23*(1), 63–83. doi: 10.1177/0893318909335417.

Stone, L. (2008, February 9). Linda Stone's thoughts on attention and specifically, continuous partial attention [Msg 1]. Message posted to http://continuouspartialattention.jot.com/WikiHome.

Thompson, E. P. (1967). Time, work-discipline, and industrial capitalism. *Past and present, 38*, 56–97.

Wallace, L. (2008, March 9, 6:07:22 PM). SXSW: Zuckerberg keynote descends into chaos as audience takes over. Wired Blog Network (Underwire), http://blog.wired.com/underwire/2008/03/sxsw-mark-zucke.html.

Waller, M. J., Conte, J. M., Gibson, C. B., & Carpenter, M. A. (2001). The effect of individual perceptions of deadlines on team performance. *Academy of Management Review, 26*(4), 586–600.

Weick, K. E. (1979). *The social psychology of organizing* (2nd ed.). New York: McGraw-Hill.

Yu, L., & Tng, T. H. (2003). Culture and design for mobile phones for China. In J. E. Katz, (Ed.), *Machines that become us: The social context of personal communication technology* (pp. 187–198). New Brunswick: Transaction Publishers.

Zerubavel, E. (1981). *Hidden rhythms: Schedules and calendars in social life.* Chicago: University of Chicago Press.

PART III

8

OCCUPATIONAL BURNOUT AND THE CASE STUDY OF PHYSICIANS

Stacey A. Passalacqua

UNIVERSITY OF TEXAS AT SAN ANTONIO

> *"This job is sucking the life out of me."*
> *"I don't know how much longer I can do this."*
> *"It's the same thing, day in and day out."*
> *"Why do I even bother?"*
> *"They're all the same ... "*
> *"At a certain point you just stop caring."*
> *"They need this, they need that ... just leave me alone, go away!"*

As many of us know far too well, chronic stress at work eventually wears a person down. Consequently, you yourself may have had some of the above thoughts about your job or the people you serve. The statements are indicative of a worker who feels emotionally drained; detached from their customers, clients, or patients; and no longer fulfilled by what they do. The phenomenon we are referring to is what laypeople and researchers call "burnout."

Occupational Burnout

Background

Burnout, a negative mental and emotional state resulting from prolonged occupational stress, was a challenge faced and identified by human service workers long before it was studied by researchers (Maslach & Jackson, 1984). Broadly understood, human services improve and preserve the well-being of people by meeting their various needs (Hasenfeld, 2010). Health care workers were the first to draw the attention of researchers because of the constant and intense emotional demands they face while on the job. Soon after, human service workers in other fields (i.e., teachers, social workers, and police officers) became the object of study as well (Schaufeli & Enzmann, 1998). Human service jobs entail a great deal of interaction between service provider (e.g., nurse) and recipient (e.g., patient). Service providers are expected to display and/or manage particular feelings as part of their job—a kind of "emotional labor" is thus required of these workers and is at the core of the burnout experience (Hochschild, 1983; Maslach, 1993).

Schaufeli, Leiter, and Maslach (2009) suggest that various systemic cultural changes ushered in the modern era of burnout. Starting in the 1950s, the human services became the subject of greater government and state influence and thus became bureaucratized; job descriptions became more formalized and often led to "frustration and disillusionment arising from a widespread institutionalized clash of utilitarian organizational values with providers' personal or professional values" (Schaufeli et al., 2009, p. 207). To provide a recent example, Sullivan (2009) found that social workers feel pressured to emphasize their organization's values of resource allocation and paternalistic (instead of client-centered) care planning over the values they, as individual trained professionals, feel are appropriate. In another example, physicians contracted by managed care organizations can be prevented from offering the highest level of care for a patient (e.g., running the most sophisticated diagnostic panels, offering cutting-edge treatment, keeping the patient in the hospital as long as needed) because it is too expensive for the organization—here, the institutional objective of cost control trumps physicians' professional goal of doing what is best for their patient. A second systemic change suggested to impact burnout was the 1960s Cultural Revolution, featuring changing attitudes toward authority and lessening the traditional prestige of professionals in law enforcement, education, and health care, while empowered recipients expected more attentive and responsive service and care than ever before (Schaufeli et al., 2009).

Two researchers independently began to document the experience of burnout in the 1970s. Freudenberger (1974) started using the term after hearing it as a reference to the consequences of long-term drug use and he applied it to the experience of the volunteers he studied at St. Mark's free clinic in New York. Freudenberger observed that as they worked with drug addicts and the homeless, these volunteers underwent "gradual emotional depletion, loss of motivation, and reduced commitment" (as cited in Schaufeli et al., 2009, p. 205). In California, Maslach and her colleagues were studying the same phenomenon in their interviews with health care workers and found that in response to the strain of their jobs, workers suffered emotional exhaustion, felt negativity toward their patients or clients, and doubted their professional competence (Maslach, Schaufeli, & Leiter, 2001). Because the concept of burnout did not originate from the theorizing of scholars but was derived from workers' own experiences, it was not initially recognized as an area of respectable academic research; however, this quickly changed with the addition of theoretical models, scores of studies, and ample empirical evidence (Maslach, Schaufeli, & Leiter, 2001).

Assessing Burnout

Burnout research shifted toward quantitative methodology and the use of larger numbers of subjects, leading to the development of several assessment instruments in the 1980s. Of the instruments, the scale with the best psychometric properties (e.g., reliability, validity, responsiveness) was Maslach and Jackson's (1981) Maslach Burnout Inventory (MBI), which has become the most well-known and widely used burnout instrument to date. The MBI is a twenty-two-item scale composed of three subscales: emotional exhaustion (feeling stretched too thin and depleted emotionally); depersonalization (treating care or service recipients impersonally and/or feeling callously toward them); and personal accomplishment (feeling skilled and effective in and fulfilled by one's work with care or service recipients) (Maslach & Jackson, 1981). Importantly, unlike the other two subscales, *lower scores* on personal accomplishment indicate higher degrees of burnout. Each of the MBI's twenty-two items is a statement about feelings or attitudes, and respondents are asked to rate the statements on dimensions of frequency (how often they experience the feeling or attitude) and intensity (how strongly they experience the feeling or attitude). The general term "recipients" is used in some statements and refers to the individuals to whom the survey respondent provides service, care, or treatment. In studies utilizing the MBI, "recipient" is often substituted with a more specific term for the sake of clarity (e.g., when surveying physicians, researchers might use the term "patients"). Technically, there are various versions of the MBI that are designed with the correct terminology for specific recipients in various human service domains—the MBI-Human Services Survey (MBI-HSS) uses the terms patients and clients and the MBI-Educators Survey (MBI-ES) refers to students (Maslach, Schaufeli, & Leiter, 2001).

The nine-item emotional exhaustion subscale consists of statements such as, "I feel emotionally drained from my work" and "Working with people all day is really a strain for me." The eight-item personal accomplishment subscale consists of such statements as, "I feel I'm positively influencing other people's lives through my work" and "I have accomplished many worthwhile things in this job." When calculating a respondent's overall MBI score, personal accomplishment items are reverse-scored so that they are scaled in the same direction as the other two subscales and can be summed up for a composite score. The five-item depersonalization subscale consists of statements such as, "I feel I treat some recipients as if they were impersonal 'objects'" and "I've become more callous toward people since I took this job." Among medical professionals, the scores considered "high" for emotional exhaustion and depersonalization are ≥ 10 and ≥ 27, respectively; a score ≤ 33 in personal accomplishment is considered low (Maslach, Jackson, & Leiter, 1996). A high emotional exhaustion score in combination with either a high depersonalization score or a low personal accomplishment score on the MBI is considered an indication of burnout (Schaufeli, Leiter, & Maslach, 2009).

The original MBI was created for human service professionals; soon after, in response to significant demand, the MBI-ES was developed for educators; then, acknowledging growing interest in assessing burnout outside of the human services, the MBI-General Survey (MBI-GS) was developed (Leiter & Schaufeli, 1996; Schaufeli, Leiter, & Maslach, 2009). The MBI-GS has been demonstrated appropriate for use across a variety of occupations that range greatly in degree of client/patient interaction (Schaufeli, Leiter, Maslach, & Jackson, 1996). The MBI-GS features three subscales (i.e., exhaustion, cynicism, and personal efficacy) that correspond to the subscales of the MBI but, unlike the MBI, does not involve mention of other people (coworkers or clients/patients) in the work environment, focusing more on an individual's feelings toward his or her work in general. The most notable difference between the MBI and the MBI-GS is that the general survey assesses cynicism instead of depersonalization, as "depersonalization refers to distancing oneself emotionally from service recipients and to the development of cynical attitudes toward them, cynicism refers to distancing oneself from work itself and to the development of negative attitudes toward work in general" (Bakker, Demerouti, & Schaufeli, 2002).

An alternative approach to studying burnout by Maslach and Leiter (1997) is based on its conceptual opposite, engagement. This perspective takes a positive psychology approach, focusing on optimal functioning and individual strengths as opposed to debilitation and shortcomings. Rather than looking at burnout, which is an inherently negative phenomenon, researchers assess varying levels of "engagement" (a positive phenomenon). Engagement manifests itself through energy (as opposed to emotional exhaustion), involvement (as opposed to depersonalization), and efficacy (as opposed to reduced sense of personal accomplishment); accordingly, engagement is measured using a reverse pattern of scores on the respective MBI subscales.

Schaufeli and colleagues also conceptualize the experience of engagement as negatively related to burnout but take the position that engagement should be assessed as a distinct construct. They argue that it should be measured using a unique set of criteria rather than the subscales created for the MBI (Bakker, Schaufeli, Leiter, & Taris, 2008; Schaufeli, Bakker, & Salanova, 2006). As such, Schaufeli and colleagues (2006) created the Utrecht Work Engagement Scale (UWES), validated in numerous countries, to assess what they see as the three primary dimensions of engagement: vigor (e.g., "At my work I feel bursting with energy"), dedication (e.g., "I find the work that I do full of meaning and purpose"), and absorption (e.g., "I feel happy when I am working intensely"). The original seventeen-item UWES was later revised to a nine-item measure assessing the same three dimensions.

Burnout Models

It is generally accepted that emotional exhaustion, depersonalization, and lack of personal accomplishment do not develop simultaneously, and some researchers have taken the associations between the dimensions as an indicator of the burnout process, though the MBI was not originally intended as a description of how burnout advances (Houkes, Winants, Twellaar, & Verdonk, 2011; Taris, Le Blanc, Schaufeli, & Schreurs, 2005). There is particular utility in identifying the causal order of burnout to enable interventions for at-risk individuals or those in the early phases of burning out (Houkes et al., 2011; Taris et al., 2005).

Taris and colleagues reviewed evidence for the three most influential models of the burnout process: Leiter and Maslach's (2004) process model; Golembiewski, Munzenrider, and Stevenson's (1986) phase model; and Lee and Ashforth's (1993) model. Leiter and Maslach propose a model in which chronic job demands evoke a stress response that creates emotional exhaustion; in an effort to cope with this exhaustion, workers begin to detach or withdraw ("depersonalization" in human services or "cynicism" in nonhuman service work) leading to diminished feelings of personal accomplishment. Golembiewski and colleagues offer the phase model in which each of the three burnout dimensions is divided into low and high levels and there are, thus, eight possible paths to burnout. A worker may take various routes to the destination of burnout, but notably in the phase model, depersonalization is first in the process, contributing to reduced feelings of personal accomplishment and finally emotional exhaustion. Lee and Ashforth's model is distinguished by the suggestion that the three burnout elements do not occur in sequence—that emotional exhaustion leads to depersonalization and reduced sense of personal accomplishment, and that depersonalization and reduced feelings of personal accomplishment develop independently from one another. More specifically, Lee and Ashforth argue that reduced sense of personal accomplishment does not occur as a result of depersonalization and arises instead directly from emotional exhaustion.

Until recently, clear support for any causal model of burnout was lacking. Ashforth and Lee (1997) brought attention to the need to elucidate the path to burnout, as few studies at that time had done so. Ashforth and Lee also made the points that some individuals burn out faster than others (or do not burn out at all while their coworkers do) and that various work stressors may burn employees out quickly whereas other stressors may evoke burnout more slowly. In the years that followed this commentary, researchers began to devote greater attention to the issues voiced by Ashforth and Lee by examining both organizational and individual predictors of burnout, and by further exploring the path of burnout development.

Organizational Predictors of Burnout

Maslach and Leiter (2008) have identified issues centering around six primary areas that stand out in the literature as significant organizational contributors to the development of burnout—workload, control, reward, community, fairness, and values. Workload is the most commonly recognized job stressor related to burnout; too much or overly difficult work without an opportunity to rest and recover is consistently associated with emotional exhaustion (Cordes & Dougherty, 1993; Leiter & Maslach, 2004). Emotional exhaustion has, in fact, been shown through structural modeling to account for the relationship between workload and depersonalization, and also for the relationship between workload and reduced sense of personal accomplishment (e.g., see Demerouti, Bakker, Nachreiner, & Schaufeli, 2001). Lack of personal control or autonomy is also problematic, role conflict being a frequent example of such (Maslach & Leiter, 2008). Role conflict exists when two or more role requirements are contradictory or in opposition to one another (Matteson & Ivancevich, 1982). Insufficient reward (i.e., financial compensation, appreciation, or social approval) also puts workers at risk for burnout, as does lack of "community" constituted by positive relationships and interactions at work, in the form of teamwork, productive conflict management, social support, and the like (Leiter & Maslach, 2004). Lastly, lack of fairness in procedures and practices contributes to burnout, as does a mismatch between the values of an individual and the organization they work for (Leiter & Maslach, 2004; Maslach & Leiter, 2008).

Based on these six domains of work life, Leiter and Maslach (2004) developed the Areas of Worklife Scale (AWS) in an attempt to identify early predictors of burnout and enable preventative interventions. The twenty-nine-item AWS (intended for a wide variety of occupations) assesses the fit between worker and job by having respondents evaluate whether their needs are met in the six areas previously discussed. Leiter and Maslach ask respondents to rate their agreement with such items as, "I have enough time to do what's important in my job" (a "workload" item) and "Working here forces me to compromise my values" (a "values" item). In tests of the AWS, greater incongruity between worker preferences and their workplace significantly predicted the worker having developed burnout one year later. The emphasis in the AWS is on the interaction between person and work environment which may avert the development of burnout. This seems to be one reason why in the same workplace, exposed to the same pressures, individuals vary in their experience of burnout. For example, in a study by Barnett, Gareis, and Brennan (1999), it was not work hours that lead to burnout; rather, the relationship between work hours and burnout was explained by worker preference for hours and the relationship between worker and spouse work schedules.

Individual Predictors of Burnout

Though there is substantial evidence for various organizational causes of burnout, there is less clear support for individual predictors of burnout. In their meta-analysis of research on personality and burnout, Alarcon, Eschleman, and Bowling (2009) reviewed 114 published studies that investigated individual characteristics and their relationship to the three burnout dimensions. Personality was found to be dependably related to burnout, but some personality features were less significant predictors than others (Alarcon et al., 2009). For example, emotional stability, positive affectivity, and negative affectivity had a stronger association with emotional exhaustion and depersonalization than other variables that were not affect-related (i.e., about emotions)—those with positive affectivity and emotional stability were less likely to suffer emotional exhaustion and depersonalization; those with negative affectivity were more likely. Many additional characteristics were found to have associations with one or more dimensions of burnout; self-esteem, self-efficacy, extraversion, locus of control, conscientiousness, agreeableness, openness, optimism, proactive and Type A personality, and hardiness were all found to be linked to lower levels of burnout (Alarcon et al., 2009).

Demographic factors that have been found to put one at increased risk for burnout associated with depersonalization/cynicism include being single rather than married, younger rather than older, and male rather than female (Maslach, 1993). Choice of coping mechanisms also varies from person to person, some techniques being effective (e.g., active coping) and others being dysfunctional (e.g., drinking or drug use), creating yet another individual-level difference that has the potential to either buffer or make a worker more susceptible to burnout (e.g., see Koeske, Kirk, & Koeske, 1993). Evidence for individual differences as significant predictors of burnout remains lacking, however, due to inconsistent findings and the size of relationships between these factors and burnout (Maslach, 1993).

Impact of Burnout

The impact of burnout is far-reaching, affecting employees, coworkers, the employee's clients/service recipients/patients, and the organization to which the employee belongs. Employees suffering from burnout are more susceptible to cardiovascular disease, high blood pressure, increased work/family conflict, poor mental health, sleep disturbance, emotional and uncontrolled eating, and more (Bacharach, Bamberger, & Conley, 1991; Maslach, 1993; Nevanperä et al., 2012). The mental, emotional, and physical impact of burnout on an individual level parallels the effects of long-term stress, as burnout is an extended stress response (Maslach, Schaufeli, & Leiter, 2001).

In terms of the consequences of burnout on service recipients (whether customers, clients, or patients), burnout inherently features suboptimal attitudes toward and treatment of recipients as articulated by its "depersonalization/cynicism" component (Maslach & Jackson, 1984). That is, a detached attitude toward and low-quality interactions with service recipients are simultaneously a qualifying condition for and a consequence of burnout. There is also some interesting evidence that burnout might be "contagious"—that the negative attitude of a burned out employee can "spread" to his or her coworkers either by adoption of attitude or via the creation of a negative working environment. A study of general practitioners (primary care doctors) by Bakker, Schaufeli, Sixma, and Bosveld (2001) found that perceived burnout complaints (from colleagues) were predictive of a practitioner's own emotional exhaustion if the practitioner was highly susceptible to emotional stimuli. Other studies have replicated the finding that burnout can be transmitted inter-personally, statistically controlling for the effect of job stressors that coworkers might have in common (e.g., see Bakker, Le Blanc, & Schaufeli, 2005).

Burnout, on an organizational level, decreases morale, organizational commit-ment, productivity, and job satisfaction; is predictive of conflict among employees and employee intention to leave; and increases absenteeism, turnover, and poor work performance (Maslach et al., 2001; Wright & Cropanzano, 1998). Further-more, burned out employees are less likely to adhere to safe work practices and thus impact an organization's safety outcomes (Nahrgang, Morgeson, & Hoffman, 2011). In terms of financial impact, it is estimated that burnout costs U.S. business up to $300 billion annually, taking into account all of the cumulative consequences of job stress (Leiter & Maslach, 2005).

The Role of Communication in Burnout

Communication occupies a central role in the creation, manifestation, prevention, and management of burnout. In the original conception of the phenomenon, a key feature of burnout was that it arose from "constant, emotional, communicative contact with individuals in need of help" (Miller, Stiff, & Ellis, 1988, p. 250). Miller and her colleagues (1988) were particularly interested in the relationship between caregiver and recipient, and hypothesized that degree of communicative responsiveness among caregivers would predict the development of burnout. They reasoned that interactions with patients either evoke emotional contagion (a "catching" or vicarious experiencing of the patient's emotions) or empathetic concern, involving perspective-taking and understanding of a patient's problem. Empathetic concern facilitates responsive communication and reduces the likelihood of depersonalization, whereas the draining experience of emotional contagion *decreases* communicative responsiveness and *increases* the likelihood that caregivers will depersonalize patients (Miller et al., 1988). In Miller's model, depersonalization is positioned as the first phase of burnout, and communication responsiveness (specifically lack thereof) is suggested to be the precursor that "kicks off" the burnout process. Frustrating communication between provider and patient can also play a role in the experience of burnout, as will be discussed later in the case study of physicians.

Lower-quality interactions with service recipients are both a qualifier for and consequence of burnout. The MBI depersonalization subscale features such statements as, "I feel I treat some recipients as if they were impersonal 'objects'" and "I've become more callous toward people since I took this job," using agreement with these items to identify burnout (Maslach & Jackson, 1981). It is accepted as a basic tenet that burnout compromises the relationship between provider and service recipient, yet few studies have examined the concrete ways that burnout impacts communication in this context. For example, what exactly does "treating recipients as if they were impersonal objects" or being "callous toward people" entail? The work that explores the impact of burnout on communication exists primarily in the realm of physician–patient interaction and will be addressed in this chapter's case study. Meanwhile, much more is known about the prophylactic functions of communication in burnout.

Communication can play an important role in preventing and coping with burnout; participation in decision-making (PDM) and social support are considered to be especially effective deterrents. In a study of hospital staff (the majority of whom were directly involved in patient care), PDM was a crucial factor in decreasing perceptions of burnout and role stress and increasing work satisfaction and sense of personal accomplishment (Miller, Ellis, Zook, & Lyles, 1990). The effect of PDM on burnout has since been replicated in numerous other studies (e.g., see Greco, Laschinger, & Wong, 2006). PDM functions to decrease burnout through several possible mechanisms. Four of Maslach and Leiter's (2008) six organizational contributors to burnout are addressed via PDM—PDM gives workers an increased sense of *control* and reduces role conflict; it fosters a sense of *community* by way of teamwork; and it enables workers to implement principles of *fairness* and facilitates a closer match between their *values* and that of the organization.

Many studies, involving a variety of occupational groups, from correctional officers (Lambert, Altheimer, & Hogan, 2010) to nurses (Ellis & Miller, 1994) and teachers (Ray & Miller, 1991), have found supportive communication to be linked to lower levels of burnout. Supportive communication may involve messages of understanding and encouragement (emotional support), or it may involve the provision of helpful information (informational support) and can be from coworkers, supervisors, or family members. However, researchers have not yet identified consistent relationships between various types of support and individual burnout dimensions (Halbesleben, 2006).

Burnout Interventions

In their examination of the efficacy of twenty-five published burnout interventions, Awa, Plaumann, and Walter (2010) found that 84 percent of interventions in their sample led to reductions in burnout, emotional exhaustion being the most impacted element of burnout, with organizational and combined interventions creating longer-lasting results than individual-level interventions. With all intervention types, intervention refresher sessions extended results longer (up to 2.5 years) compared to similar programs without refreshers.

Interventions to prevent or reduce burnout can be directed toward individuals, an organization, or both. Interventions that offer individual-level strategies aim to assist workers in coping with burnout via increased awareness and stress reduction, involving such techniques as self-monitoring, relaxation exercises, cognitive restructuring, and skills training (Awa et al., 2010; Le Blanc & Schaufeli, 2008).

Interventions at an organizational level involve such changes as task restructuring, attempts to decrease job demands, and increasing workers' control over their jobs and their participation in decision-making (Awa et al., 2010). The bulk of interventions have targeted individual workers rather than organizations; this emphasis on individuals reflects the conceptualization of burnout as an individual stress response and that there is a widespread belief that it is easier and less expensive to change people rather than organizations (Le Blanc & Schaufeli, 2008). The neglect of organizational factors in intervention efforts is unfortunate, as there is substantial evidence that organizational factors are more influential than individual factors in the experience of burnout, and interventions that target both the individual and organization produce longer-lasting outcomes (Awa et al., 2010; Le Blanc & Schaufeli, 2008). But organizational change involves employees at all levels, intensive time and effort, and requires financial investment, which is often not feasible.

One of the challenges in organizational burnout interventions is that stressors often vary from organization to organization; there is, thus, no universally effective intervention. In recognition of the need for customized interventions, "action research" has become increasingly popular. Action research entails workers identifying the causes of burnout in their own organization and developing and implementing a tailored intervention with the help of expert researchers (Le Blanc & Schaufeli, 2008). This approach has been implemented with success in various organizations ranging from elementary schools to oncology centers to the Federal Fire Service.

Physician Burnout

Background

Physicians suffer from the highest levels of burnout across occupations; as burnout is associated with increased risk of suicide, it is not surprising that physicians have also had the highest suicide rates out of all professions for decades (Gold, Sen, & Schwenk, 2013; Wallace, Lemaire, & Ghali, 2009). For example, in 2005, a male physician had a 70 percent higher chance of committing suicide than a non-physician male, and a female physician had between 250 percent to 400 percent higher chance of committing suicide than a non-physician female (Hampton, 2005). Sadly, it is estimated that even more physicians commit suicide than what is reported, given that their cause of death may be mislabeled, sometimes purposefully so. In their analysis of data from the National Violent Death Reporting System, Gold et al. (2013) found that non-physicians are more likely to have had a recent crisis or death of a loved one that contributed to their suicide; physicians, however, were more likely to have had a job problem contribute to their suicide.

Shanafelt and colleagues (2012) conducted the first national study assessing physician burnout by specialty and compared to the general U.S. population— once public, their findings quickly made national news headlines. Out of the

7,288 physicians that Shanafelt et al. surveyed, 45.8 percent met the criteria for burnout based on high emotional exhaustion or depersonalization scores. Relative to the control group consisting of a national sample of non-physician working adults, physicians experienced higher levels of emotional exhaustion (32.1 percent versus 23.5 percent), depersonalization (19.4 percent versus 15.0 percent), and burnout overall (37.9 percent versus 27.8 percent). Physicians in specialties providing front line care—family medicine, general internal medicine, and emergency medicine—suffered from the highest burnout levels. There are many reasons why physicians experience greater burnout than workers in other professions.

Contributing Factors

Professional influences. Decreased control, administrative requirements, loss of autonomy, long hours and lack of sleep, high patient volume, and difficulty balancing personal and professional life are the most frequently identified factors that contribute to physician burnout (Shanafelt, Sloan, & Habermann, 2003). Increasingly, physicians are expected to see too many patients in too little time. For example, 40 percent of hospitalists in a study by Michtalik, Yeh, Pronovost, and Brotman (2013) reported that their average inpatient count surpassed safe levels at least monthly; 36 percent of these physicians reported patient counts exceeding safety levels at least once a week. These heavy caseloads (number of patients) and long hours can make it extremely difficult for physicians to have time for a personal life. In Shanafelt et al.'s (2012) study, physicians worked significantly more than those in other occupations—they worked a median of ten hours more than non-physicians (fifty hours versus forty hours), and 37.9 percent of physicians worked sixty or more hours per week (versus 10.6 percent of non-physicians). In a study of surgeons, 89 percent of surgical oncologists worked more than fifty hours a week, 60 percent worked more than sixty hours a week, and 24 percent worked more than seventy hours a week (Kuerer et al., 2007). Consequently, work–life balance can be a significant problem for physicians, with 40.1 percent in Shanafelt et al.'s study indicating that their work schedule failed to allow enough time for family life or personal time, whereas only 23.1 percent of non-physician working adults felt this way.

Individual-Level Influences

Gender. The findings on gender differences in physician burnout are intriguing but not conclusive. While in some studies there are no differences in the prevalence of burnout between male and female physicians, in other studies female physicians report significantly higher levels of burnout (e.g., see Linzer et al., 2002; McMurray et al., 2000). The female physicians in McMurray et al.'s sample were 1.6 times more likely to indicate that they were burned out, with their chance of burnout increasing by 12 percent to 15 percent with every additional 5 hours they worked per week over 40 hours.

Shanafelt et al. (2012) found female physicians to be more dissatisfied with their work–life balance than their male counterparts. When surveyed, 43.1 percent of female physicians felt that their schedule left no time for family or personal time; 38.9 percent of male physicians felt the same (Shanafelt et al., 2012). The greater work–life strain felt by female physicians has been suggested to be one reason that the increased risk of suicide for female physicians compared to non-physician females is even higher than the increased risk of male physicians compared to non-physician males (Pompili, Mancinelli, Girardi, & Tatarelli, 2004; Schernhammer & Colditz, 2004). Female physicians take on greater responsibility for child care and domestic duties in their household, earn less on average, and are more likely to experience sexual harassment at work than male physicians (Gautam, 2001). Female physicians also tend to spend more time with patients than male physicians, which can exacerbate feelings of stress from time pressures and workload (Gautam, 2001; Medscape, 2012). In Dyrbye et al.'s (2011) study of work–home conflict and burnout among surgeons, female surgeons reported more work–home conflict, were more likely to feel that having children had negatively impacted their career, and experienced more conflicts between their and their spouse's career compared to male surgeons. These challenges are not exclusive to female physicians— they are shared by other working women—but they are especially present for women in medicine due to the intensely demanding nature of their job.

Some research also suggests gender differences in the psychological path to burnout. For example, a longitudinal study of Dutch physicians by Houkes, Winants, Twellaar, and Verdonk (2011) found sex differences in the development of burnout, with emotional exhaustion appearing to trigger the burnout process for female physicians, and depersonalization signaling the onset of burnout for male physicians. Furthermore, the experience of reduced personal accomplishment appeared to differ among the physicians in Houkes et al.'s study, with female physicians' feelings of personal accomplishment being impacted by the other burnout dimensions (emotional exhaustion and depersonalization) whereas male physicians' feelings of personal accomplishment were independent from the other dimensions, actually increasing over time in the face of emotional exhaustion and depersonalization.

Personality. Several personality characteristics, such as neuroticism and compulsiveness, have been found to increase the likelihood of burnout among physicians (McManus, Keeling, & Palce, 2004; Spickard, Gabbe, & Christensen, 2002). In an ironic twist, the most conscientious, dedicated, and motivated individuals appear to be at higher risk for burnout—these physicians typically devote themselves to their work and patients until they are depleted (Balch, Freischlag, & Shanafelt, 2009). For example, surgeons who pay attention to detail, are committed to patients, and feel a sense of responsibility associated with patients' trust are more likely to burn out because of these qualities (Shanafelt, 2007). In the physician burnout literature, however, the emphasis is less on personality and more on contextual and systemic forces. As Shanafelt and colleagues (2012) point out, given that half of U.S. physicians suffer from burnout, their high rates of burnout can be primarily attributed to our present health care environment and care delivery system.

Consequences of Burnout

The impact of burnout extends beyond individual physicians to their patients and the health care organization for which they work. On a personal level, burnout among physicians contributes to stress-related health issues, depression, substance abuse, relationship and family problems, and suicidal ideation (Gunderson, 2001; Krasner et al., 2009; Shanafelt et al., 2012). Professionally, physicians who are burned out are more likely to make medical errors, get sued, and leave the medical profession; they are also at risk to be less productive and efficient, be less professional, experience and express less empathy, and engage in less patient-centered communication (Shanafelt et al., 2010; Wallace, Lemaire, & Ghali, 2009). The impact of physician burnout on patients includes decreased adherence to treatment recommendations, diminished satisfaction and degree of trust and confidence in their physician, compromised quality of care, and longer recovery time and hospital stays (Halbesleben & Rathert, 2008; Wallace et al., 2009).

Burnout is also inherently damaging to the physician–patient relationship. The focus of burnout work has traditionally been on the internal experience of the sufferer; what has received much less attention is the specific ways in which burnout impacts interactions between provider and client/patient, or even provider and provider. When being assessed for burnout via the MBI, respondents are asked to self-report the degree and frequency with which they identify with statements such as, "I feel I treat some patients as if they were impersonal objects" and "I've become more callous toward people since I took this job" (Maslach & Jackson, 1984). Respondents' own perceptions of their interactions are a fundamental component of establishing the existence of burnout, but there has been a distinct lack of information on the ways in which burnout manifests itself communicatively. In Williams, Savage, and Linzer's (2006) physician–patient cycle model, the communication between physician and patient is the point at which physicians' emotional and mental states (e.g., emotional exhaustion, depersonalization) become observable via behavior. Research which examines the interpersonal effects of physicians' internal experience is lacking; in particular, the impact of burnout on specific communication practices has received inadequate attention (Williams et al., 2006).

A study by Shanafelt, Bradley, Wipf, and Back (2002) was the first that sought to assess the impact of burnout on patient care. Surveying physicians in an internal medicine residency program, Shanafelt and colleagues found that 76 percent of their sample met the criteria for burnout. Residency training (the postgraduate medical training that occurs following medical school) is well known for being a time during which there is a sharp increase in burnout. Young physicians are in a high-pressure environment, working long hours, caring for a large number of patients, and getting very little sleep (Rockey, 2011). Importantly, the burned out physicians in Shanafelt et al.'s study were two to three times more likely to engage in self-reported suboptimal patient care practices. Some of the physicians' suboptimal practices involved such things as neglecting to fully discuss treatment options or answer patients' questions and feeling guilty about how they treated a patient from a humanitarian standpoint. High scores on the depersonalization subscale of the MBI were the most predictive (out of the three subscales) of self-reported suboptimal patient care. Consequently, studies have found physician burnout, particularly depersonalization and emotional exhaustion, to be predictive of low patient satisfaction (e.g., Anagnostopoulous et al., 2012; Halbesleben & Rathert, 2008).

Passalacqua and Segrin (2012) investigated burnout among resident physicians, examining the effect of burnout on empathy and patient-centered communication during thirty-hour ("long-call") hospital shifts. Patient-centered communication is a key component of quality care and involves such concrete communication behaviors as eliciting and addressing patients' concerns and making eye contact during conversation. The physicians who were burned out according to their scores on the MBI were more likely to experience a decline in empathy toward patients as their shift wore on and reported using less patient-centered communication with patients. This was the first study to investigate the impact of burnout on physician attitudes and communicative behaviors during a hospital shift and served to illustrate how burnout can impact the ability of physicians to effectively cope with the challenge of maintaining empathy and patient-centered communication while on call. Furthermore, the findings of this study indicate that patient-centered communication (or lack thereof) may be one factor which can help explain the path from burnout to lower patient satisfaction.

Travado et al. (2005) were interested in the influence of oncologist burnout on physician–patient communication, as it is well-documented that physicians' communication skills have a significant effect on cancer patients' satisfaction (e.g., Baile & Aaron, 2005; Zachariae et al., 2003). Findings revealed that oncologists with burnout symptoms were less confident about their communication skills and had more negative expectations about the outcome of their communication with patients (Travado et al., 2005). These negative expectations are not unfounded—burnout can and does lead to more dissatisfying physician–patient interactions.

Bakker, Schaufeli, Sixma, Bosveld, and Van Dierendonck (2000) conducted a five-year longitudinal study of general practitioners and found that among physicians who suffered from burnout, depersonalization led to demanding and threatening patient behaviors. These findings are echoed in the work of Williams, Savage, and Linzer (2006). In their physician–patient cycle model, Williams et al. explain that in encounters where a provider seems inadequately concerned or involved (i.e., exhibiting "depersonalization"), some patients respond by being increasingly demanding. Demanding patient behaviors are a stressor that contributes to burnout; burned out physicians then respond in a manner that evokes more demanding behavior, thus exacerbating the physician's burnout and perpetuating the cycle.

Interventions

The majority of burnout interventions for physicians target individual coping ability rather than attempting to change problematic organizational factors. These individual-level interventions include such things as stress management, seminars, group writing workshops, and resilience, self-care, and mindfulness training (e.g., Beach et al., 2013; Ospina-Kammerer & Figley, 2003). Many intervention studies, however, have suffered from a number of issues including small sample size, lack of random assignment to conditions, and failure of results to persist over time. Of the various individual-level interventions, mindfulness training (helping physicians be present and attentive in the moment) appears to be particularly promising. In Krasner et al.'s (2009) mindfulness program administered to primary care physicians over a span of a year, burnout was significantly reduced up to fifteen months afterward. The interventions that produce the longest-lasting effects, however, are those that target both individuals and their organizations (Awa et al., 2010). Unfortunately, such combination interventions are uncommon, particularly in health care.

The Future

There have been concerns that implementation of the Patient Protection and Affordable Care Act might worsen the incidence of burnout among physicians via increased workload, administrative duties, and financial restrictions (Dyrbye & Shanafelt, 2011). Several years after their initial investigation (Shanafelt et al., 2012), Shanafelt and colleagues (2015) again assessed the prevalence of burnout among U.S. physicians to find out if it had become more pervasive in the current health care environment. In 2011, 45.5% of physicians sampled met the criteria for burnout; by 2014, the rate had risen to 54.4% (Shanafelt et al., 2015). Rates of burnout had increased across all 24 specialties studied and jumped up by over 10% in 9 of them. Burnout among workers in the general population, however, did not change significantly from 2011 to 2014, further widening the gap between the rates of burnout in physicians and non-physicians. The 2016 Medscape Physician Lifestyle Report, based on data gathered from 15,800 physicians, echoes the warning that physician burnout is progressively worsening—burnout in all 25 specialties was both more widespread and more severe than the previous year's report (Peckham, 2016). Physicians in the 2016 report ranked causes of burnout, with the top three causes being too many bureaucratic tasks, too many work hours, and increasing computerization. These features of medical practice are ones unlikely to abate in the present health care environment.

Wallace, Lemaire, and Ghali (2009) argue that physician wellness, or lack thereof, should serve as an indicator of the quality of patient care and the health care system as a whole. Given that over half of U.S. physicians are now estimated to suffer from burnout, plus the host of negative outcomes burnout has for physicians and their patients, it is clear that something must change. We will all be the

patients of physicians at some point in our lives; physician burnout is, consequently, everyone's problem.

References

Alarcon, G., Eschleman, K. J., & Bowling, N. A. (2009). Relationships between personality variables and burnout: A meta-analysis. *Work and Stress, 23*, 244–263. doi: http://dx.doi.org/10.1080/02678370903282600.

Anagnostopoulous, F., Liolios, E., Persenfonis, G., Slater, J., Kafetsios, K., & Niakas, D. (2012) Physician burnout and patient satisfaction with consultation in primary health care settings: Evidence of relationships from a one-with-many design. *Journal of Clinical Psychology in Medical Settings, 19*, 401–410. doi: 10.1007/s10880-011-9278-8.

Ashforth, B. E., & Lee, R. T. (1997). Burnout as a process: Commentary on Cordes, Doughtery, and Blum. *Journal of Organizational Behavior, 18*, 703–708. doi: 10.1002/(SICI)1099-1379(199711)18:6<703::AID-JOB847>3.0.CO;2-1.

Awa, W. L., Plaumann, M., & Walter, U. (2010). Burnout prevention: A review of intervention programs. *Patient Education and Counseling, 78*, 184–190. Retrieved from http://dx.doi.org/10.1016/j.pec.2009.04.008.

Bacharach, S. B., Bamberger, P., & Conley, S. (1991). Work–home conflict among nurses and engineers: Mediating the impact of role stress on burnout and satisfaction at work. *Journal of Organizational Behavior, 12*, 39–53. doi: 10.1002/job.4030 120104.

Baile, W. F., & Aaron, J. (2005). Patient–physician communication in oncology: Past, present, and future. *Current Opinion in Oncology, 17*, 331–335. doi: 10.1097/01.cco.0000167738.49325.2c.

Bakker, A. B., Demerouti, E., & Schaufeli, W. B. (2002). Validation of the Maslach Burnout Inventory–General Survey: An Internet study. *Anxiety, Stress, and Coping, 15*, 245–260. doi: 10.1080/1061580021000020716.

Bakker, A. B., Le Blanc, P. M., & Schaufeli, W. B. (2005). Burnout contagion among intensive care nurses. *Journal of Advanced Nursing, 51*, 276–287.

Bakker, A. B., Schaufeli, W. B., Leiter, M. P., & Taris, T. W. (2008). Work engagement: An emerging concept in occupational health psychology. *Work and Stress, 22*, 187–200. doi: 10.1080/02678370802393649.

Bakker, A. B., Schaufeli, W. B., Sixma, H. J., & Bosveld, W. (2001). Burnout contagion among general practitioners. *Journal of Social and Clinical Psychology, 20*, 82–98. doi:10.1521/jscp.20.1.82.22251.

Bakker, A. B., Schaufeli, W. B., Sixma, H. J., Bosveld, W., & Van Dierendonck, D. (2000). *Patient demands, lack of reciprocity, and burnout: A five-year longitudinal study among general practitioners. Journal of Organizational Behavior, 21*, 425–441. doi: 10.1002/(SICI)1099-1379(200006)21:4<425::AID-JOB21>3.0.CO;2-#.

Balch, C. M., Freischlag, J. A., & Shanafelt, T. D. (2009). Stress and burnout among surgeons: Understanding and managing the syndrome and avoiding the adverse consequences. *Archives of Surgery, 144*, 371–376. doi: 10.1001/archsurg.2008.575.

Barnett, R. C., Gareis, K. C., & Brennan, R. T. (1999). Fit as a mediator of the relationship between work hours and burnout. *Journal of Occupational Health Psychology, 4*, 307–317. doi: 10.1037/1076-8998.4.4.307.

Beach, M. C., Roter, D., Korthuis, P. T., Epstein, R. M., Sharp, V., Ratanawongsa, N., … Saha, S. (2013). A multicenter study of physician mindfulness and health care quality. *Annals of Family Medicine, 11*, 421–428. doi: 10.1370/afm.1507.

Cordes, C. L., & Dougherty, T. W. (1993). A review and integration of research on job burnout. *Academy of Management Review, 18*, 621–656. doi: 10.5465/AMR.1993. 9402210153.

Demerouti, E., Bakker, A. B., Nachreiner, F., & Schaufeli, W. B. (2001). The job demands–resources model of burnout. *Journal of Applied Psychology, 86*, 499–512. doi: 10.1037/0021-9010.86.3.499.

Dyrbye, L. N., & Shanafelt, T. D. (2011). Physician burnout: A potential threat to healthcare reform. *JAMA, 305*, 2009–2010. doi:10.1001/jama.2011.652.

Dyrbye, L. N., Shanafelt, T. D., Balch, C. M., Satele, D., Sloan, J., & Freischlag, J. (2011). Relationship between work–home conflicts and burnout among American surgeons. *JAMA Surgery, 146*, 211–217. doi:10.1001/archsurg.2010.310.

Ellis, B. H., & Miller, K. I. (1994). Supportive communication among nurses: Effects on commitment, burnout, and retention. *Health Communication, 6*, 77–96. doi: 10.1207/s15327027hc0602_1.

Freudenberger, H. J. (1974). Staff burn-out. *Journal of Social Issues, 30*, 159–165.

Gautam, M. (2001). Women in medicine: Stresses and solutions. *Western Journal of Medicine, 174*, 37–41. Retrieved from http://www.ncbi.nlm.nih.gov/pmc/articles/PMC1071229/pdf/wjm17400037.pdf.

Gold, K. J., Sen., A., & Schwenk, T. L. (2013). Details on suicide among US physicians: Data from the National Violent Death Reporting System. *General Hospital Psychiatry, 35*, 45–49. doi:10.1016/j.genhosppsych.2012.08.005.

Golembiewski, R. T., Munzenrider, R. F., & Stevenson, J. G. (1986). *Stress in organizations: Toward a phase model of burnout.* New York, NY: Praeger.

Greco, P., Laschinger, H. K. S., & Wong, C. (2006). Leader empowering behaviors, staff nurse empowerment, and work engagement/burnout. *Nursing Research, 19*(4), 41–56. doi:10.12927/cjnl.2006.18599.

Gunderson, L. (2001). Physician burnout. *Annals of Internal Medicine, 135*, 145–148. doi: 10.7326/0003-4819-135-2-2001107170-00023.

Halbesleben, J. R. (2006). Source of social support and burnout: A meta-analytic test of the conservation of resources model. *Journal of Applied Psychology, 91*, 1134–1145. doi: 10.1037/0021-9010.91.5.1134.

Halbesleben, J. R., & Rathert, C. (2008). Linking physician burnout and patient outcomes: Exploring the dyadic relationship between physicians and patients. *Health Care Management Review, 33*, 29–39. doi: 10.1097/01.HMR.0000304493.87898.72.

Hampton, T. (2005). Experts address risk of physician suicide. *JAMA, 294*, 1189–1191. Retrieved from: http://jama.jamanetwork.com/article.aspx?articleid=201513.

Hasenfeld, Y. (2010). The attributes of human service organizations. In Y. Hasenfeld (Ed.), *Human services as complex organizations* (pp. 9–32). Newbury Park, CA: Sage.

Hochschild, A. R. (1983). *The managed heart: Commercialization of human feeling.* Berkeley, CA: University of California Press.

Houkes, I., Winants, Y., Twellaar, M., & Verdonk, P. (2011). Development of burnout over time and the causal order of the three dimensions of burnout among male and female GPs: A three-wave panel study. *BMC Public Health, 11*, 240. Retrieved from http://www.biomedcentral.com/1471-2458/11/240.

Koeske, G. F., Kirk, S. A, & Koeske, R. D. (1993). Coping with job stress: Which strategies work best? *Journal of Occupational and Organizational Psychology, 66*, 319–335. doi: 10.1111/j.2044-8325.1993.tb00542.x.

Krasner, M. S., Epstein, R. M., Beckman, H., Suchman, A. L., Chapman, B., Mooney, C. J., & Quill, T. E. (2009). Association of an educational program in mindful communication with burnout, empathy, and attitudes among primary care physicians. *JAMA, 302,* 1284–1293. doi: 10.1001/jama.2009.1384.

Kuerer, H. M., Eberlein, T. J., Pollock, R. E., Huschka, M., Baile, W. F., Morrow, M., … Shanafelt, T. D. (2007). Career satisfaction, practice patterns and burnout among surgical oncologists: Report on the quality of life of members of the Society of Surgical Oncology. *Annals of Surgical Oncology, 14,* 3043–3053. doi: 10.1245/s10434-007-9579-1.

Lambert, E. G., Altheimer, I., & Hogan, N. L. (2010). Exploring the relationship between social support and job burnout among correctional staff. *Criminal Justice and Behavior, 37,* 1217–1236. doi: 10.1177/0093854810379552.

Le Blanc, P. M., & Schaufeli, W. B. (2008). *Burnout interventions: An overview and illustration.* In J. R. B. Halbesleben (Ed.), *Handbook of stress and burnout in healthcare* (pp. 201–216). New York: Nova Science Publishers. Retrieved from http://www.wilmarschaufeli.nl/publica tions/Schaufeli/319.pdf.

Lee, R. T., & Ashforth, B. E. (1996). A meta-analytic examination of the correlated of the three dimensions of job burnout. *Journal of Applied Psychology, 8,* 123–133.

Leiter, M. P., & Maslach, C. (2004). Areas of worklife: A structured approach to organiza- tional predictors of job burnout. *Research in Occupational Stress and Well Being, 3,* 91–134. doi: 10.1016/S1479-3555(03)03003-8.

Leiter, M. P., & Maslach, C. (2005). *Banishing burnout: Six strategies for improving your rela- tionship with work.* San Francisco: Jossey-Bass.

Leiter, M. P., & Schaufeli, W. B. (1996). Consistency of the burnout construct across occupations. *Anxiety, Stress, & Coping, 9,* 229–243. doi:10.1080/10615809608249404.

Linzer, M., McMurray, J. E., Visser, M. R., Oort, F. J., Smets, E., & de Haes, H. C. (2002). Sex differences in physician burnout in the United States and the Netherlands. *Journal of the American Medical Women's Association, 57,* 191–193. Retrieved from http:// www.ncbi.nlm.nih.gov/pubmed/12405233.

Maslach, C. (1993). Burnout: A multidimensional perspective. In W. B. Schaufeli, C. Maslach, & T. Marek (Eds.), *Professional burnout: Recent developments in theory and research* (pp. 19–32). New York: Taylor & Francis.

Maslach, C., & Jackson, S. E. (1981). The measurement of experienced burnout. *Journal of Occupational Behavior, 2,* 99–113. doi: 10.1002/job.4030020205.

Maslach, C., & Jackson, S. E. (1984). Burnout in organizational settings. *Applied Social Psychology Annual, 5,* 133–153. Retrieved from smlr.rutgers.edu/Jackson-burnout.

Maslach, C., Jackson, S. E., & Leiter, M. P. (1996). *MBI: The Maslach Burnout Inventory: Manual.* Consulting Psychologists Press: Palo Alto, CA.

Maslach, C., & Leiter, M. P. (1997). *The truth about burnout.* San Francisco: Jossey-Bass.

Maslach, C., & Leiter, M. P. (2008). Early predictors of job burnout and engagement. *Journal of Applied Psychology, 93,* 498–512.

Maslach, C., Schaufeli, W. B., & Leiter, M. P. (2001). Job burnout. *Annual Review of Psychology, 52,* 397–422. doi: 10.1146/annurev.psych.52.1.397.

Maslach, C., Schaufeli, W. B., & Leiter, M. P. (2008). Early predictors of job burnout and engagement. *Journal of Applied Psychology, 93,* 498–512. doi: 10.1037/0021-9010.93.3.498.

Matteson, M. T., & Ivancevich, J. M. (1982). *Managing job stress and worker health.* New York: Free Press.

McManus, I. C., Keeling, A., & Palce, E. (2004). Stress, burnout, and doctors' attitudes to work are determined by personality and learning style: A twelve year longitudinal study of UK medical graduates. *BioMed Central Medicine, 2,* 29–31. doi: 10.1186/1741- 7015-2-29.

McMurray, J. E., Linzer, M., Konrad, T. R., Douglass, J., Shugerman, R., & Nelson, K. (2000). The work lives of women physicians: Results from the physician worklife study. *Journal of General Internal Medicine, 15,* 372–380. doi: 10.1111/j.1525–1497.2000.im9908009.x.

Medscape (2012). Medscape physician compensation report: 2012 results. Retrieved November 20, 2013, from http://www.medscape.com/features/slideshow/compensa tion/2012/public.

Michtalik, H. J., Yeh, H., Pronovost, P. J., & Brotman, D. J. (2013). Impact of physician workload on patient care: A survey of hospitalists. *JAMA Internal Medicine, 173,* 375–377. doi: 10.1001/jamainternmed.2013.1864.

Miller, K. I., Ellis, B. H., Zook, E. G., & Lyles, J. S. (1990). An integrated model of communication, stress, and burnout in the workplace. *Communication Research, 17,* 300–326. doi: 10.1177/009365095022002001.

Miller, K. I., Stiff, J. B., & Ellis, B. H. (1988). Communication and empathy as precursors to burnout among human service workers. *Communication Monographs, 55,* 250–265. doi: 10.1080/03637758809376171.

Nahrgang, J. D., Morgeson, F. P., & Hoffman, D. A. (2011). Safety at work: A meta-analytic investigation of the link between job demands, job resources, burnout, engagement, and safety outcomes. *Journal of Applied Psychology, 96,* 71–94. doi: 10.1037/a0021484.

Nevanperä, N. J., Hopsu, L., Kuosma, E., Ukkola, O., Utti, J., & Laitinen, J. H. (2012). Occupational burnout, eating behavior, and weight among working women. *American Journal of Nutrition, 95,* 934–943. doi: 10.3945/ajcn.111.014191.

Ospina-Kammerer, V., & Figley, C. R. (2003). An evaluation of the Respiratory One Method (ROM) in reducing emotional exhaustion among family physician residents. *International Journal of Emergency Mental Health, 5,* 29–32. Retrieved from www.ncbi. nlm.nih.gov/pubmed/12722487.

Passalacqua, S. A., & Segrin, C. (2012). The effect of resident physician stress, burnout, and empathy on patient-centered communication during the long-call shift. *Health Communication, 27,* 449–456. doi: 10.1080/10410236.2011.606527.

Peckham, C. (2016). *Medscape Lifestyle Report 2016: Bias and Burnout.* Retrieved from http:// www.medscape.com/features/slideshow/lifestyle/2016/public/overview#page=1.

Pompili, M., Mancinelli, I., Girardi, P., & Tatarelli, R. (2004). Letter to the editor: On female physicians committing suicide. *Medscape General Medicine, 6*(2), 60. Published online. Retrieved from http://www.ncbi.nlm.nih.gov/pmc/articles/PMC1395804/.

Ray, E. B., & Miller, K. I. (1991). The influence of communication structure and social support on job stress and burnout. *Management Communication Quarterly, 4,* 506–527. doi: 10.1177/0021886394303007.

Rockey, P. H. (2011). Duty hours: Where do we go from here? *Mayo Clinic Proceedings, 86,* 176–178. doi: 10.4065/mcp.2011.0086.

Schaufeli, W. B., & Bakker, A. B. (2004). Job demands, job resources, and their relation-ship with burnout and engagement: A multi-sample study. *Journal of Organizational Behavior, 25,* 293–315. doi: 10.1002/job.248.

Schaufeli, W. B., Bakker, A. B., & Salanova, M. (2006). The measurement of work engagement with a short questionnaire: A cross-national study. *Educational and Psychological Measurement, 66,* 701–716. doi: 10.1177/0013164405282471.

Schaufeli, W. B., & Enzmann, D. (1998). *The burnout companion to study and practice: A critical analysis.* London: Taylor & Francis.

Schaufeli, W. B., Leiter, M. P., & Maslach, C. (2009). Burnout: 35 years of research and practice. *Career Development International, 14,* 204–220. doi: 10.1108/13620430910966406.

Schaufeli, W. B., Leiter, M. P., Maslach, C., & Jackson, S. E. (1996). Maslach Burnout Inventory–General Survey. In C. Maslach, S. E. Jackson, & M. P. Leiter (Eds.), *The Maslach Burnout Inventory: Test manual* (3rd ed., pp. 22–26). Palo Alto, CA: Consulting Psychologists Press.

Schernhammer, E. S., & Colditz, G. A. (2004). Suicide rates among physicians: A quantitative and gender assessment (meta-analysis). *American Journal of Psychiatry, 161*, 2295–2302. doi:10.1176/appi.ajp.161.12.2295.

Shanafelt, T. D. (2007). A career in surgical oncology: Finding meaning, balance, and personal satisfaction. *Annals of Surgical Oncology, 15*, 400–406. doi: 10.1245/s10434-007-9725-9.

Shanafelt, T. D., Balch, C. M., Bechamps, G., Russell, T., Dyrbye, L., Satele, D., ... Freischlag, J. (2010). Burnout and medical error among American surgeons. *Annals of Surgery, 251*, 995–1000. doi: 10.1097/SLA.0b013e3181bfdab3.

Shanafelt, T. D., Boone, S., Tan, L., Dyrbye, L. N., Stoile, W., Satele, D., ... Oreskovich, M. R. (2012). Burnout and satisfaction with work–life balance among US physicians relative to the general US population. *JAMA Internal Medicine, 172*, 1377–1385. doi: 10.1001/archinternmed.2012.3199.

Shanafelt, T. D., Bradley, K. A., Wipf, J. E., & Back, A. L. (2002). Burnout and self-reported patient care in an internal medicine residency program. *Annals of Internal Medicine, 136*, 358–367. Retrieved from http://annals.org/article.aspx?articleid=715151.

Shanafelt, T. D., Hasan, O., Dyrbye, L. N., Sinsky, C., Satele, D., Sloan, J., & West, C. P. (2015). Changes in burnout and satisfaction with work-life balance in physicians and the general US working population between 2011 and 2014. *Mayo Clinic Proceedings 90*(12), 1600–1613. Retrieved from http://dx.doi.org/10.1016/j.mayocp.2015.08.023.

Shanafelt, T. D., Sloan, J. A., & Habermann, T. M. (2003). The well-being of physicians. *American Journal of Medicine, 114*, 513–519. doi: 10.1016/S0002-9343(03)00117-7.

Spickard, A., Gabbe, S. G., & Christensen, J. F. (2002). Mid-career burnout in generalist and specialist physicians. *JAMA, 288*, 1447–1550. doi: 10.1001/jama.288.12.1447.

Sullivan, M. P. (2009). Social workers in community care practice: Ideologies and interactions with older people. *British Journal of Social Work, 39*, 1306–1325. doi: 10.1093/bjsw/bcn059.

Taris, T. W., Le Blanc, P. M., Schaufeli, W. B., & Schreurs, P. J. G. (2005). Are there causal relationships between the dimensions of the Maslach Burnout Inventory? A review and two longitudinal tests. *Work and Stress, 19*, 238–255. doi: 10.1080/02678370500270453.

Travado, L., Grassi, L., Gil, F., Ventura, C., Martins, C., & Southern European Psycho-Oncology Study (SEPOS) Group (2005). Physician–patient communication among Southern European cancer physicians: The influence of psycho-social orientation and burnout. *Psycho-Oncology, 14*, 661–670. doi: 10.1002/pon.890.

Wallace, J. E., Lemaire, J. B., & Ghali, W. A. (2009). Physician wellness: A missing quality indicator. *Lancet, 374*, 1714–1721. doi: 10.1016/S0140-6736(09)61424-0.

Williams, E. S., Savage, G. T., & Linzer, M. (2006). Short communication: A proposed physician–patient cycle model. *Stress and Health, 22*, 131–137. doi: 10.1002/smi.1088.

Wright, T., & Cropanzano, R. (1998). Emotional exhaustion as a predictor of job performance and voluntary turnover. *Journal of Applied Psychology, 83*, 486–493. doi: 10.1037/0021–9010.83.3.486.

Zachariae, R., Pedersen, C. G., Jensen, A. B., Ehrnrooth, E., Rossen, P. B., & von der Maase, H. (2003). Association of perceived physician communication style with patient satisfaction, distress, cancer-related self-efficacy, and perceived control over the disease. *British Journal of Cancer, 88*, 658–665. doi: 10.1038/sj.bjc.6600798.

9

TIME IS NOT ON OUR SIDE

Temporal Agency and Affective Orientation in the Enron Email Corpus

Matthew S. McGlone, Joseph McGlynn, III, and Nicholas A. Merola

UNIVERSITY OF TEXAS AT AUSTIN

Time Is Not on Our Side: Temporal Agency Language in the Enron Email Corpus

Analyses of organizational email corpora have demonstrated that language patterns in email reflect employees' identities in an organization (Oberlander & Gill, 2006), their relationships with peers, superiors, and subordinates (McArthur & Bruza, 2003), and their sensitivity to organizational change (Carley & Reminga, 2004). These analyses have focused chiefly on explicit, intentional communication between employees. However, implicit and nonstrategic word use patterns in email may also reflect organizational dynamics (e.g., Keila & Skillicorn, 2005; Kessler, 2010). In this chapter, we describe the study exploring a documented nonconscious word use pattern—grammatical agency assignment in temporal language (McGlone & Pfiester, 2009; Chen, McGlone, & Bell, 2015)—in the Enron email corpus released by the U.S. Federal Energy Regulatory Commission in 2002 (and refined by Klimt & Yang, 2004). Our study demonstrates the diagnostic value of analyzing temporal agency to gauge changes in the affective tenor of organizational discourse.

In a span of roughly fifteen years, the Enron Corporation ("Enron" hereafter) grew from a merger of two local gas supply companies into the seventh-largest business organization by revenue in the United States. By 2001, the company employed 21,000 people in over forty countries (Fusaro and Miller, 2002). From Enron's inception, CEO Kenneth Lay and other senior management aggressively sought growth and profit by selling off key petrochemical assets, taking on silent partners, and rebranding the company to take advantage of the burgeoning deregulated energy market. After constructing the first nationwide natural gas pipeline in the United States, Enron promptly transformed the company's core business into global commodity and options trading. They deftly created a successful global financial powerhouse from very simple beginnings. By taking this course, Enron quickly became beloved to its devoted employees, its unswerving stakeholders, and the broader stock market community.

Enron's soaring success came crashing down late in 2001 when the mammoth organization suddenly found itself insolvent, causing senior management to file for Chapter 13 bankruptcy. Financial tragedy, public outcry, and scandal quickly followed. Under heavy stakeholder uproar and political pressure, the U.S. Securities and Exchange Commission (SEC) (SEC Spotlight on Enron) and the Federal Energy Regulatory Commission (FERC) (FERCWestern Energy Markets—Enron Investigation) conducted simultaneous independent inquiries into the sudden collapse. In May 2002, FERC publicly released a corpus of actual emails from 158 employees—including those produced by top executives such as the company's very public CEOs, Kenneth Lay and Jeffrey Skilling. The FERC took this unusual step in order to improve the public's understanding of the various reasons for their investigation of Enron. The full corpus represents a large collection (~500,000 emails) and temporal record of email conversations over a period of 3.5 years.

For researchers focusing on social networks and organizational behavior, the Enron corpus is alluring because it enables the examination of communication and social processes in a real-world organization over a long period of time. It provides researchers a rare, authentic glimpse into the social network of an actual business organization. The Enron corpus also contains a large amount of raw data on organizational discourse during a *crisis*. We believe that scientific analysis of this data can provide insight into the communicative relationship within and among the social and formal networks in this particular organization.

Our focus here is on the communicative patterns Enron executives used in their correspondence to describe the passage of time. Although the language people use to describe temporal passage is typically idiomatic and composed with little deliberation, research suggests that time language can reflect one's emotional and attitudinal orientation toward events that are not always apparent from more deliberate and considered word choices (McGlone & Pfiester, 2009; McGlone & Giles, 2011). In the next section, we describe this research on the "affective embodiment" of time language and discuss how it might be tracked in employee communication to gauge changes in organizational climate. In the following section, we apply an analytic scheme based on this research to samples of correspondence in the Enron email database. In the final section, we draw conclusions regarding the utility of this analysis and delineate its implications for future research on time language patterns in organizational correspondence.

Time, Affect, and Embodiment

Scholars have long observed that humans' sense of time is mediated by their communication patterns. Leibniz famously rejected Newton's notion of "absolute time" in favor of a relative temporality people employ to represent order relations (before, after, during) between events (Vailati, 1997). Bergson (1889) characterized temporal change as a perceptual illusion produced by imposing the analytic medium of language on a physical dimension we grasp intuitively. Idealist philosophers such as McTaggart (1908) took this reasoning even further, asserting that time is entirely an illusion resulting from humans' inclination to anchor sensory experience in a "specious present." Few contemporary scholars question time's very existence, but most continue to treat it as a highly mediated, context-sensitive concept.

Communication research on time has been heavily influenced by the idea of "social time" (Sorokin & Merton, 1937), which emphasizes the link between interpersonal interactions and the temporal intervals they occupy. In the 1970s, Bruneau (1977) introduced an area of communication inquiry he dubbed "chronemics" with the express purpose of studying this link. Since then, communication scholars have examined people's intersubjective experience of time primarily in organizational settings (e.g., Ballard & Seibold, 2003; Shockley-Zalabak, 2002). This work has demonstrated that our interactions in various social, cultural, and occupational groups engender a plurality of temporal frames of reference that we experience in parallel. Researchers have also investigated people's use of monotemporal artifacts (timelines and calendars, in particular) to concretize and simplify their complex temporal experiences in the service of communicating and coordinating with others. One commonly overlooked set of such artifacts—linguistic conventions for describing temporal change—plays a subtle but nonetheless significant role in temporal communication.

Like many other abstract, non-sensorial concepts, time is linguistically structured by analogical extension from more concrete concepts grounded in physical experience (Lakoff & Johnson, 1980; Miller & Johnson-Laird, 1976). The primary source analog for time is space. The linguistic correspondences between time and space are reflected in the common phrasal lexicon used to denote relations in the two domains. Table 9.1 presents a sample of parallel spatial and temporal sentence constructions in the English language.

These parallels occur because temporal relations are predicated on a subset of those used for the analysis of spatial location and motion. Clark (1973) argued

TABLE 9.1 Parallel Spatial and Temporal Constructions in English

Space	Time
from Los Angeles to San Francisco	*from 9 a.m. to 5 p.m.*
in San Antonio	*in 1976*
The border lies ahead of us.	*The future lies ahead of us.*
They are two miles behind us.	*They are two hours behind us.*
We're getting close to the city limits.	*We're getting close to spring break.*
The train is fast approaching.	*Spring break is fast approaching.*

that the applicable subset of spatial relations is determined by conceiving time as a unidimensional, directional, and dynamic entity. Because time is typically thought of as unidimensional, only those spatial terms that presuppose one dimension (e.g., *long–short*) also appear in the temporal lexicon, but those that presuppose two or more dimensions (e.g., *deep–shallow*) do not. Because time is directional, ordered spatial terms (e.g., *before–after*) have temporal senses, but symmetric terms (e.g., *left–right*) do not. We will focus here on terms used to convey time's dynamic quality. Numerous terms that denote physical movement are also used to describe the passage of time, as in *the weekend flew by, we're getting close to Thanksgiving,* and so forth.

English and most other languages use two distinct spatial metaphors to encode temporal change. These metaphors are grounded in our experience of bodily movement, and consequently provide linguistic evidence of time's status as an "embodied" concept (Clark, 1973; Johnson, 1990). To illustrate, compare the assertions *we have passed the due date* and *the due date has passed.* These statements differ in two important respects. First, they imply opposite directions of symbolic movement. The former implies a future-bound (past → future) direction of temporal passage, but the latter implies a past-bound (past ← future) direction. Second, the sentences attribute agency—i.e., the instrumentality of temporal change—to different entities. The former implies that humans (the referents of *we*) are the agents of temporal change, moving away from inert events in the past and present toward others in the future. In contrast, the latter attributes agency to the event (*due date*) itself, which has moved from the future beyond present-dwelling human observers into the past. The spatiotemporal relations implied by the human-agent and event-agent metaphors are illustrated in Figure 9.1.

As vehicles for conveying temporal sequencing and change, human- and event-agent expressions are functionally equivalent. Thus *we are approaching spring break* and *spring break is approaching* both convey the same temporal relation (future) between the observer and the event, albeit from different spatiotemporal perspectives. Given their ostensible equivalence, under what circumstances are

FIGURE 9.1 Two metaphors of temporal passage in English.

people inclined to use one type of expression or the other? To date, studies of temporal language have focused exclusively on the comprehension of idiomatic time expressions (Boroditsky & Ramscar, 2002; McGlone & Harding, 1998), not their production. This research has demonstrated that the context in which temporal expressions are encountered can have a significant impact on the ease and manner with which they are comprehended. McGlone and Harding (1998) observed that people's comprehension of temporal sentences was facilitated when they were presented in perspectivally consistent blocks (i.e., all human- or event-agent sentences) relative to inconsistent (the two types juxtaposed) blocks. People also used the perspectival information available in these blocks to interpret ambiguous temporal sentences in a contextually consistent manner. For example, when people encountered the ambiguous sentence *The meeting scheduled for next Wednesday has been moved forward two days* in the context of human-agent sentences, most inferred that the meeting had been postponed to Friday, consistent with the human-agent entailment directing temporal movement toward the future (see Figure 9.1). In contrast, when this sentence appeared in the context of event-agent sentences, the majority inferred that the meeting had been moved earlier in the week to Monday, consistent with the event-agent entailment directing temporal movement toward the past. The influence of linguistic context on temporal thinking is paralleled by spatial context effects documented by Boroditsky and Ramscar (2002), who posed the aforementioned proposition about rescheduling a meeting to people in a variety of situations involving physical movement. When interpreters engaged in forward physical movement themselves (e.g., moving through a lunch line), they preferred the human-agent reading of the proposition; however, when they observed an object moving toward them (e.g., a wheeled chair moving across the room), they preferred the event-agent reading. Taken together, the effects of linguistic and spatial context on temporal language comprehension suggest that the human- and event-agent perspectives are not "dead metaphors" of mere etymological interest, but active cognitive constructs that mediate people's thinking about time.

Another contextual factor that may influence temporal communication is the speaker's affective orientation toward the event being described. In everyday discourse, people express their feelings about conversational topics in many ways, not just direct declarations like *I'm really into Facebook* or *I hate my job*. Sociolinguists have identified a variety of subtle linguistic markers that reflect one's affect, attitude, or stance toward a topic (Berman, 2005; Wiener & Mehrabian, 1968). One such marker is the grammatical passive voice. Communicators opt for passive constructions (e.g., *Louise was helped by John*) over parallel active constructions (e.g., *John helped Louise*) to direct causal attribution away from the thematic agent to the patient (Brown & Fish, 1983). This choice may reflect their attitudes and beliefs about the agent (e.g., John is nurturing) or the patient (e.g., Louise is weak), and in turn may implicitly encourage addressees to form consonant impressions of these parties (LaFrance, Brownell, & Hahn, 1997).

Like passive voice, the manner in which people encode their temporal experiences constitutes another potential linguistic marker of their affective orientation toward life events. In particular, the metaphor one uses to frame temporal passage constitutes a vehicle for manipulating agency akin to grammatical voice. When communicators assign temporal agency to humans (*we're approaching the weekend*) or events (*the weekend is approaching*), the assignment reflects different spatial entailments of time's embodied conceptual structure (Clark, 1973). However, affect is also grounded in bodily experience and poses spatial entailments of its own. These entailments are reflected in the etymology of the term *emotion*, which derives from the Latin verb *emovere* denoting "moving out, or migration from one place to another." Embodiment theorists argue that humans' understanding of emotion is predicated on a symbolic relationship between affect and movement, in which we equate positive affect with approach and negative affect with avoidance or passivity (Johnson, 1990; Kovecses, 2000). This relationship is presumed to underlie a variety of behavioral phenomena associated with emotional processing. For example, Cacioppo, Priester, and Berntson (1993) observed that novel pictorial stimuli presented while participants were engaged in arm flexion (a motor action associated with approach) were subsequently evaluated more favorably than stimuli presented during arm extension (associated with avoidance). In recent years, numerous studies employing variants of Cacioppo et al.'s (1993) methodology have demonstrated that approach/avoidance motor actions differentially modulate the affective appraisal of many classes of stimuli, including words, names, faces, and songs (Niedenthal, Barsalou, Winkielman, Krauth-Gruber, & Ric, 2005; Puca, Rinkenauer, & Breidenstein, 2006).

The motion–emotion link is also evident among the various figurative expressions we use to talk about emotional experience (Gibbs, 1994; Kovecses, 2000). Likes and loves are commonly framed in terms of approach (*I'm leaning towards Obama, we've become so close since we first met,* etc.), while disaffections and detestations are equated with physical withdrawal (*we're far apart on that issue, she pushed me away,* etc.). McGlone and Pfiester (2009) explored the possibility that the conceptual correspondences between motion and emotion influence the way communicators encode the temporal passage of emotionally valenced events. For example, consider the different ways one might talk about a prospective event expected to be pleasant, such as a birthday. The human- and event-agent metaphors provide functionally equivalent ways to articulate the birthday's temporal status. However, our desire to encounter pleasant events—i.e., the ones we "look forward to"—may predispose us to conceive them in terms of approach, and accordingly attribute temporal agency to ourselves (e.g., *we're getting close to my birthday*). In contrast, our trepidation about experiencing an unpleasant event may incline us to deemphasize our symbolic role in temporal change by instead assigning agency to the event itself (e.g., *the April 15 tax filing deadline is fast approaching*). In this manner, the language we use to encode temporal change may reflect an embodied "approach/avoidance" affective schema in which communicators symbolically move toward pleasant events but passively observe the arrival of unpleasant ones via agency manipulation.

McGlone and Pfiester (2009) report linguistic evidence for this affective schema using two different methodologies. In their first study, they searched a large corpus (~14 million words) of written and spoken English for the occurrence of key spatial terms used in a temporal sense (e.g., *come*). Independent coders then examined the immediate discourse context of each identified linguistic token and judged whether the affective valence of the encoded event was positive, negative, or neutral. This analysis indicated that communicators describing temporal passage associated with ostensibly positive events (a wedding anniversary, a noteworthy scientific discovery, etc.) modally characterized themselves as the symbolic locus of temporal change (*we are coming up on our tenth anniversary; we might be coming to the culminating stage of our search*). In contrast, communicators preferred to encode the passage of negative events (age-related health problems, a projected increase in traffic volume on urban roads, etc.) by assigning the agency of change not to themselves, but to the event (*when the time comes [that] she can't do things; average speeds for major arterial roads are expected to decline significantly in coming years*). A similar pattern of agency assignment was observed for temporal expressions employing the other key terms.

A second study employed an experimental methodology to explore the motion–emotion link. Participants were asked to describe positive or negative experiences in the recent past. These accounts were then analyzed for the presence of key spatiotemporal terms used in human- and event-agent expressions. These analyses corroborated the correlational findings of the aforementioned corpus study. When recounting positive past experiences, people modally encoded temporal passage using human-agent metaphors. For example, consider the temporal expressions one participant used to describe a positive experience of duck hunting with friends:

> *We stayed at my cousin's cabin Friday night and got up early Saturday morning. We* <u>*began the day*</u> *[human agent] at about 4 a.m. with a little breakfast and coffee. Next we spread the decoys out and then got in our blinds. We shot for about 5 hours. It was amazing. Everybody got something except this new guy who hadn't ever been out with us. I bagged two pintails. Had a bufflehead in my sights once, but didn't connect. It was great hanging out in the blind and* <u>*passing the time*</u> *[human agent] drinking beer and listening to the outdoors. I needed to unwind after a hard week at school and this was perfect. When we left the lake we got stopped by a Game Warden and he gave my buddy a ticket b/c he didn't have his safety card. He was mad, but it was funny to me b/c he knew better. We went back to the cabin and cleaned the ducks and then got something to eat.* <u>*After dinner was done*</u> *[event agent] not much else happened.*

Of the three spatiotemporal expressions in this account, two of the three are human-agent and one is event-agent. The narratives participants generated for negative events, in contrast, were dominated by event-agent metaphors. The following account was offered by a participant describing a bad day at work:

> It normally takes me about 30 minutes to get to [nearby city] where I work, so I got in my car and headed out around 2:30 to make it there by 3:00. But I hit a major traffic jam on [nearby interstate highway] and nothing was moving. I called to let my boss know I was going to be late and she sounded pretty p.o.'ed. Practically an entire hour passed [event agent] while I just sat there with nothing to do. I finally was able to make it to my exit and then blast through town to work. When I finally got there 45 minutes late, my boss dumped a bunch of things on me just to be mean, I'm pretty sure. I went through the rest of the day [human agent]with like a cloud over my head because she was in a bad mood and kept criticizing me. My shift was only supposed to go until 9 [event agent], but I didn't get done with half what I was supposed to, so I stayed another hour but still didn't getting [sic] everything done. After that, I just drove home and slept.

These findings suggest that the conceptual correspondences between motion and emotion identified by embodiment theorists (Gibbs, 2006; Niedenthal et al., 2005) are operative when people describe the symbolic motion of temporal passage. Anecdotally, the operation of these correspondences appears to have occurred largely outside of awareness. After the researchers informed participants at the beginning of the debriefing that our study examined "differences in the way people talk about time when recalling positive and negative experiences," participants were then asked to speculate about what these differences might be. Although many hypotheses were offered (e.g., people talk about time as elapsing more quickly for positive than negative events), no one spontaneously generated ideas that bore any resemblance to the notion of temporal agency that was the actual focus. Moreover, when the researchers did eventually describe the difference between human- and event-agent metaphors and provided examples, many participants expressed puzzlement and confusion about the distinction.

Spatiotemporal Language in the Enron Email Corpus

The research we report here extended McGlone and Pfiester's (2009) analysis of temporal agency assignments to an investigation of longitudinal trends in temporal language used by employees in professional correspondence contained in the Enron email corpus. This corpus offers not only the largest extant collection of internal electronic correspondence within a large and prominent corporation, but also constitutes a rich temporal record of dramatic organizational change. Over the 3.5 years of correspondence included in the corpus (1999–2002), Enron descended from its peak as a global financial powerhouse named "America's Most Innovative Company" by *Fortune* magazine six years in a row to a scandal-ridden, bankrupt company that became a popular symbol for corporate fraud and corruption.

Several studies have mined the Enron email corpus to investigate social networks among employees (e.g., Keila & Skillicorn, 2005), dissemination of proprietary neologisms (Kessler, 2010), and message clustering during critical incidents in the company's downfall (e.g., Berry & Browne, 2005). However, the metaphoric content of the corpus has not been explored heretofore. Our analysis focused specifically on metaphoric language used to describe the passage of time by members of Enron's senior management. Using an incident timeline metric suggested by Berry and Browne (2005), we explored the relative frequency of human and event temporal agency assignments in executive correspondence before and after ostensibly positive and negative critical incidents during the 1999–2002 corpus coverage period. Three positive and negative incidents—valenced as such from the perspective of a present-oriented Enron executive with a profit motive, albeit not from that of consumers nor a government agency, nor from that of the executives in hindsight—were selected. These events were selected not only for their affective valence but also because they were relatively discrete events that occurred within a single day, thus allowing us to distinguish between correspondence occurring before or after the event with some precision. These critical incidents are described in Table 9.2. The key spatiotemporal terms employed in our analysis of the correspondence are presented in Table 9.3.

TABLE 9.2 Critical Incidents at Enron Used as Event Anchors for the Corpus Analysis

Date	Valence	Incident Description
January 19, 2000	Positive	Enron rolls out broadband plan; stocks rise 26 percent in a single day to record high of $67.25.
May 5, 2000	Positive	Enron energy analyst describes "Deathstar Strategy" to executive board for gaming the California energy market in an email; according to the memo, Enron would be paid "for moving energy to relieve congestion, without actually moving any energy or relieving any congestion."
August 23, 2000	Positive	Stock rises 10 percent in a single day to hit all-time high of $90.56 with a market valuation of $70 billion.
February 19, 2001	Negative	Fortune article by Bethany McLean released, "Is Enron Overpriced?"; stocks drop 8 percent in a single day; Skilling calls employee meeting to discuss "blackbox" strategy.
August 22, 2001	Negative	Sherron Watkins, executive VP, writes letter to Lay expressing concern about accounting practices; she provides a letter in which she describes suspicion that these practices are an "elaborate hoax."
October 17, 2001	Negative	*Wall Street Journal* article describing CFO Fastow's shell company accounting strategy coincides with "surprise" announcement of SEC inquiry; Lay allegedly caught off guard.

TABLE 9.3 Key Terms and Examples of Their Occurrence in Human- and Event-Agent Temporal Expressions

Term	Human Agent Expressions	Event Agent Expressions
ahead	We went ahead with the renovation plan.	The renovation plan is ahead of schedule.
approach	We are approaching the summer.	The summer is approaching.
begin	We began the meeting at 3 p.m.	The meeting began at 6 p.m.
behind	Let's put the matter behind us.	All our troubles are behind us.
close	We're getting close to kickoff time.	Kickoff time is getting closer.
come	We have come to the end of the regular season.	The playoffs are coming up soon.
done	When I'm done with dinner, I'll drive home.	When dinner is done, I'll drive home.
end	We ended the meeting at 6.	The meeting ended at 6.
enter	We are entering the last month of the fiscal year.	The fiscal year is entering its last month.
finish	When I've finished dinner, I'll drive home.	When dinner is finished, I'll drive home.
forward	We are moving forward with the project.	The project is moving forward.
from ... to/until	I was in a meeting from 2 to/until 4 p.m.	My meeting was from 2 to/until 4 p.m.
go	I went through the day feeling tired.	As the day went on, I grew tired.
move	We are moving quickly through our meeting agenda.	The meeting is moving quickly.
near	We are nearing the filing date.	The filing date is drawing near.
pass	We passed the due date on Thursday.	The due date passed on Thursday.
reach	We have reached the last week of the election season.	The election season has reached its last week.
run	We are running a few minutes late.	The meeting is running a few minutes late.
start	We started the fiscal year with a bang.	The fiscal year started with a bang.

We examined the pre- and post-incident correspondence generated by members of Enron's Corporate Policy Committee in 2000, consisting of thirteen influential executives. These executives included the CEO (Skilling), Chairman (Lay), Vice-Chairman (Baxter), CFO (Fastow), CAO (Causey), a number of heads from different Enron divisions, and an in-house lawyer. One member from this committee has since committed suicide (Baxter), one died of a heart attack (Lay), and eight have been charged and found guilty of various accounting and securities frauds. All correspondence generated by committee members within seven days prior to and seven days following each critical incident were inspected for the presence of key spatiotemporal terms. Because the temporal agency assignment process appears to be unconscious rather than strategic (McGlone & Pfiester, 2009), we analyzed all correspondence regardless of intended recipient, reasoning that the emotional valence of the incident would "color" post-incident correspondence attributes regardless of recipient. The percentages of human- and event-agency expressions in pre- and post-incident email messages are presented in Figures 9.2 and 9.3.

This analysis revealed significant, contrasting shifts in temporal agency assignment based on incident valence. When the incidents were positive, executives' use of

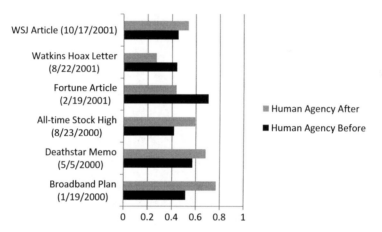

FIGURE 9.2 Proportions of Human Agency Expressions in Pre- and Post-Critical Incident Correspondence.

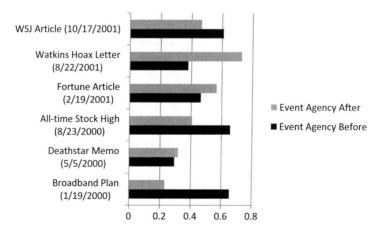

FIGURE 9.3 Proportions of Event Agency Expressions in Pre- and Post-Critical Incidence Correspondence.

human agency assignments (e.g., *Look how far we have come in just a few months!*) increased and event assignments declined; however, when the incidents were negative, event assignments (e.g., *the time for doing that has already come and gone*) increased and human assignments declined. Interestingly, the shifts in temporal agency assignment we observed align better with Berry and Browne's (2005) timeline than with former CEO Jeffrey Skilling's testimony at his 2006 trial about the time course with which he and other senior executives became aware of accounting irregularities and other problems that ultimately led to Enron's downfall. Skilling's testimony was disputed by attorneys for the prosecution, who claimed he and his senior colleagues were aware of these problems far earlier than they claimed. Given that temporal agency assignments are typically made outside of conscious awareness, our findings suggest that affect-driven temporal agency assignments may constitute a cue to emotional leakage in managerial discourse (Keila & Skillicorn, 2005).

Conclusions

One of the most generative theoretical constructs to emerge from embodiment theory has been the idea of "embodied simulation," according to which the bodily states we experience when engaging in action are reactivated to some degree when we encounter cues—images, sounds, words, etc.—associated with these actions (Niedenthal et al., 2005). For example, when people merely listen to words describing actions such as *chew* or *kick*, the areas of the motor cortex that control associated body parts (mouth and leg) exhibit greater activation (Hauk, Johnsrude, & Pulvermuller, 2004). Performing physical actions such as forming a fist or pulling a lever toward the body has been shown to impair people's ability to process messages describing conflicting actions such as *aiming a dart* or *closing the drawer* (Glenberg & Kaschak, 2002). Interestingly, simulation effects of this sort are not restricted to simple literal messages. Matlock (2004) demonstrated that people understand sentences describing "fictive motion" (i.e., locative descriptions metaphorically framed as motion, such as *the road runs along the coast*) in terms of implicit physical sensations of movement. People do not, however, report being aware of these sensations, so fictive motion processing does not appear to be dependent on deliberate thought about motion.

We contend that the pattern of metaphorical agency assignment we have documented in the Enron email database derives from the interaction of tacit embodied simulations underlying people's understanding of time and emotion. Time's grounding in the perceptual experience of movement in space creates two perspectives of temporal passage, one in which people are the agents of passage (*we're approaching the end of the fiscal year*) and another in which events are the agents (*the end of the fiscal year is approaching*). The symbolic human activity implied by the former and passivity by the latter map onto the motion entailments underlying emotion, whereby we move toward affectively positive stimuli, but either withdraw from negative stimuli we can avoid or resignedly observe the arrival of those we can't. The interaction of the entailments inclines us to symbolically assume the agent role for the passage of a pleasant event but to abdicate it when faced with an unpleasant one. The resulting pattern of agency assignments constitutes a temporal analog of the self-serving attributional bias studied by social psychologists, whereby people prefer to make internal attributions for successes and external attributions for failures (Miller & Ross, 1975).

Our conclusions are qualified by two important limitations of the reported research. First, we have no direct evidence of embodiment's role in temporal agency assignment beyond the documented assignment patterns. Although the conceptual correspondences between time, motion, and emotion constitute a plausible substrate for these patterns, future research employing direct measures of these hypothesized mediators (e.g., a measure of cortical activity) is necessary to substantiate this substrate. Second, the generalizability of our findings is obviously limited by the characteristics of the language sample we examined. Most known human languages employ some form of human- and event-agent expressions to describe temporal passage (Boroditsky, 2001; Clark, 1973; Núñez & Sweetser, 2006), but we have only explored their correspondence with event valence in a sample of well-educated, high SES American English speakers. Whether this correspondence generalizes to other English-speaking groups or other languages remains an open question.

Finally, our study highlights the analytic value of examining symbolic agency in communication, a topic that has received considerable attention in recent years but is rarely portrayed in precise linguistic terms. In particular, Cooren, Fairhurst, Putnam, and their colleagues have explored the ascription of agency to nonhuman entities such as machines (e.g., *my computer doesn't like the file you just sent me*), texts (e.g., *Leaked Memo Unmasks Duplicity of Enron Executives*), and even directional signs (e.g., *the yellow arrows will direct you to the waiting room*) in organizational discourse (Cooren, 2004; Fairhurst & Putnam, 2004). The interplay of human and nonhuman agency, Castor and Cooren (2006) argue, discursively constitutes organizations as "hybrid" forms, whose hybridity is most salient when they confront institutional problems. The present results hint at a similarly hybrid construction of human temporal experience: Enron executives generally ascribed temporal agency to themselves when times were good, but abdicated it to events when times were bad.

References

Ballard, D. I. (2009). Organizational temporality over time: Activity cycles as sources of entrainment. In R. Roe, M. J. Waller, & S. Clegg (Eds.), *Time in organizational research* (pp. 204–219). London: Routledge.

Ballard, D. I., & Seibold, D. R. (2003). Communicating and organizing in time: A meso-level model of organizational temporality. *Management Communication Quarterly, 16*, 380–415.

Bergson, H. (1889). *Time and free will: An essay on the immediate data of consciousness.* London, UK: Allen & Unwin.

Berman, R. A. (2005). Developing discourse stance in different text types and languages. *Journal of Pragmatics, 37,* 105–124.

Berry, M. W., & Browne, M. (2005). Email surveillance using nonnegative matrix factorization, *Proceedings of workshop on link analysis, counterterrorism and security,* SIAM International Conference on Data Mining, 2005. Newport Beach, CA, April 2005, 45–54.

Boroditsky, L. (2001). Does language shape thought? Mandarin and English speakers' conceptions of time. *Cognitive Psychology, 43,* 1–22.

Boroditsky, L., & Ramscar, M. (2002). The roles of body and mind in abstract thought. *Psychological Science, 13,* 185–189.

Brown, R., & Fish, D. (1983). The psychological causality implicit in language. *Cognition, 14,* 237–273.

Bruneau, T. (1977). Chronemics: The study of time in human interaction (with a glossary of chronemic terminology). *Journal of the Communication Association of the Pacific, 6,* 1–30.

Cacioppo, J. T., Priester, J. R., & Bernston, G. G. (1993). Rudimentary determination of attitudes II: Arm flexion and extension have differential effects on attitudes. *Journal of Personality and Social Psychology, 65,* 5–17.

Carley, K. M., & Reminga, J. (2004). *ORA: Organization risk analyzer.* Technical report, Carnegie Mellon University, School of Computer Science, Institute for Software Research International, Retrieved July 6, 2008, from: http://www.casos.cs.cmu.edu/projects/ora/publications.html.

Castor, T., & Cooren, F. (2006). Organizations as hybrid forms of life: The implications of the selection of agency in problem formulation. *Management Communication Quarterly, 19,* 570–600.

Chen, M., McGlone, M. S., & Bell, R. A. (2015). Persuasive effects of linguistic agency assignments and point of view in narrative health messages about colon cancer. *Journal of Health Communication, 20,* 977–988.

Clark, H. H. (1973). Space, time, semantics, and the child. In T. E. Moore (Ed.), *Cognitive development and the acquisition of language* (pp. 27–63). New York: Academic Press.

Cooren, F. (2004). Textual agency: How texts do things in organizational settings. *Organization, 11,* 373–393.

Fairhurst, G. T., & Putnam, L. (2004). Organizations as discursive constructions. *Communication Theory, 14,* 5–26.

Fusaro, P.C., & Miller, R.M. (2002). *What went wrong at Enron.* New York: John Wiley & Sons.

Gibbs, R. W., Jr. (1994). *The poetics of mind: Figurative thought, language, and understanding.* Cambridge, UK: Cambridge University Press.

Gibbs, R. W., Jr. (2006). *Embodiment and cognitive science.* Cambridge, UK: Cambridge University Press.

Glenberg, A. M., & Kaschak, M. P. (2002). Grounding language in action. *Psychonomic Bulletin and Review, 9,* 558–565.

Hauk, O., Johnsrude, I., & Pulvermuller, F. (2004). Somatotopic representation of action words in human motor and premotor cortex. *Neuron, 41,* 301–307.

Johnson, M. (1990). *The body in the mind: The bodily basis of meaning, imagination, and reason.* Chicago, IL: University of Chicago Press.

Keila, P. S., & Skillicorn, D. B. (2005). Structure in the Enron email dataset. *Computational and Mathematical Organization Theory, 11,* 183–199.

Kessler, G. (2010). Virtual business: An Enron email corpus study. *Journal of Pragmatics, 42,* 262–270.

Klimt, B., & Yang, Y. (2004). Introducing the Enron corpus. First conference on email and anti-spam (CEAS), Mountain View, CA. Retrieved October 14, 2010, from http://www.ceas.cc/papers-2004/168.pdf.

Kovecses, Z. (2000). *Metaphor and emotion: Language, culture, and body in human feeling.* New York: Cambridge University Press.

LaFrance, M., Brownell, H., & Hahn, E. (1997). Interpersonal verbs, gender, and implicit causality. *Social Psychology Quarterly, 60,* 138–152.

Lakoff, G., & Johnson, M. (1980). *Metaphors we live by.* Chicago: University of Chicago Press.

Lakoff, G., & Johnson, M. (1999). *Philosophy in the flesh: The embodied mind and its challenge to Western thought.* New York NY: Basic Books.

Matlock, T. (2004). Fictive motion as simulation. *Memory and Cognition, 32,* 1389–1400.

McArthur, R., & Bruza, P. (2003). Discovery of implicit and explicit connections between people using email utterances. In *Proceedings of the Eighth European Conference of Computer-Supported Cooperative Work, Helsinki,* pp. 21–40.

McGlone, M. S., & Giles, H. (2011). Language and interpersonal communication. In M. L. Knapp & J. A. Daly (Eds.), *Handbook of interpersonal communication* (4th Ed., pp. 201–237). Thousand Oaks, CA: Sage.

McGlone, M. S., & Harding, J. L. (1998). Back (or forward?) to the future: The role of perspective in temporal language comprehension. *Journal of Experimental Psychology: Learning, Memory, and Cognition, 24,* 1211–1223.

McGlone, M. S., Harding, J. L., & Glucksberg, S. (1995). Time marches on: Understanding time-as-movement expressions. In P. Amsili, M. Borillo, & L. Vieu (Eds.), *Time, space, and movement: Meaning and knowledge in the sensible world* (p. 21–38). Toulouse, France: Groupe LRC.

McGlone, M. S., & Pfiester, R. A. (2009). Does time fly when you're having fun, or do you?: Affect, agency, and embodiment in temporal communication. *Journal of Language and Social Psychology, 28,* 3–31.

McTaggart, J. M. E. (1908). The unreality of time. *Mind, 17,* 457–474.

Miller, G. A., & Johnson-Laird, P. N. (1976). *Language and perception.* Cambridge, MA: Harvard University Press.

Miller, D. T., & Ross, M. (1975). Self-serving biases in the attribution of causality: Fact or fiction? *Psychological Bulletin, 82,* 213–225.

Niedenthal, P. M., Barsalou, L. W., Winkielman, P., Krauth-Gruber, S., & Ric, F. (2005). Embodiment in attitudes, social perception, and emotion. *Personality and Social Psychology Review, 9,* 184–211.

Núñez, R., & Sweetser, E. (2006). With the future behind them: Convergent evidence from Aymara language and gesture in the crosslinguistic comparison of spatial construals of time. *Cognitive Science, 30,* 401–450.

Oberlander, J., & Gill, A. J. (2006). Language with character: A stratified corpus comparison of individual differences in e-mail communication. *Discourse Processes, 42,* 239–270.

Puca, R. M., Rinkenauer, G., Breidenstein, C. (2006). Individual differences to approach and avoidance movements: How the avoidance motive influences response force. *Journal of Personality, 74,* 979–1014.

Shockley-Zalabak, P. (2002). Protean places: Teams across time and space. *Journal of Applied Communication Research, 30,* 231–250.

Sorokin, P. A., & Merton, R. K. (1937). Social time: A methodological and functional analysis. *American Journal of Sociology, 46,* 615–629.

Vailati, E. (1997). *Leibniz and Clarke: A study of their correspondence.* New York, NY: Oxford University Press.

Wiener, M., & Mehrabian, A. (1968). *Language within language: Immediacy, a channel in verbal communication.* New York: Appleton Century Crofts.

10

MULTI-METHODOLOGICAL APPROACHES FOR STUDYING EMOTION IN COMPUTER-MEDIATED COMMUNICATION

Mark S. Pfaff and Afarin Pirzadeh

INDIANA UNIVERSITY—PURDUE UNIVERSITY INDIANAPOLIS

Introduction

Computer-mediated communication (CMC) sits at the crux of a number of interesting cognitive, behavioral, and organizational research domains. Communication analysis has led to countless insights within these domains by functioning as a window into real-world processes within small and large groups. Specific methods abound for communication analysis, which poses a challenge to researchers both in terms of selecting the right tools for the job, as well as implementing them correctly and consistently. The dramatically increasing use of computer-mediated communication in casual and organizational settings presents a variety of new challenges and opportunities for researchers. One challenge is the wide variety of technological alternatives to face-to-face (FTF) communication, each of which has unique features to consider, such as emoticons, avatars, and other novel nonverbal modes of expression. On the other hand, by virtue of being computer-mediated, gathering, organizing, and analyzing communication data has become more efficient and in many cases automatable.

Fundamental cognitive processes, such as memory, attention, and decision-making, can be placed under the microscope, so to speak, using a variety of reliable and well-validated stimuli and measurement methods. Communication, however, as a macrocognitive activity (involving concurrent use of multiple cognitive functions in naturalistic settings), is often more difficult to examine as precisely, or under such controlled laboratory conditions. As a result, many communication-related research questions require concurrent use of multiple methods in order to locate and evaluate a phenomenon of interest. For the research discussed in this chapter, the phenomenon of interest is the role of mood in computer-mediated communication. This chapter illustrates a selection of methods, some more commonly applied to communication research than others, through a sequence of studies conducted with small physically distributed teams performing communication-heavy tasks in various induced mood states. These methods include simulated task environments, mood and stress inductions, quantitative and qualitative communication analyses, and a variety of measures including traditional self-report and psychological surveys, as well as psychophysiological data. These studies integrated multiple methods in order to achieve a whole that was greater than the sum of its parts. In addition to communication and psychological measures, these studies employed individual and team task performance metrics, such as decision-making speed and accuracy, team dynamics, and problem-solving strategies. Fusing the results from task performance (the "what") and communication (the "how") produced new insights into teamwork in stressful and emotionally charged environments (Pfaff & McNeese, 2010).

This chapter begins with a brief summary of the history and significance of CMC, followed by examples of the experimental methods and measures available for studying it. In the interest of brevity, only a sampling of representative results is presented here. The goal of this chapter is to demonstrate some of the opportunities for researchers to expand their methodological toolkits and further advance knowledge in the field of communication, computer-mediated and otherwise.

Computer-Mediated Communication (CMC)

CMC arose from linking computers to one another in networks, and consequently operators found that in addition to sharing data, they also could send simple messages to one another. From there, CMC grew from simple message dispatch systems to multimedia group communication applications (Walther, 1996). Early research on CMC focused on different communication modalities and mainly argued that, regardless of task, the more similar CMC is to face-to-face communication, the more efficient the communication will be. This is referred to as the *bandwidth hypothesis* (Whittaker, 2002), which itself is rooted in information theory (Shannon & Weaver, 1949).

Further research on CMC began to reject the bandwidth hypothesis, leading to a wave of studies examining the exchange of cognitive information and cueing. Many studies (e.g. Chapanis, Ochsman, Parrish, & Weeks, 1972; Chapanis, Parrish, Ochsman, & Weeks, 1977) demonstrated that face-to-face interaction does not necessarily increase the efficiency of communication. In fact, several studies showed that CMC could be more efficient than face-to-face in some task-oriented communication, including cognitive problem-solving tasks and team coordination. Reid (1977) reviewed the results of twenty-eight studies providing evidence that partners performing primarily cognitive tasks through spoken communication performed the same in terms of task efficiency and performance whether using the telephone, video communication, or face-to-face. Findings of other studies in this line demonstrated the efficiency of CMC in the area of cognitive cueing and information exchange, ultimately characterizing CMC as an impersonal and task-oriented communication, unable to convey emotional and social information.

The main cause of the impersonality of CMC in earlier research was explained by the absence of nonverbal cues, which convey personal and emotional information in face-to-face communication (Kiesler, Siegel, & McGuire, 1984; Culnan & Markus, 1987). According to Mehrabian (1972), in everyday communications, only 7 percent of the people's emotional understanding stemmed from the words spoken, whereas 38 percent was attributed to verbal tone and 55 percent was related to facial expression. Culnan and Markus (1987) refer to this as the *cues-filtered-out* perspective.

Social presence theory (Short, Williams, & Christie, 1976) characterizes technological differences in terms of how they present a sense of other communication participants' goals, attitudes, and motives. Face-to-face communication and video/speech methods (e.g. Skype™) provide rich visual interpersonal information afforded by gaze and facial expressions, making them high on the scale of social presence, with text-based communication at the low end of this scale. According to this theory, technologies that fail to communicate social presence will negatively affect social and emotional communication.

Over time, CMC flourished in additional contexts such as social chat groups and online forums. Researchers began finding that CMC could indeed be more interpersonal than previously thought, as communicators discovered new ways to express emotional and social information in text. One of the main theories representing this perspective is Social Information Processing (SIP; Walther, 1992). SIP argues that people are able to employ different active and passive strategies to convey nonverbal behaviors in text-based CMC. In addition, it asserts that communicators can develop social relationships via CMC as well as through face-to-face interaction (Walther, 1996). This perspective acknowledges that the rate of social information cues exchange may be less in CMC compared to face-to-face communication due to the absence of explicit and visible nonverbal cues, but the interpersonal relationship formed over CMC may eventually exhibit the same qualities of a face-to-face interaction (Walther, 1993).

Compared to prior views of CMC as an impersonal mode of communication, these studies demonstrated that CMC can be highly interpersonal. CMC can indeed convey emotional and social information when desired and appropriate, or it can remain impersonal and task-oriented when that is the desired interactive setting. For example, to conduct brainstorming, group coordination, or decision-making through CMC, strategies such as time pressure, reduced periods for discussion, anonymous interaction, turn-taking, or floor-sharing techniques can be applied to encourage task-oriented communication. Although the above strategies might be helpful to impersonalize CMC, they may also affect task outcomes if social or emotional information is necessary to reach the best results. Hence, careful judgment should be applied when selecting communication tools for a given task.

To conclude, computer mediation alone does not determine whether communication is impersonal or interpersonal. The specific technical implementation of a CMC system provides a basis for communicators to set their communication tone as preferred. Impersonal CMC may be desired when users wish to capitalize on its strengths for task-focused communication. On the other hand, CMC can also be a highly interpersonal means of communication when users have the time and technological affordances to build and express their emotions while exchanging information (Whittaker, 2002). Walther (1992) went even further and offered a new perspective explaining that at high levels of intimacy, emotions and affinity via CMC could exceed face-to-face interpersonal communication.

Emotional Communication in Text-Based CMC

Emotional communication in CMC is a relatively new research area (Derks, Fischer, & Bos, 2008), but the number of studies focusing on social-emotional aspects of text-based CMC is growing. The lens model (Brunswik, 1956) is frequently used to conceptually frame research on emotional communication (e.g. Aronoff, Woike, & Hyman, 1992; Scherer, 2003).

Figure 10.1 shows the modified version of the lens model applied in our studies. This approach models the process of encoding (expression) and decoding (impression) of emotional communication. As the diagram shows, factors such as individual differences, culture, social rules, and situational context can affect all communication, including instant messaging (IM).

In studies of text-based CMC, the lack of nonverbal behaviors is one of the main issues discussed, (e.g. Walther, Loh, & Granka, 2005; Derks, Fischer, & Bos, 2008), since when communicating face-to-face, people apply nonverbal behaviors (e.g. facial, vocal, and body movements), in addition to verbal cues, to communicate their emotions (Scherer, 2005). Those deeply ingrained social behaviors and expectations do not simply disappear when a person begins communicating with someone via a computer.

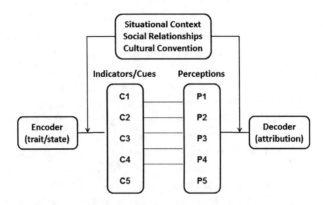

FIGURE 10.1 The modified lens model (adapted from Scherer, 2003).

Several studies have examined the variety of strategies people use to convey nonverbal behaviors via text-based CMC, supporting the SIP theory (Walther, 1992). Walther, Loh, and Granka (2005) showed that likable and dislikable partners can be identified in text-based CMC as accurately as face-to-face. Hancock, Landrigan, and Silver (2007) investigated the mechanisms people apply to convey their emotions in CMC. In their study, participants developed five types of emotional cues (degree of agreement, negative affect terms, punctuation, speed of response, and verbosity) to adapt their emotion expression to a text-based communication environment. Hancock, Gee, Ciaccio, and Lin (2008) also showed that participants in a negative mood used more negative terms and produced fewer words than participants in a positive mood.

An ongoing problem in this area of research is identifying the specific cues and strategies people rely upon in the cyclical process of emotion expression and perception in text-based CMC, though a lexicon of emotional cues in text-based CMC is emerging. Boonthanom (2004) applied the lens model to study different cues in the context of asynchronous text-based CMC (email messages) into two main categories of verbal and nonverbal emotional cues. Verbal cues include *emotion words* (e.g. happy, angry) and *linguistic markers* (e.g. "I could punch him a million times."). Linguistic markers consist of cues that express emotion without containing emotion words, but rather via rhetorical devices such as hyperbole or understatement. Nonverbal or paralinguistic cues in text-based CMC include cues normally transferred by nonverbal behaviors in face-to-face communication, such as facial expression, tone of voice, body gesture, or posture. The nonverbal cues identified by Boonthanom (2004) include *vocal spelling* (altering spelling to mimic a specific vocal inflection, e.g. "weeeell" or "soooo"), *lexical surrogates* (textual representations of vocal sounds that are not words, e.g. "uh huh" or "haha"), *spatial arrays* (also known as *emoticons*, pictographs constructed from punctuation and letters, e.g.:- (for a sad face, or :-D to indicate laughing), *manipulation of grammatical markers* (altering the presentation of words, e.g. all capital letters, strings of periods or commas), and *minus features* (deliberate or inadvertent neglect of conventional formatting elements, e.g. lack of capitalization or paragraphing).

As anyone who has used synchronous text-based CMC such as IM knows, these cues are not exclusive to asynchronous methods such as email or posts to online forums. However, the ways they are used to express emotional dynamics conversationally in synchronous media like IM is still unclear, and potentially quite different for certain emotions or situations. Producing new knowledge about these problems has implications in two main areas. The first is a better understanding of people's needs to express their emotions via CMC under a variety of circumstances, and their strategies for doing so with current technologies. The second is for the design of new procedures and tools to support those needs in the next generation of CMC systems.

Multi-Methodological Investigation of Emotion in Instant Messaging (IM)

In pursuit of the goals described above, we conducted a series of studies that demonstrate different ways of combining multiple methods to study CMC in general, and IM in particular. The first study demonstrates how analysis of text-based chat logs helps explain differences in team decision-making behaviors under different mood and stress conditions, in a way that is not possible through performance measurement and self-reports alone. A second study analyzed this same corpus of data to see whether different mood and stress states affected the usage of a variety of verbal and nonverbal emotional cues in text-based chat. Finally, building upon these findings, a third study conducted a new experiment to examine the specific verbal and nonverbal cues used to express emotion in informal text-based chat during different mood states.

Study I: Effects of mood and stress on text-based communication in a team decision-making task

In this study (Pfaff, 2012), undergraduate students worked in distributed teams of six in an emergency management simulation called NeoCITIES (McNeese et al., 2005), designed after the problem-solving and decision-making activities of 911 dispatchers. Within each team, members were assigned in pairs to one of three emergency services: Police, Fire/EMS, or Hazardous Materials. The task requires teams to monitor the occurrence of emergency events in a simulated city, determine which of the three services are responsible for addressing the event, and track the escalation and resolution of ongoing events.

All communication in NeoCITIES is via text-based chat; only the within-pair communication was analyzed for the study described here. Each pair consists of an information manager (IM) and resource manager (RM). The IMs from all three services can chat with each other as they receive information about new events and negotiate whose team should respond. IMs may chat with their own RM as well, but the RMs may only chat with their respective IM. This structured set of communication channels enables the experimenter to present information to one particular team member and observe whether and how that information is distributed to the team. The communication between IM and RM occurs primarily after the IMs determine responsibility for a given event. IMs and RMs discuss the right number and type of resources to dispatch (e.g. fire trucks, ambulances, etc.) and the ongoing status of the event. The RM is the only member who can dispatch resources to the field and receive status updates about the progress of the response to the event. This information may be conveyed to the IM if further discussion is desired to modify their response. The conversations analyzed for this study were ten minutes in duration, the length of a NeoCITIES session for each condition in the experiment.

The experiment employed mood and stress manipulations in a within-subjects factorial design, with two levels of stress (normal/high) and two levels of mood (sad/happy). Stress was manipulated in the form of time pressure (eighteen versus thirty events addressed during a ten-minute session), and mood was manipulated by showing participants pretested happy or sad movie clips prior to the task. This is a commonly used approach to induce a mood lasting at least for the ten-minute duration of the experiment.

A hybrid approach was taken for analyzing the 168 chat logs produced by the participants across all four conditions in the experiment. Strictly quantitative methods of communication analysis are fast and often automatable, but can oversimplify the meaning of the discussion. Qualitative methods can preserve the complexity and richness of the content, but are generally labor-intensive and time-consuming manual processes. Hybrid approaches aim to employ the strengths of quantitative and qualitative methods by using a strongly defined and comprehensive set of coding categories capturing both the *meaning* and *quantity* of messages relevant to the research question at hand. This study used the Adaptive Architectures for Command and Control (A2C2; Entin & Entin, 2001) coding scheme, modified to fit the specific activities in the NeoCITIES simulation. This coding scheme breaks communications down into requests and transfers in three categories: information (facts about the situation), action (ground-level activities), and coordination (higher-level activities of delegating and accepting responsibility for action). Additional categories included acknowledgments ("OK") and off-task messages, totaling eight message types that comprehensively captured all statements made among team members during the task. Tuning the coding scheme to the specific task helps ensure the categories are as mutually exclusive as possible, supporting high inter-rater reliability. In addition, this scheme defines *anticipation ratios*, which are the ratio of transfers to requests in each of the three categories. For example, teams that transfer information proactively, without waiting for the information to be requested, will have a high information anticipation ratio (greater than 1.0). Teams that tend to only transfer information when requested, or even defer or ignore such requests, will have a low anticipation ratio, which is diagnostic of poor communication efficiency. Once coded, the proportions of each message type and the anticipation ratios can then be statistically analyzed.

Analysis of the coded data revealed a number of interesting results. Under the stress of time pressure, the proportions of information requests and transfers significantly increased, indicating that the teams were generally unable to streamline their communication to cope with the increased pace of the task. In fact, the proportion of information requests was inversely correlated with task score, suggesting that the increased communication overhead was one contributing factor toward diminished team performance. This result demonstrates how this type of hybrid communication analysis can be diagnostic of specific problems in the training, systems, or procedures associated with the task under investigation. In this case, high numbers of information requests highlights problems attending to and remembering important facts about the situation. Further analysis of the content of statements in this category can help with designing solutions to cope with frequent task-switching and interruptions, by revealing exactly what the individuals were having problems attending to in the situation.

With respect to mood, the happy mood improved team awareness, as shown by significantly increased action anticipation ratios. In the sad mood, participants were less likely to announce their actions, requiring their teammates to ask what they were doing about a particular event. The sad mood also increased the use of acknowledgements (e.g. "OK") rather than explicit statements of action (e.g. "I'm sending a police car"). Both of these results reveal an inward focus induced by the sad mood, reducing awareness of the actions of other team members, leading to potentially disastrous misunderstandings and mistakes. One possible way to address this problem is communication training that encourages teams to improve their action anticipation in general, but also to be aware that during times when the task is going poorly and some members may be experiencing a negative mood, other team members should be prepared to recognize the symptoms of a sad team member turning away from the group.

This sampling of findings from Study I demonstrates how mood and stress inductions in a realistic simulated task can elicit interesting and actionable changes in communication behaviors, when captured and analyzed using a well-designed hybrid coding scheme. It also demonstrated how emotional states influence the use of CMC, even in strictly task-focused contexts.

Study II: Analysis of Text-Based Emotional Cues in a Team Decision-Making Task

This exploratory study (Pirzadeh & Pfaff, 2012) was the next step to investigate emotion communication in IM. Controlling for personality traits of the participants, we explored the relationships between induced psychological states (mood and stress) and emotional cues they used in IM in the context of the NeoCITIES team decision-making task. Comparing IM communication with vocal or face-to-face communication, Johnstone and Scherer (2000) described how stress produces changes in speech and vocal communication of emotion. They showed that intensity and fundamental frequency are significantly higher in vocal communication of emotion under stress; analogous cues may be evident in IM. The inclusion of personality trait measures was motivated by a wealth of studies exploring the relationships between personality traits and verbal and nonverbal behaviors in traditional face-to-face settings. For example, Scherer (1978) showed that extraversion could be recognized through certain vocal cues: extraverted individuals tend to speak with a louder and often more nasal voice. However, there is much less known about the influence of personality traits on CMC.

Study II employed a different methodological approach than Study I. Using both manual and automated text analysis methods, we searched for specific emotional cues within the 168 chat conversations from the previous study (Pfaff, 2012). The advantage of these quantitative approaches is their speed and efficiency to mine large data sets, though they only capture content, not context. In this case, our goal was to see whether predefined cues, such as those provided by Boonthanom (2004), would appear in different proportions under different emotional conditions. If so, this would provide an objective measure of IM's capacity for emotion expression, specifically whether it supports some emotions more richly than others. Future research could then focus more intently on the emotions and cues of greatest interest.

The factorial structure of the previous experimental design was maintained: Stress (normal/high) X Mood (happy/sad). Emotion words were analyzed using Linguistic Inquiry and Word Count software (LIWC; Tausczik & Pennebaker, 2010). Nonverbal cues (Boonthanom, 2004) were counted manually by the researchers. As LIWC also supports text analysis for attentional focus, social relationships, cognitive styles, and individual differences, we also analyzed text for other potentially relevant cues including self-references (I, me, my), social words (indicating relationships or interactions), big words (more than six characters), and cognitive or thinking words (causal and insight words).

According to the lens model, psychological state and personality traits of the sender and receiver may both affect emotion communication. All "big five" personality factors were assessed in the original NeoCITIES experiment (openness to experience, extraversion, conscientiousness, agreeableness, neuroticism) using the NEO PI-R™ Five-Factor Personality Inventory (Goldberg et al., 2006). This provided an opportunity for us to explore the relationship between those personality traits and emotional cues used in the chat logs by participants.

Some example findings from Study II illustrate the kinds of insights this approach can provide about emotion communication via IM. The only cue affected by mood was the use of big words, with sad participants using big words nearly twice as often as happy participants. A possible explanation for this increase may be the effect of a negative mood to focus attention on local details rather than the big picture (Gasper, 2003). In a negative mood, participants may dwell longer on technical specifics, such as the names of resources, locations, and operations in the NeoCITIES task, which often require longer words. In a study on cockpit communication, Sexton and Helmreich (2000) found that flight engineers used more big words than captains and first officers. They explained that this effect is possibly because the information they communicate is necessarily more technical than the others. However, they also found that using big words negatively correlated with performance in the cockpit overall, possibly due to either the lack of a succinct and concise vocabulary for the same information, or a tradeoff between the ability to maintain effective situation awareness and the cognitive effort to speak elaborately. In either case, in a time-sensitive task, inefficient and overly verbose communication is cause for serious concern.

The absence of significant effects for mood on any of the other text-based cues was somewhat surprising. Given the result of the Hancock et al. (2008) study, in which there was an increase of negative terms used by participants in a negative mood, we expected to see some significant effect for mood in the use of positive or negative emotion words. Instead, stress produced significantly more negative emotion words than under normal conditions, as well as fewer vocal spellings. An increase in negative emotion words under stress was expected, as the time pressure stressor was designed to frustrate the participants through frequent task-switching. However, the decrease in the number of vocal spelling cues was unexpected. This result suggests that the use of vocal spelling needs additional time and cognitive effort to consider and execute. It may also indicate that vocal spelling, as a strategy for coping with the restricted emotional bandwidth of IM, is of limited use under stress in a task-based context when users need time and cognitive effort to accomplish their tasks.

Stress also led participants to use more self-references and cognitive words than under normal conditions. This seemed consistent with the results of Study I above (Pfaff, 2012) that participants under stress engaged in greater amounts of sense-making behavior. Statements related to sense-making are part of figuring out the situation on a certain event and explaining or justifying actions taken, which seems likely to account for the increase in self-references and cognitive words (e.g. "I sent two fire trucks because I thought the fire was too big for just one.").

With respect to personality traits, extraversion produced the most interesting results. Extraversion predicted increased use of positive emotion words, social words, and articles among the verbal cues, and vocal spelling, lexical surrogates, and minus features among the nonverbal cues. Although extraversion might be expected to increase talkativeness in general, there was no significant correlation between extraversion and the overall amount of chat. Therefore, there is some-thing about these specific six cues that extraverts appeared to employ more than introverts. The use of vocal spelling and lexical surrogates are especially intriguing as nonverbal cues that mimic real speech. As such, the correlation between extraversion and vocal spelling and lexical surrogates in this study corresponds to the findings of Scherer (1978), which detected extraversion from an assessment of voice quality, specifically dynamic range and vocal effort.

Openness to experience predicted increased usage of minus features. Individuals high on the openness scale are more likely to use richer vocabularies and have vivid imaginations. They also tend to be more sensitive to emotion and creative ideas. Individuals low on the openness scale are more likely to favor conventional approaches. Individuals low on this scale may adhere more to conventions of punctuation and formatting in text, while those high on the openness scale may be less diligent about their typography in text-based IM.

The results of Study II supported the application of Brunswik's lens model (1956) in synchronous text-based CMC by providing evidence of the psychological state (mood), situational context (stress), and trait characteristics of participants affecting different cues they used in IM. Though no interactions were found between the personality measures and the effects of mood or stress on any of the emotional cues, the task was not specifically designed to elicit any particular results related to personality, and such individual difference measures are often unable to detect differences with samples as small as this. Given the structured task of the NeoCITIES simulation, it is not entirely surprising that the chat logs were not especially rich in emotion expression. Therefore, the results of this study offered evidence that studying text-based emotional cues in IM merited further study and led us to design a new experiment using informal open-ended chat between friends.

Study III: Emotion Expression during Informal Chat

Armed with the exploratory findings from Study II, Study III explored text-based IM communication within a wider range of emotional states by cultivating controlled emotionally laden situations in which participants were more likely to apply text-based emotional message cues to express their emotions, compared to the preceding study, which was more task-focused.

This study employed Russell's (1980) circumplex model of emotion to define the four emotional states examined: relaxed, angry, happy, and sad. These four major emotional states occur frequently in human's daily life, and users of IM are likely to chat in any of them. In Russell's circumplex model of affect, different emotions are arranged in a two-dimensional space defined by pleasure–displeasure on the horizontal axis, and degree of activation on the vertical axis. The four chosen emotions each occupy a different quadrant of this space, providing an opportunity to explore a wider range of emotional states than the preceding two studies.

Besides investigating a range of emotions, we also made a few more changes to the analytic methods. First, we subdivided negative emotion words into three categories of sadness, anger, and anxiety emotion words. Next, we selected extraversion as the only trait among the "big five" personality traits for this study, as Study II showed it was the most dominant personality influence on the emotional cues used in IM. Lastly, we included a measure for trait emotional intelligence (EI) (Petrides, Furnham, & Mavroveli, 2007). Trait EI measures individual differences in affective self-evaluations and integrates the emotion-related facets of basic personality dimensions (Petrides, Pita, & Kokkinaki, 2007). Compared to *ability EI*, which measures emotion-related cognitive abilities by performance tests, *trait EI* concentrates on emotion-related dispositions and self-perceptions via self-report.

Therefore, this study specifically measured the influence of four emotional states (relaxed, angry, happy, sad), extraversion, and emotional intelligence of individuals on the type and quantity of emotion-related cues used during informal conversations between friends in IM, in controlled emotionally laden situations.

Ten pairs of friends (three males and seventeen females, ranging from eighteen to thirty-one years old) participated in this study. Because the conversations had to be between people who were friendly and familiar with each other (and likely to IM each other in real life), partners had to know each other for at least six months. The study used a within-subjects design. For the mood induction, four short video clips were selected to elicit the relaxed, angry, happy, and sad moods. Seated in two different rooms, partners watched each of these movies, followed by a manipulation check (using Russell's (1980) twenty-eight emotion items). They then chatted with their partner for ten minutes via IM (Google Chat) before watching the next movie. They were given some sample questions to use if desired (e.g. How do you feel about the video? Have you had any similar experiences?), but the chat session was left open-ended for the participants to chat freely.

The mood manipulation was successful, with the levels of each emotion (relaxed, angry, happy, and sad) significantly higher than the other three for each of the corresponding mood inductions. As expected, by conducting the study in informal chat rather than a structured task, there was noticeably more use of emotion words. There were more negative and angry words in the angry and sad conditions, and more positive and assent words in the happy condition. Of course, this is partially influenced by the topics of their conversation in those conditions, which were movie scenes specifically portraying events that would be described with those words.

The nonverbal cues were more interesting. Overall, the happy condition led to more use of nonverbal cues than the other three conditions, including more vocal spellings, lexical surrogates, emoticons, punctuation, and manipulation of grammatical markers. The increase of vocal spellings in the happy mood supports the finding in Study II of decreased vocal spellings due to the frustrations of the stress condition. As with Study II, these particular cues are noteworthy in how they attempt to mimic real speech (Hancock, 2004). Participants seem to apply these mechanisms to adapt the prosody of face-to-face communication to text-based CMC. As such, these results correspond to the findings of Scherer (1978) and Ekman (1982), which showed prosody (e.g. tone of voice, frequency, pitch) is one of the main cues to emotional expression in face-to-face communication, and is exhibited differently across various emotions.

The absence of significant patterns of cues for the other three emotions suggests that a happy mood promotes an overall increase in emotional expressivity in IM, which has two potential explanations. The first is that IM, as it is currently implemented in common desktop and web-based applications such as Google Chat, may not provide sufficient support to express negative emotions. The manipulation check confirmed that participants were in the desired mood at the beginning of the chat session, and concurrent psychophysiological measures (heart rate and galvanic skin response collected for another study) confirmed that the mood inductions persisted throughout each chat session. Yet the only manifestation of the negative moods (angry and sad) in the chat logs was simply a reduction in the number of cues used in the happy condition. This is either because letters, numbers, punctuation, and even emoticons are ill-suited to express negative emotions, or participants expressed negative emotions using cues not among those captured in this analysis. Alternately, in line with the results of Study I showing an increased inward focus of participants in a negative mood (in NeoCITIES, this was manifest as reduced attentiveness to their partners), perhaps sad partners chatting informally also turn inward and become less expressive overall. Both findings have implications for future research on emotion communication via CMC, as well as for the design of the next generation of IM tools that can facilitate a wider range of emotional expression. One caveat is that future studies must reexamine these findings with chat data from a more diverse participant pool (in terms of age, gender, and ethnicity) than this primarily young and female sample.

Conclusion

Supporting the social information processing theory (Walther, 1992), the results of these three studies demonstrate a range of strategies for expressing different emotions in text-based CMC. The level of detail of these findings is the result of both deliberate and opportunistic combinations of multiple methods. Conducting the first study in a simulated task environment provided a reliable and engaging experimental platform that encouraged realistic communication behaviors, while capturing all communication and participant actions in real time. Because IM is increasingly used in organizational contexts, it is important to continue examining emotion expression in structured tasks like NeoCITIES, as well as everyday work tasks like planning and brainstorming. Though higher levels of emotion expression are found in informal chat than in the structured task, the same off-the-shelf IM tools are commonly used in both contexts, and therefore the design implications apply broadly across all formal and informal uses of IM.

Though laboratory research necessarily introduces some degree of artificiality in the communication activities between individuals, this can be addressed through thoughtful and creative design of the setting and cover story given to participants at the time of the experiment. The increase in experimental control is arguably well worth the decrease in the naturalistic characteristics of real IM conditions. Mining a corpus of real-world IM data poses a host of ethical and methodological problems, such as privacy concerns of the communicators, as well as increased difficulty determining the emotional state of the communicators from the text alone. However, the studies described above can help refine the automated extraction of emotional cues for sentiment analysis of text (Alm, Roth, & Sproat, 2005; Pang & Lee, 2008), which provides a step toward solving that problem. This is a growing area of research with implications for a variety of applications, from product marketing to managing political unrest.

Our next steps are addressing how to design the next generation of CMC tools that can better support the emotional expression needs of the users. Many studies in the field of affective computing are designing innovative ways of automatically detecting the emotional state of the communicator. In some cases, this is to make the system adapt to the user's emotional state, while in others this is to show more emotional information to the receiver of the communication than is embedded in the text itself, for example by using avatars (Neviarouskaya, Prendinger, & Ishizuka, 2010). However, these automated system-driven approaches are not truly "user-centered" in the strictest sense of the term. We believe the users of CMC systems should have primary control over whether and how they express their emotional states. Therefore, our focus moving forward, and our recommendation to the CMC research community, is to continue developing our understanding of the emotion expression needs of CMC users and apply that knowledge toward enhancing existing systems and envisioning CMC systems of the future.

References

Alm, C. O., Roth, D., & Sproat, R. (2005). Emotions from text: Machine learning for text-based emotion prediction. *Proceedings from the conference on human language technology and empirical methods in natural language processing* (pp. 579–586). Vancouver, British Columbia, Canada: Association for Computational Linguistics.

Aronoff, J., Woike, B. A., & Hyman, L. M. (1992). Which are the stimuli in facial displays of anger and happiness—Configurational bases of emotion recognition. *Journal of Personality and Social Psychology, 62,* 1050–1066.

Barchard, K. A. (2001). Emotional and social intelligence: Examining its place in the nomological network. Unpublished doctoral thesis, University of British Columbia, Vancouver.

Boonthanom, R. (2004). *Computer-mediated communication of emotions: A lens model approach.* (Doctoral dissertation). Retrieved from http://hdl.handle.net/123456789/398.

Brunswik, E. (1956). *Perception and the representative design of psychological experiments.* Berkeley, CA: University of California Press.

Chapanis, A., Ochsman, R., Parrish, R., & Weeks, G. (1972). Studies in interactive communication I: The effects of four communication modes on the behavior of teams during cooperative problem solving. *Human Factors, 14,* 487–509.

Chapanis, A., Parrish R., Ochsman, R., & Weeks, G. (1977). Studies in interactive communication II: The effects of four communication modes on the linguistic performance of teams during cooperative problem solving, *Human Factors, 19,* 101–126.

Culnan, M. J., & Markus, M. L. (1987). Information technologies. In F. M. Jablin, L. L. Putnam, K. H. Roberts, & L. W. Porter (Eds.), *Handbook of organizational communication: An interdisciplinary perspective* (pp. 421–443). Newbury Park, CA: Sage Publications.

Derks, D., Fischer, A. H., & Bos, A. E. R. (2008). The role of emotion in computer-mediated communication: A review. *Computer Human Behavior, 24,* 766–785.

Ekman, P. (1982). *Emotion in the human face.* Cambridge, UK: Cambridge University Press.

Entin, E. E., & Entin, E. B. (2001, June). *Measures for evaluation of team processes and performance in experiments and exercises.* Paper presented at the 6th International Command and Control Research and Technology Symposium. Annapolis, MD.

Gasper, K. (2003). When necessity is the mother of invention: Mood and problem solving. *Journal of Experimental Social Psychology, 39*, 248–262.

Goldberg, L. R., Johnson, J. A., Eber, H. W., Hogan, R., Ashton, M. C., Cloniger, C. R., & Gough, H. G. (2006). The international personality item pool and the future of public-domain personality measures. *Journal of Research in Personality, 40*, 84–96.

Hancock, J. T. (2004). Verbal irony use in computer-mediated and face-to-face conversations. *Journal of Language and Social Psychology, 23*, 447–463.

Hancock, J. T., Landrigan, C., & Silver, C. (2007). Expressing emotion in text-based communication. *Proceedings of SIGCHI '07: ACM conference on human factors in computing systems*, 929–932.

Hancock, J. T., Gee, K., Ciaccio, K., & Lin, J. M. H. (2008). I'm sad you're sad: Emotional contagion in CMC. *Proceedings of CSCW '08: ACM conference on computer-supported cooperative work*, 295–298.

Johnstone, T., & Scherer, K. R. (2000). Vocal communication of emotion. In M. Lewis & J. Haviland, (Eds.), *Handbook of emotion* (2nd ed., pp. 220–235). New York, NY: Guilford Press.

Kiesler, S., Siegel, J., & McGuire, T. (1984). Social psychological aspects of computer-mediated communication. *American Psychologist, 39*, 1123–1134.

McNeese, M. D., Bains, P., Brewer, I., Brown, C., Connors, E. S., Jefferson, T., … Terrell, I. S. (2005). The NeoCITIES simulation: Understanding the design and experimental methodology used to develop a team emergency management simulation. In *Proceedings of the 49th annual meeting of the human factors and ergonomics society* (pp. 591–594). Santa Monica, CA: Human Factors and Ergonomics Society.

Mehrabian, A. (1972). *Nonverbal communication*. Chicago: Aldine-Atherton.

Neviarouskaya, A., Prendinger, H., & Ishizuka, M. (2010). User study on AffectIM, an avatar-based instant messaging system employing rule-based affect sensing from text. *International Journal of Human-Computer Studies, 68*, 432–450.

Pang, B., & Lee, L. (2008). *Opinion mining and sentiment analysis*. Now Publishers Inc.

Petrides, K. V., Furnham, A., & Mavroveli, S. (2007). Trait emotional intelligence: Moving forward in the field of EI. In G. Matthews, M. Zeidner, & R. Roberts (Eds.), *Emotional intelligence: Knowns and unknowns—Series in affective science* (pp.151–166). Oxford: Oxford University Press.

Petrides, K. V., Pita, R., & Kokkinaki, F. (2007). The location of trait emotional intelligence in personality factor space. *British Journal of Psychology, 98*, 273–289.

Pfaff, M. S., & McNeese, M. D. (2010). Effects of mood and stress on distributed team cognition. *Theoretical Issues in Ergonomics Science, 11*, 321–339.

Pfaff, M. S. (2012). Negative affect reduces team awareness: The effects of mood and stress on computer-mediated team communication. *Human Factors: The Journal of the Human Factors and Ergonomics Society, 54*, 560–571.

Pirzadeh, A., & Pfaff, M. S. (2012). Emotion expression under stress in instant messaging. In *Proceedings of the human factors and ergonomics society annual meeting* (pp. 493–497). Santa Monica, CA: Human Factors and Ergonomics Society.

Reid, A. (1977). *Comparing the telephone with face-to-face interaction*. In I. Pool (Ed.), *The social impact of the telephone* (pp. 386–414). Cambridge, MA: MIT Press.

Russell, J. A. (1980). A circumplex model of affect. *Journal of Personality and Social Psychology, 39*, 1161–1178.

Scherer, K. R. (1978). Personality inference from voice quality: The loud voice of extroversion. *European Journal of Social Psychology, 8*, 467–487.

Scherer, K. R. (1985). Vocal affect signalling: A comparative approach. In J. Rosenblatt, C. Beer, M. Busnel, P. J. B. Slater (Eds.), *Advances in the study of behavior* (pp. 189–244). New York: Academic Press.

Scherer, K. R. (2003). Vocal communication of emotion: A review of research paradigms. *Speech Communication, 40*, 227–256.

Scherer, K. R. (2005). What are emotions? And how can they be measured? *Social Science Information, 44*, 695–729.

Sexton, J. B., & Helmreich, R. L. (2000). Analyzing cockpit communication: The links between language, performance, error, and workload. *Human Performance in Extreme Environments, 5*, 63–68.

Shannon, C. E., & Weaver, W. (1949). *The mathematical theory of information*. Champaign, IL: University of Illinois Press.

Short, J., Williams, E., & Christie, B. (1976). *The social psychology of telecommunications*. London: Wiley Press.

Spector, P. E. (1982). Behavior in organizations as a function of employee's locus of control. *Psychological Bulletin, 91*(3), 482–497.

Tausczik, Y. R., & Pennebaker, J. W. (2010). The psychological meaning of words: LIWC and computerized text analysis methods. *Journal of Language and Social Psychology, 29*, 24–54.

Walther, J. B. (1992). Interpersonal effects in computer-mediated interaction: A relational perspective. *Communication Research, 19*, 52–60.

Walther, J. B. (1993). Impression development in computer-mediated interaction. *Western Journal of Communication, 57*, 381–398.

Walther, J. B. (1996). Computer-mediated communication: Impersonal, interpersonal and hyperpersonal interaction. *Communication Research, 23*, 3–43.

Walther, J. B., Loh, T., & Granka, L. (2005). Let me count the ways: The interchange of verbal and nonverbal cues in computer-mediated and face-to-face affinity. *Journal of Language and Social Psychology, 24*, 36–65.

Whittaker, S. (2002). Theories and methods in mediated communication. In A. Graesser (Ed.), *The handbook of discourse processes* (pp. 243–286). Hillsdale, NJ: Erlbaum.

INDEX

Taylor & Francis eBooks

Helping you to choose the right eBooks for your Library

Add Routledge titles to your library's digital collection today. Taylor and Francis ebooks contains over 50,000 titles in the Humanities, Social Sciences, Behavioural Sciences, Built Environment and Law.

Choose from a range of subject packages or create your own!

Benefits for you

» Free MARC records
» COUNTER-compliant usage statistics
» Flexible purchase and pricing options
» All titles DRM-free.

REQUEST YOUR FREE INSTITUTIONAL TRIAL TODAY

Free Trials Available
We offer free trials to qualifying academic, corporate and government customers.

Benefits for your user

» Off-site, anytime access via Athens or referring URL
» Print or copy pages or chapters
» Full content search
» Bookmark, highlight and annotate text
» Access to thousands of pages of quality research at the click of a button.

eCollections – Choose from over 30 subject eCollections, including:

Archaeology	Language Learning
Architecture	Law
Asian Studies	Literature
Business & Management	Media & Communication
Classical Studies	Middle East Studies
Construction	Music
Creative & Media Arts	Philosophy
Criminology & Criminal Justice	Planning
Economics	Politics
Education	Psychology & Mental Health
Energy	Religion
Engineering	Security
English Language & Linguistics	Social Work
Environment & Sustainability	Sociology
Geography	Sport
Health Studies	Theatre & Performance
History	Tourism, Hospitality & Events

For more information, pricing enquiries or to order a free trial, please contact your local sales team: www.tandfebooks.com/page/sales

Routledge
Taylor & Francis Group

The home of Routledge books

www.tandfebooks.com